# Industrial Economics

## A Critical Introduction to Corporate Enterprise in Europe and America

W. Duncan Reekie
*E. P. Bradlow Professor*
*University of the Witwatersrand*
*South Africa*

Edward Elgar

Published by
Edward Elgar Publishing Limited
Gower House
Croft Road
Aldershot
Hants GU11 3HR
England

Gower Publishing Company
Old Post Road
Brookfield
Vermont 05036
USA

**British Library Cataloguing in Publication Data**

Reekie, W. Duncan (William Duncan), *1942–*
  Industrial economics: a critical introduction
  to corporate enterprise in Europe and America
  1. Industries. Economic aspects
  I. Title
  338

Printed and bound in Great Britain
by the Camelot Press Ltd, Southampton

ISBN  1 85278 074 6 ✓
       1 85278 075 4 (pbk)

# Contents

1 **Introduction, Plan and Purpose**                                      1
  1.1  Background                                      1
  1.2  Overview                                        2

2 **Industrial Organization, Microtheory and Policy Options**            5
  2.1  Review of basic microeconomics                 5
  2.2  Perfect competition and Pareto optimality      8
  2.3  Policy alternatives                            23
  2.4  From elegance to pragmatism                    35

3 **The SCP Rationale and Obstacles to its Application**                38
  3.1  The SCP paradigm                              38
  3.2  Measures of structure                         45
  3.3  Problems of structural measurement            50
  3.4  Measures of conduct                           54
  3.5  Criteria of performance                       56

4 **Monopoly Gains and Losses**                                         59
  4.1  Deadweight social loss                        59
  4.2  X-inefficiency                                65
  4.3  Monopoly and cost-reduction                   69

5 **Business and its Organization**                                     73
  5.1  The mixed economy                             73
  5.2  Business in the economy                       77
  5.3  Industrial structure and morphology           81
  5.4  Cost implications of company size             91
  5.5  More notes of caution                         94

6 **The Issue of International Business**                               96
  6.1  Foreign trade                                 96
  6.2  Foreign direct investment                     99
  6.3  Tariffs and FDI                              107
  6.4  FDI trade-offs and industrial organization   109

**7  Costs and Market Structure** 116
7.1  Multiproduct costs 116
7.2  Multiplant costs 121
7.3  Industry lifecycle costs 123
7.4  Product lifecycle costs 125
7.5  Transaction costs 129
7.6  Pragmatism again 137

**8  Transaction Costs: A Closer Look** 139
8.1  The entrepreneur and transaction costs 139
8.2  The entrepreneur as a transactions facilitator 142
8.3  The transacting process 145
8.4  Who is the entrepreneur? 151

**9  The Firm, the Manager and the Entrepreneur** 153
9.1  The manager is not (necessarily) the entrepreneur 154
9.2  The reason the firm exists 159
9.3  Transaction costs and the firm 161
9.4  The divorce of ownership from control 169

**10  Principal/Agent and Corporate Control** 174
10.1  Principal and agent 174
10.2  Agency theory and industrial organization 184
10.3  The internal management market 184
10.4  Entrepreneurship and the market for corporate control 187
10.5  The management/shareholder contract 191

**11  Competition Policy** 199
11.1  Monopoly policy in the USA 199
11.2  Monopoly policy in the UK 201
11.3  Restrictive practices legislation 205
11.4  Merger policy in the USA 209
11.5  Merger policy in the UK 212
11.6  Assessment of industrial policy 216

**12  The Consumers' Interest** 223
12.1  Theories of regulation 224
12.2  Information and market imperfections 228
12.3  The labour-managed firm 231
12.4  Conclusions 233

*Index* 237

# 1.   Introduction, Plan and Purpose

## 1.1   BACKGROUND

This text is designed for senior undergraduate/graduate students of industrial economics or, as it is sometimes termed, industrial organization. Public policy towards business has become a major field of study in universities worldwide. This has paralleled the growing controversy over the role of the state in industrial life. Privatization, conservation, full employment, 'rust belts', 'two nations', inflation, 'technological unemployment', multinational investment, insider-trading, merger 'waves', monopoly profits and other catch-phrases invoke concern in the daily press. Such topics typify the issues dealt with in industrial organization. The debates which these issues have generated are not confined to any one national economy; nor are they the preserve of any one school of economic thought. Indeed, a recent theoretical text in the area (Reid, 1987) identifies three 'Schools', three 'Approaches' and two 'New Departures'.[1]

There have been major advances in economics in the last two to three decades from which industrial organization has benefited. Important contributions have been made in the economics of information, of property rights, of bureaucracy and regulation, of transactions costs analysis, of public choice, of agency, and emphases have been placed on competition as a process and on the importance of entry and contestability. These various building-blocks can be subdivided into a range of 'schools', 'approaches' and 'new departures'.

In a conceptual work such a subdivision is no doubt correct and indeed even beneficial. How else can the development of thought be studied? The applied business economist studying the issues (rather than the concepts) from the viewpoint of either policy-maker, corporation or trade association, however, must be able to draw on the totality of the discipline as and when it is appropriate. If he does not, then from a purely pragmatic view he could find himself

1

positing propositions incomprehensible to or irreconcilable with those put forward by his opposite numbers in the policy debate.

The intellectual validity of an eclectic approach is not difficult to sustain. Most, if not all, of the concepts industrial economists draw on are but variations of received price theory. Emphases differ by writer and the breadth of applicability varies with vintage but essentially there are no major paradigm differences (unless one moves into the neo-Marxian framework). I have expanded else-where (1986) on this, and argued that the differences between, for example, Marshall's approach to the entrepreneur and that of the Austrians are more apparent than real.[2] If so then it can be mis-leading to isolate different schools of thought. Rather, what theories are known and generally agreed upon should be integrated or selected, as the case may be, and applied to the issues at hand.

An eclectic stance is taken here towards the approaches of study. Early texts in the field were purely descriptive. These were succeeded by analytical case studies, while for the last fifteen years, economists have relied heavily on the structure/conduct/performance paradigm. This book rejects no approach but rather builds on each, using the differing but compatible insights from recent advances or shifts in emphasis of the modern received price theory. A particular doctrinal posture is thus not taken, but rather a stance of eclectic agnosticism is adopted in order to give the comprehensive exposition demanded by the broad and ever-changing nature of the subject. The debates in industrial organization are obviously unsettled. In a dynamic world they probably always will be. This book outlines some boundaries of the debates, specifies the terminology and relates the current state of play.

## 1.2 OVERVIEW

Chapter 2 reviews mainstream price theory, shows how the structure/conduct/performance paradigm is inferred from it, and then details the theoretically logical policy alternatives which exist. Already, in Chapter 2 itself, the reader will notice how dif-ficult it is (if not impossible) to carry pure theory over into the real world. The following chapters serve to emphasize this truth and, by extension, underscore the need for a practically informed, eclectic and pragmatic approach to industrial organization. Chapter 3 formally links the SCP modes of industrial economics to price theory — a linkage which is only assumed in Chapter 2. The apparent formal linkages of firm numbers and elasticities, collusion and profit margins suggest that there might well be empirical yardsticks for the industrial economist to use in his assessments of structure, conduct or performance. There are, but again they are imperfect at best, and misleading at worst. Chapter 3 appraises many of the measures commonly used for statistically describing industrial organization. Chapter 4 looks at the broadest picture of industrial organization's impact on the economy — deadweight welfare loss. This topic, which has now been researched for some decades, is still a source of controversy given the recent introduction of rent-seeking behaviour into the analysis. This issue, that of X-inefficiency, and that of technical progress leading to cost reduction are discussed.

Chapter 5 examines UK and US statistics showing the importance and nature of industries and firms to the economy. Empirical yardsticks discussed in earlier chapters are applied to the data, and concepts such as minimum efficient scale are expanded upon. Chapter 6 outlines evidence indicating that corporations are not confined within national boundaries, and asks why firms become multinational in operation. The theory of comparative advantage is questioned, but on closer analysis the existence of multinational enterprises is found not to contradict it. Foreign direct investment is often a least-cost way of carrying out international trade. Costs move to centre stage in Chapter 7. In particular recent or less conventional approaches to cost such as multiproduct and multiplant costs, product and industry life-cycle costs and transactions costs are examined.

Chapter 8 develops the latter with particular emphasis placed on the entrepreneur as a transactions facilitator moving sellers and buyers each to higher positions on their respective utility functions. This then begs several questions. Who is the entrepreneur? How does an entrepreneur differ from a manager? What is the linkage between managers, owners and entrepreneurs?

Chapters 9 and 10 examine these questions looking in particular at the divorce of ownership from control and how recent developments in agency theory and in the understanding of the market in corporate control are helping to provide answers to such questions.

Chapters 11 and 12 conclude the book. Chapter 11 examines the regulation of industry in Europe and the USA at the level of managers and competition policy. Emphasis is placed on evaluating current trends against recent theory rather than on the oft-repeated historical review of the legislation. Chapter 12 examines regulation of industry in general in the light of regulation theory, the scope (or lack of it) which markets have for internalizing external costs, and the role information plays in this process of optimal market satisfaction of consumer wants.

## NOTES

1.  Reid identifies the SCP paradigm, the case study 'approach' and the model-building 'approach' as 'Schools'. He views as 'Approaches' the Marshallian tradition, Austrianism and workable competition. 'New Departures' include contestability and the organizational view of the firm.
2.  For example, I argued that Marshall's 'undertaker' and the Austrian 'entrepreneur' are very similar and indeed that their motivational spur, pure profit resulting from alertness to opportunity, is the same. Thus my eclectic approach differs from Reid who in his Preface argues that '[no] one could legitimately dispute that there are Marshallian and Austrian approaches to industrial organisation . . . proponents of the two views would wish to see fostered . . . worlds (which would be quite different, and immediately recognisable as such)'. This book is predicated on the contrary view that the differences are of emphases only and that in the practical world these differences taken together enrich our understanding.

## REFERENCES

Reekie, W.D. (1986), 'The Economics of Business and the Business of Economics', *South African Journal of Economics*.
Reid, G.C. (1987), *Theories of Industrial Organisation* (Oxford: Blackwell).

# 2. Industrial Organization, Micro-theory and Policy Options

## 2.1 REVIEW OF BASIC MICROECONOMICS

Public policy towards industry is always explicitly or implicitly directed at maximizing social welfare. Social welfare in turn depends on the three efficiencies: allocative, technical and distributive. *Allocative efficiency* relates to the extent to which existing output combinations maximize aggregate individual satisfactions; *technical efficiency* relates to the extent to which these are being produced with the least-cost combination of inputs; while *distributive efficiency* is concerned with how any particular aggregate output could be reallocated between individuals in order to maximize welfare.

Welfare is clearly not maximized if it is possible to improve one person's welfare by altering the existing pattern of inputs and outputs without harming another. If such a special situation is achieved however, as will be explained, it still may not be a welfare maximizing position. This situation — where any reallocation of inputs or outputs would harm at least one person — is known as *Pareto optimality*.

Three conditions are necessary for Pareto optimality to hold:

1. the marginal rate of substitution (MRS) between any pair of goods (X and Y) should be the same for *all* consumers;
2. the marginal rate of substitution (MRS) between any pair of factor inputs (say K and L) should be the same in the production of all goods; and
3. the MRS (which by (1) is the same for all consumers) should be the same as the marginal rate of product transformation (MRT) in production.

The rationales for each of these conditions are illustrated in Figure 2.1 (see also Bator, 1957).

*Figure 2.1*

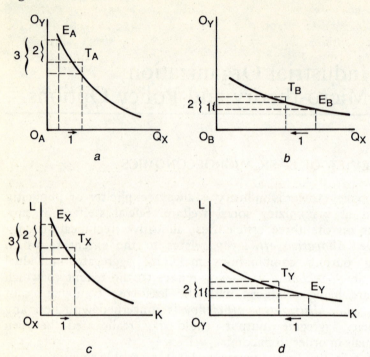

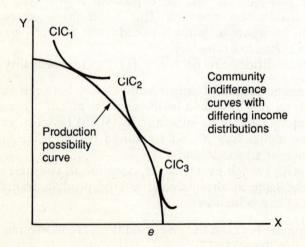

Community
indifference
curves with
differing income
distributions

Consider Figures 2.1a and 2.1b. Assume two individuals A and B, in a two-good, Y and X, world, with different tastes as indicated by their respective indifference curves. Each currently possesses bundles of Y and X as indicated by their original endowment points $E_A$ and $E_B$. Their marginal valuations of Y and X are not the same. A values 1X at 3Y (or 1Y at 1/3X), but B thinks 1X is only worth 1Y (or 1Y is only worth 1X). Both individuals can be made better off if each acquires some of the good he values more highly from the other. For example, if B gives 1X to A in exchange for 2Y, B moves to $T_B$ and A to $T_A$ (where $T_A$ and $T_B$ represent transaction or trade points).

B would have been willing to accept anything over 1Y (to induce him to give up an X) and in fact receives 2Y. Figure 2.1 does not explicitly imply that points $T_B$ and $T_A$ will be the trades actually negotiated. It does not definitely state what exchange prices will be agreed upon, but the trades will take place in the direction of the arrows, and the price will be somewhere between 1Y and 3Y for the traded X. Any price (in terms of Y) between these limits will result in both A and B becoming better off (moving to a higher indifference curve). As they trade, their marginal evaluations come closer to each other. A's MRS declines from 3:1 of X for Y and B's MRS rises from its original 1:1 ratio. Trading continues until no further mutual gains are possible, that is until their respective MRSs are equal (at 2:1 in this instance).

So under condition 1:

$$MRS^A_{XY} = MRS^B_{XY} \qquad (1)$$

By analogous reasoning (Figures 2.1c and 2.1d replicate Figures 2.1a and 2.1b, the only alternation is in the labelling, and the diagrams now show production isoquants not indifference curves):

$$MRS^X_{KL} = MRS^Y_{KL} \qquad (2)$$

If this condition did not hold then an appropriate reallocation of capital and labour could increase the output of both X and Y. In this case increasing the capital devoted to production of X (with a corresponding reduction in the amount devoted to Y) while increasing the labour devoted to Y (and reducing the amount involved in producing X) would lift the outputs of X and Y above the levels shown by the isoquants to (for example) $T_x$ and $T_y$, respectively.

Finally condition 3 states:

$$MRS_{XY} = MRT_{YX} \qquad (3)$$

This holds when the (community's) indifference curve has the same slope as the (economy's) production possibility frontier, as in Figure 2.1e. (A community indifference curve is a line joining points where all members of society have unchanged levels of utility or satisfaction.) For example, if the amount of X that *any* consumer would be prepared to forgo to obtain $1Y(MRS_{XY})$ is, say, 3X, then this marginal valuation is greater than the amount of X that must be given up to produce $1Y(MRT_{XY})$, say 1X, and so it would be worthwhile to reallocate resources to produce 1Y. 1X would be removed from a consumer, and an additional 1Y would be produced. That 1Y would be traded with a (different) consumer for 3X, the original consumer would be returned his 1X and the remaining 2X could be distributed among some or all of the community. A Pareto improvement would have occurred. Conversely, if $MRS_{XY} < MRT_{YX}$, it would be Pareto optimal to transfer resources from Y to X.

We have now established the three basic conditions which underlie Paretian economic efficiency. These conditions hold in the particular market structure of perfect competition.

## 2.2  PERFECT COMPETITION AND PARETO OPTIMALITY

Given the equilibrium of perfect competition, the three Pareto optimum conditions hold. This is shown in the following figures. Figure 2.2a shows the familiar situation where one consumer allocates his budget optimally between two goods, Y and X, each of which have given prices. Consumer equilibrium and utility maximization occur at the point of tangency where:

$$MU_X/MU_Y = MRS_{XY} = P_X/P_Y \qquad (4)$$

Analogously a producer of a given product, with two inputs at given prices, will minimize production costs for a given output (or maximize output for a given total cost) at the point of tangency shown in Figure 2.2b where:

$$MP_K/MP_L = MRS_{KL} = P_K/P_L \qquad (5)$$

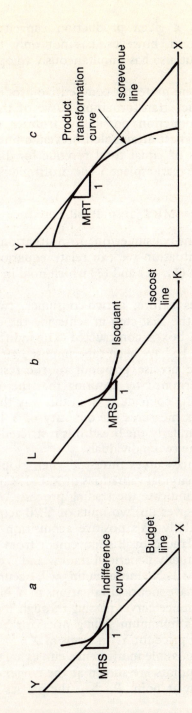

*Figure 2.2*

A two-good producer with a given production capacity in a perfectly competitive situation, however, has not only to mix resource inputs optimally, but also has simultaneously to optimize his output mix.

Figure 2.2c, relating to one perfectly competitive producer of X and Y, shows the product transformation curve of the firm (which is akin to the production possibility frontier of the economy) and the firm's highest attainable isorevenue line. (The isorevenue line joints points of equal total revenue for different mixes of Y and X sold on the marketplace.) The profit-maximizing position is where:

$$MC_X/MC_Y = MRT_{YX} = P_X/P_Y \qquad (6)$$

If we now move from the one-consumer/one-firm situation to the multi-consumer/multi-firm situation we can relate equations (4), (5) and (6) to the equations (1), (2) and (3) which hold in Pareto optimality.

For simplicity assume, as before, a two-consumer, two-firm situation. Figure 2.3 shows the first step in achieving the desired result. A Bowley–Edgeworth box is constructed. The indifference curves of Figures 2.1a and 2.1b have been superimposed after first swivelling B's by 180°. The precise positions of the respective origins $O_A$ and $O_B$ are determined by ensuring that the original endowment points $E_A$ and $E_B$ coincide at E. In this way the total height of the Edgeworth box measures the quantity of Y held in aggregate by A and B, and similarly the breadth is restricted to the limited total of Xs held by the two individuals.

At E, since the indifference curves intersect, their slopes and hence their $MRS_S$ and the marginal valuations of X and Y held by A and B differ. The arrows indicate the trading process. When A moves from $Y_A$ to $Y'_A$ and gives up two units of Y, B acquires a corresponding amount. Similarly, A's positive acquisition of 1X from B is exactly counterbalanced by B's movement from $X_B$ to $X'_B$. T will be a point of mutually beneficial trading and is equivalent to $T_A$ and $T_B$ in Figure 2.1. No more trading will occur since, at this point, both A and B have identical valuations of Y in terms of X. Their respective indifference curves passing through T will be tangential to each other. A's minimum selling price for Y is the same as B's maximum buying price for Y (in terms of X).

In Figure 2.4a a series of possible indifference curves are shown for A and B. Possible trade points are shown at the tangencies. If initial endowments had been at point P, then the parties would

*Figure 2.3*

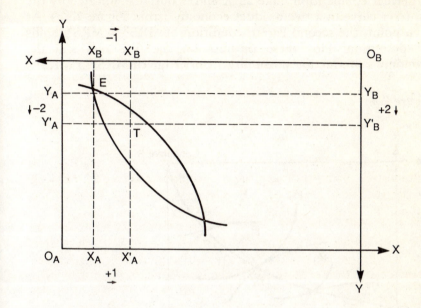

have exchanged and traded to end up between curves $I_1^B$ and $I_2^A$. In fact, they would trade until they arrived somewhere on the line segment RS. This line is the contract curve and is drawn in such a way that it connects all points of tangency between indifference curves, that is all points of equal marginal rates of substitution. That is, in perfectly competitive equilibrium, not only is equation (4) satisfied but so also is equation (1), the first required condition of Pareto optimality.

In like manner Figure 2.4b is a Bowley–Edgeworth box constructed from Figures 2.1c and 2.1d for two producers (one of X and one of Y) or for a two-division firm (one producing X and one Y). Capital and labour will be reallocated between the producers (or divisions) until the aggregate outputs of X and Y are above the original totals indicated by the endowment points (given that the endowment points, $E_Y$ and $E_X$ were neither originally identical nor on the contract curve). Again, the contract curve joins points of tangency and hence not only is equation (5) satisfied but so also is equation (2), the second required condition for Pareto optimality.

To show that all three required conditions hold simultaneously in perfect competition, take all X and Y outputs indicated by the contract curve in a two-product economy (from Figure 2.4b). At each point, the second Pareto condition of $MRS^X = MRS^Y$ holds by definition. Plot these outputs on the YX axes and the economy's production possibility frontier (given $MRS^X = MRS^Y$)

*Figure 2.4*

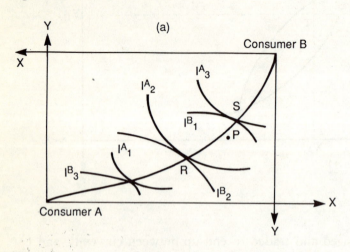

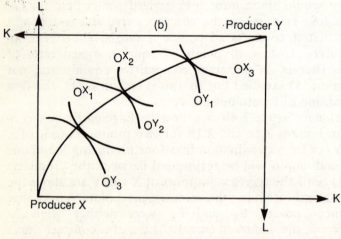

is obtained as in Figure 2.5. Now locate point S where $MRT_{YX} = P_X/P_Y = MC_X/MC_Y$. That is, where equation (6) and the third Pareto condition is satisfied. From point S construct a Bowley–Edgeworth box originating at O for consumers in a two-person economy and find the *unique* point in that box where $MRS^A = MRS^B = P_X/P_Y$. That occurs where the consumer's budget line is parallel to the isorevenue line. Hence at point T all three Pareto conditions hold, the economy's total output of Y and X is indicated by the verticals drawn from S to the axes and these totals are divided between consumers as shown by T in relation to the sides of the Bowley–Edgeworth box.

*Figure 2.5*

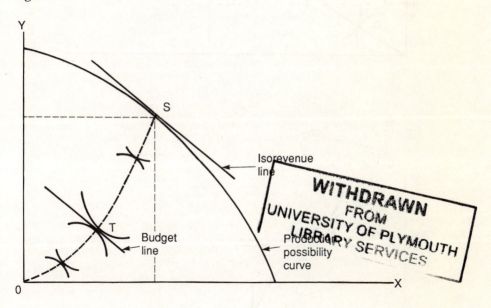

T is certainly Pareto optimal: all three conditions hold but as Figure 2.6 (which is derived from Figure 2.5) shows, not all community indifference curves at S are necessarily tangential to the production possibility frontier. $CIC_C$ and $CIC_D$ are the community indifference curves relating to the output distributions associated with points C and D, respectively. Both pass through S

*Figure 2.6*

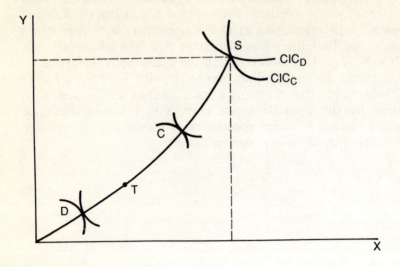

*Figure 2.7*

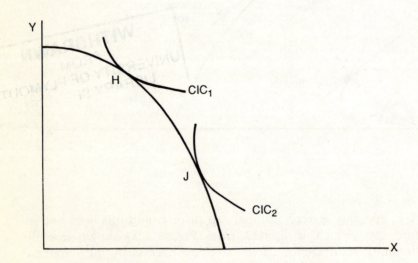

*Figure 2.8*

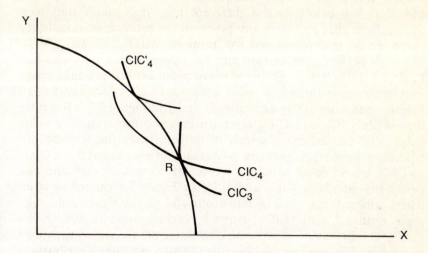

*Figure 2.9*

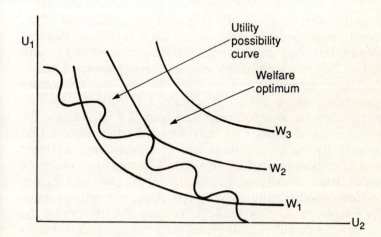

but neither would be tangential to the production possibility curve. Only point T would provide a CIC satisfying all three conditions. But point T is *only* unique given that the output mix of X and Y at S is selected. If a different mix of X and Y had been chosen from that at S then any point on the production possibility curve would have possessed the property $MRT_{YX} = MC_X/MC_Y$ and with perfect competition any such point would have also had $P_X/P_Y = MC_X/MC_Y$. Thus for every point on the product transformation curve there is a point analogous to T which satisfies all Pareto conditions. (For example, H and J in Figure 2.7.) But note that while $CIC_1$ and $CIC_2$ are both Pareto optimal, only a value judgement can ascertain which is 'better', since the welfare distributions implicit in each are different, and movement from $CIC_1$ to $CIC_2$ would make someone worse off, as well as someone else better off. Similarly $CIC_3$ and $CIC_4$ in Figure 2.8 cannot be compared, albeit from $CIC_4$ a move out and to the right could take place until a higher ($CIC_1$) curve is reached compatible with the Pareto conditions of making no one worse off (provided the move is within the production frontier). Only welfare distributions (CICs) where no one is worse off but someone is possibly better off are Pareto comparable.

We now take every point on a given production possibility frontier which satisfies the Pareto conditions (e.g. H, J and R in Figures 2.7 and 2.8). We select only those points which also maximize consumer welfare or utility (e.g. at $CIC_1$, $CIC_2$ and $CIC_3$, respectively). Bear in mind that these CICs represent Paretian optimal conditions but do so under differing income and wealth distributions. The resulting utility values for two persons, 1 and 2, in a two-person economy can be used to plot the economy's utility possibility curve shown in Figure 2.9. A social welfare function can then be superimposed on Figure 2.9 to indicate the point where societal welfare is maximized. Each point on that curve satisfies Paretian conditions and each represents different allocations of consumption decisions and of factors of production. The function itself, illustrated graphically by $W_1$, $W_2$ and $W_3$ can be represented algebraically as $W = f(U_1, U_2)$; but only if some subjective judgement is first made as to how the utilities of the two individuals should be weighted can the graphical values actually be plotted. Figure 2.9 makes such a hypothetical value judgement. The utility possibility curve, however, which was only the penultimate step, is as far as marginal analysis can take us.

Some philosophers have attempted to give normative social

*Figure 2.10*

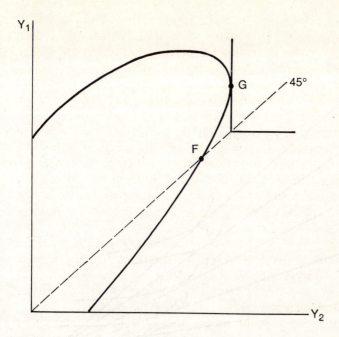

answers which go beyond this penultimate stage. Egalitarians, for example, if confronted with an income possibility curve in a two-person economy as in Figure 2.10 (and given identical cardinal utility functions for both individuals) would allocate incomes equally as at point F. More recent philosophers such as John Rawls would apply a 'maximin criterion of social justice' so that incomes would be allocated in such a way that the least well off (for whatever reason) received maximum benefit (as at point G).[1] Neither of these points, of course, need maximize the sum of $Y_1$ plus $Y_2$ which could be above and to the left of G. Thus a still higher income for 1, the more monetarily productive individual, could induce him to devote less of his time to leisure and more to income-generation. Total income would then rise provided only the lower incentive to work for individual 2 results in a reduction of $Y_2$ smaller than the increase in $Y_1$.

Figure 2.11 shows how one individual can allocate his time between work and leisure. Given a 24-hour day and that people prefer leisure to work then income is required to compensate for

*Figure 2.11*

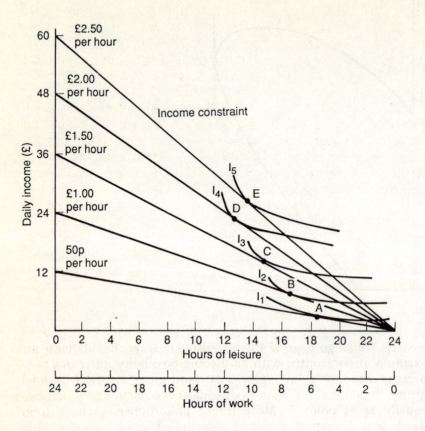

labour services provided (i.e. for leisure forgone). The extent to which the individual is prepared to trade off the one against the other is given by the shape and position of the indifference curves. The straight lines assume a perfectly competitive labour market at five alternative wage rates of 50p, £1 (and so on) to £2.50 per hour. Each originates at the extreme of the abcissa (only 24 hours can be worked in a day). For any number of hours worked the individual's income can be derived from these lines. Thus at point A, given a 50p rate six hours would be worked and £3 earned, at C at £1.50 ten hours would be worked and £15 earned, and so on. Points A–E if plotted against the wage rate would provide the individual's labour supply curve. As can be seen, after D such a curve would be backward-bending indicating a lower quantity of labour supplied as the wage rate rose. This, of course, is apparently contrary to the first law of demand, namely that as the price of a good falls the quantity demanded will rise. Here as the price of leisure falls (the hourly wage given up by working) the hours of leisure 'bought' also fall, at least between E and D. The reason, of course, is that Figure 2.11 has not disaggregated the income and substitution effects. If income had been held constant then a falling leisure price would invariably have resulted in more leisure being consumed.

This complication is not of consequence to this discussion. It need merely be noted that not only does a consumer allocate his income between goods but he also allocates his time between income earning and leisure. Thus we know in a two-good world

$$MU_X/MU_Y = MRS_{XY} = P_X/P_Y \qquad (4)$$

but we can also now state that in consumer equilibrium

$$MU_I/MU_L = MRS_{IL} = P_I/P_L \qquad (7)$$

where I is income, L is leisure and the 'price' of income and of leisure is the wage rate.[2] Leisure is simply another commodity, so for the last pound spent on all goods in a multi-good world the consumer will, in perfectly competitive Pareto optimality allocate his income and his labour services such that

$$MU_X = MU_Y = MU_L \ldots = MU_n \qquad (8)$$

Any monopoly power in the system shifts it away from Pareto optimality with resulting inefficiencies. This is explained by the fact that departures from perfectly competitive behaviour by firms may violate the three conditions of Pareto optimality as follows:

1.  If a firm has sufficient market power to charge differing prices for the same product then since each consumer equates his own MU/P ratios between all goods these ratios will differ between individuals and arbitrage between consumers would make all parties better off (i.e. equation 3 is violated).
2.  Similarly a larger firm may have 'buying power' in input markets such that it can influence the price for inputs *vis-à-vis* competitors. But since each firm sets each of its MP/P ratios equal in order to minimize costs it follows that the MP/P ratios differ between firms and hence products. Reallocation of resources between firms would consequently raise total product, by shifting inputs from firms with lower marginal productivity to those with higher marginal productivities (equation (2) is unfulfilled).
3.  Finally, restating equation (3), we have $P_X/MC_X = P_Y/MC_Y$. Only in perfect competition will these ratios hold across all goods and then those ratios must be unity (i.e. $P = MC$). The reason is that in perfect competition firms will produce until $P = MC$ and if any market departs from such a state the ratios will be unequal. It would then pay to reallocate resources from industries where the ratio P/MC is lower to where it is higher.

From this framework of Paretian optimality industrial organization theorists have developed what is called the structure/conduct/performance (or SCP) paradigm. The standard neo-classical market structure model stretches from monopoly through oligopoly and monopolistic competition. In perfectly competitive equilibrium each transaction price equals marginal cost and allocative efficiency obtains.

The importance of price derives from the Marshallian theory of value and the idea of consumer surplus. These rest on the basic postulate of demand that the lower the price of the good, the more of it any group of consumers will purchase. The demand function contains information about the value customers attach to their use of the good in question. As the price is lowered either existing consumers increase consumption and/or new consumers commence to purchase the good for the first time.

In a system where the concept of consumers' sovereignty is meaningful the demand curve for a good shows the net social benefits which can be obtained from consumption of that good (geometrically these are represented by the consumer surplus triangle). At the margin market price is the reservation price of the marginal consumer. It is that price just low enough to overcome his reservations about purchasing an extra unit. It indicates in monetary terms how much an incremental unit is worth to him. (In equilibrium, price = marginal utility, provided marginal utility is modified by dividing it by the marginal utility of money.)

What distinguishes perfect competition from monopoly and monopolistic competition? The unique answer is that only in perfect competition is price equated with marginal cost. In addition, in perfect competition price equals average cost and does so at a minimum. Thus there are no supra-normal profits and the output level is where productive efficiency is maximized. But equity (in terms of an absence of monopoly or supra-normal profits) is also present in the Chamberlinian tangency situation; and it is possible for a monopolist to construct a plant which has a short-run average cost curve tangential to the horizontal portion of an L-shaped or flat-bottomed U-shaped long-run average cost curve, and so operate at optimal size. Figure 2.12 illustrates these three alternatives. The only *unique* attribute of perfect competition is P = MC.

Why, to cite Scherer, is the condition of P > MC the 'basis of the economist's most general condemnation of monopoly'? How does it lead to 'an allocation of resources which is inefficient in the sense of satisfying consumer wants with less than maximum effectiveness'? Consider Figure 2.13 where the only two industries in a hypothetical economy are depicted. X is a monopoly, Y is perfectly competitive. (The axes scales for X and Y are not identical.)[3]

If a price of £10 is charged for a unit of X (profit-maximizing MR = MC) only 2 million units will be produced. Consumers who consider a unit of X is worth £9.99 but no more than that will be excluded from the market. But such an extra unit worth £9.99 can be produced with resources costing only £5. That is, marginal social value exceeds marginal social costs, and this inequality would continue through to an output of 4 million units where P = MC.

Given full employment, the resources necessary to produce an extra unit of X must come from industry Y. In Y output is 50 million units, price is £4. Now transfer an insignificant but positive amount of resources from Y to X, say £20 in monetary terms. Four extra units of X would be produced for £5 per unit and sold

*Figure 2.12*

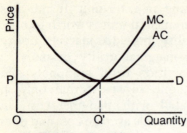

(a) Perfect competition
   P = MC
   P = AC
   Q at minimum AC

*Figure 2.13*

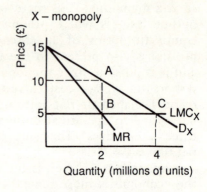

X – monopoly

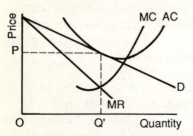

(b) Monopolistic competition
   P > MC
   P = AC
   Q < minimum AC

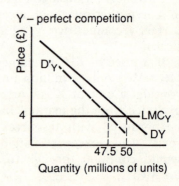

Y – perfect competition

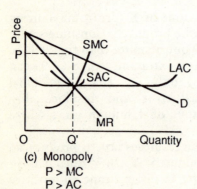

(c) Monopoly
   P > MC
   P > AC
   Q at minimum AC

for (say) £9.99. A social gain of $(4 \times £9.99) - £20 = £19.96$ would be realized in X. In Y five units would be forgone due to the £20 reduction in resources. Y's price might have to be raised to £4.01 to avoid the presence of unsatisfied willing buyers at a selling price of £4. A social cost of $(5 \times £4.01) - £20 = £0.05$ would be incurred in Y. A net social gain of £19.91 would be realized by this transfer of resources from Y towards X.

Thus in a situation like Figure 2.13 there is inefficient allocation of resources. Too few are being utilized by the monopolist and too many by the perfect competitor. If X can be transformed in some way into a perfectly competitive industry this inefficiency would cease to exist. If the profits to be made in X attract entrepreneurs from Y resources will be shifted from Y to X. The price of X will fall to clear the increased output. $D_Y$ will be shifted down and to the left to $D^1_Y$ as a result of the substitution effect (some people now buy X who previously bought Y). £10 million of resources will shift to X in order to increase output from X (as valued by consumers) by £10 million $(4 \times 2.5$ million), resulting in a net social gain of ABC, the original deadweight loss which resulted from the monopolistic behaviour of industry X.

After this point a resource transfer in either direction will represent a net loss to society.


## 2.3  POLICY ALTERNATIVES

The SCP paradigm and the resulting misallocation problems it apparently highlights gives rise to several possible policy alternatives which could be aimed at correcting any apparent sub-optimal situation. For example, *should government edict compel the existence of perfect competition*? The apparent answer would be in the affirmative (if optimal resource allocation is the objective of society). Our discussion of perfect competition would seem to indicate that it results in an optimal pricing pattern provided it holds in each and every industry. The actual answer should probably (indeed almost certainly) be negative. One main reason is that in many countries scale economies are present and over a range larger firms have lower costs than smaller. Then monopoly or oligopoly may more closely approximate the 'ideal' (i.e. social welfare maximization) than would perfect competition.

Consider Figure 2.14 where economies of scale are reflected in the lower level of a constant cost function. DD is the industry

*Figure 2.14*

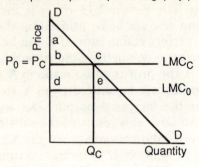

Competitive price equal to oligopoly price

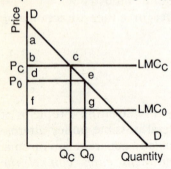

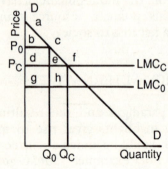

Competitive price above oligopoly price  Competitive price below oligopoly price

demand curve for a homogeneous product. $LMC_0$ is the minimum attainable long-run average and marginal cost curve. Assume it can only exist when firms are so large that the industry is oligopolistic. $LMC_c$ is the equivalent cost schedule if the industry was atomistic in structure and perfectly competitive in behaviour.[4] $P_c$ is the price which would rule in the latter conditions. $P_0$ can conceivably be the same as, lower than, or higher than the competitive ($P = MC$) price. These three alternatives are indicated in Figure 2.14.

When $P_c = P_0$, consumer surplus is abc for either market structure. The consumer is as well off under either, but the producer is better off by profits amounting to bcde. Unless the object of government is simply to punish producers, there is no reason to compel perfect competition. Society would lose by such a change in industrial structure. Society consists of both customers and producers. When price under oligopoly is below $LMC_c$ then consumers' surplus increases to ade from abc and producers' surplus rises from zero to defg. Again it is hard to justify compulsion of perfect competition. The third case is more complex, however. When prices under oligopoly are higher than $P_c$ even though costs are lower we have what Williamson (1968) termed the trade-off case. Consumer surplus would be larger under competition by an amount equal to bcdef, but profits are larger under oligopoly by amount bcgh. Under oligopoly, in overall social terms the amount bcde cancels; it is gained by producers and lost by consumers. The amount abc is common to both situations. The overall issue is whether the sum of 'net' profits due to technical efficiency under oligopoly is greater than the resulting deadweight allocative loss. The trade-off is degh against cef. Before recommending perfect competition this trade-off must be made even though price is assumed higher than marginal cost would be in an atomistic situation.

Even in this latter instance, a negative answer to our original question may have to be given. Williamson's trade-off theory, as McGee (1971) has pointed out, ignores entry. Provided that entry to the industry is not barred, any firm which can achieve cost conditions of $LMC_c$ will be attracted to enter the industry if price is $P_0$. This will ultimately force price down from $P_0$ to $P_c$. In the short run the size of cef will be reduced, making the trade-off appear more favourable. In the long run cef will be eliminated completely leaving only the two cases of $P_c = P_0$ or $P_c > P_0$.

A second policy option would be to encourage the practice of *pricing at long-run marginal cost*. This may be both a more practical and a more meaningful solution than to ask whether or not the fragmented industrial structure of perfect competition should be fostered everywhere in the economy. The main attraction of perfect competition is, after all, not its atomistic structure but its outcome, P = MC. Moreover, if industries are not permitted to take advantage of scale economies, the result, as we have seen, is that scarce social resources, which could have been used elsewhere, are diverted towards producing commodities at a higher cost than is necessary.

At least two problems arise with this option. First, there is the difficulty of how to recoup total costs from the marketplace when scale economies have still to be exhausted. Second, there is the problem of non-allocable joint costs which must also somehow be recouped from the market but which cannot be attributed directly to any particular product.

Figure 2.15 is the standard model used to show the optimal price and output position for a decreasing cost industry. With plant size $SAC_1$, pricing at SMC results in a profit-earning $P_1 Q_1$ price–output combination. But SMC > LMC at $P_1 Q_1$ and economic welfare will only be maximized when investment takes place and a plant size with a cost structure of $SAC_2$ is attained.[5] Then P = AMC = LMC, but although welfare is then maximized the firm is making a loss. Subsidies and two-part tariffs are practical methods which have been suggested by which industries can meet such deficits. Inevitably, however, such techniques also distort resource allocation. Marginal consumers may be deterred by a flat fee at the margin although quite willing to pay their reservation price. Equity may be disturbed unless those subsidized also contribute the tax revenue from which the subsidy is paid. The ideal solution (if it were costless to implement) is for each person to pay the same price at the margin (P = MC) and for the deficit to be made up by each consumer somehow accepting a share of it according to the valuation he places on intra-marginal units as indicated by the consumer's surplus of his own unique demand curve. This whole topic has spawned a proliferation of literature. None of the various practical 'solutions' to the problem, however, approaches the apparent ideal of a perfectly competitive equilibrium. This problem is unique to decreasing-cost industries.

The second problem — that of common costs — is similar in complexity and is present in virtually all productive activity. The price of any product must exceed its marginal cost of production in order to contain its own assignable overhead costs and also that

*Figure 2.15*

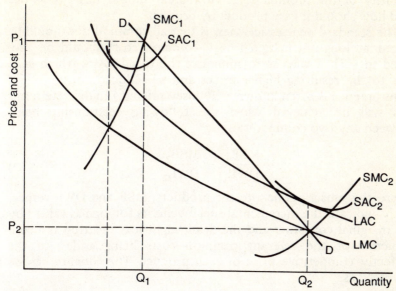

*Figure 2.16*

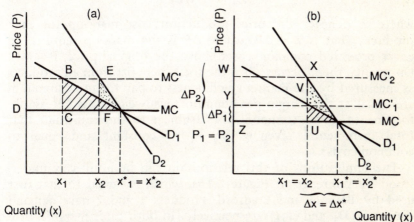

Demand curves for products with differing price elasticities.
(Price set to reflect differing mark-ups.)

Note: Price are set so that:

$$ABCD + AEFD = WXUZ + YVUZ$$

i.e. so that total incremental revenue equals common costs.

portion of common costs allocated to it both apportioned over the quantity of the product sold. How great should this excess be? And how should it vary product by product?

The standard neoclassical view is that all commodities should be priced at long-run marginal cost, common costs should be allocated in such a way as to minimize the social losses which arise due to the resulting higher prices and so reduced consumption. (This practice is often known as Ramsey pricing.) In discrete terms this will be achieved when the following relationship holds between any two commodities:

$$\frac{MSB_1}{DWL_1} = \frac{MSB_2}{DWL_2} \qquad (9)$$

where the subscripts denote the products, MSB and DWL respectively indicate the incremental social benefits forgone as valued by the marginal consumer and the deadweight loss incurred as a consequence of the relevant common costs being added to the perfectly competitive price of each product. The equality can be rewritten as:

$$\frac{Z_1}{Z_2} = \frac{DWL_1}{DWL_2}$$

where Z denotes the price–production cost mark-up for each product. That is $Z = \Delta P$, where $\Delta P$ is the mark-up required to cover pro-rated common costs above the original price, $P = MC$. Optimality then, occurs when the social benefits from all products as measured by the market's willingness to pay the price premium are equal at the margin per pound of deadweight loss necessarily forgone to cover common costs (subject to the constraint that total incremental revenue, $\Sigma_{i=1}^2 R_i$, is constant and equal to common costs).

The implications of this relationship can be intuitively understood by reference to Figure 2.16a, which is similar to that first used by Baumol and Bradford. Products 1 and 2 have demand curves, $D_1 D_1$ and $D_2 D_2$ respectively. In both cases marginal production costs equal MC. If the share of common costs allocated to each product is the same then MC rises to $MC_1$ and the original competitive output levels of $x_1{}^* = x_2{}^*$ fall to $x_1$ and $x_2$. The respective deadweight losses are given by the shaded and by the dotted regions. It is clear that minimization of the aggregate deadweight losses implies that products with a relatively price-elastic demand should bear a relatively smaller share of common costs than those with an inelastic demand, other things equal.

Prices should be set in such a way that the proportionate change in output from the original competitive levels should be the same for all products, irrespective of market size. This can be shown diagrammatically at the expense only of some generalization. Figure 2.16b is restricted to the same two-product case, and equivalent competitive output levels of $x_1^* = x_2^*$ and MC levels of $P_1 = P_2$ are assumed. Total incremental revenue required to cover common costs, $\Sigma_{i=1}^{2} R_i$, is ABCD + AEFD (as indicated in Figure 2.16a). In the optimal situation $\Sigma_{i=1}^{2} R_i$ must be constant and equation (1) satisfied. Thus ABCD + AEFD must equal WXUZ + YVUD in Figure 2.16b. Clearly, the sum of the dead-weight losses (the dotted plus the shaded triangles) is less in Figure 2.16b. No other pricing policy would result in a smaller aggregate deadweight loss. It can readily be inferred that the optimal allocation of common costs is such that $P_1$ and $P_2$ should be raised by $\Delta P_1$ and $\Delta P_2$ respectively, and output should be reduced by the equal proportions $\Delta x = \Delta x^*$.

To prove this, assume that the price elevations are sufficiently small so that elasticities are constant over the relevant range. Then:

$$DWL_1 = \tfrac{1}{2}\Delta P_1 \cdot \Delta x_1 \qquad (10)$$

But elasticity of demand for product 1, $e_1 = P_1 \cdot \Delta x_1 / x_1^* \cdot \Delta P_1$. So:

$$\Delta P_1 = P_1 \Delta x_1 / x_1^* e_1 \qquad (11)$$

Now substitute (4) in (3):

$$DWL_1 = \tfrac{1}{2}(P_1 \Delta x_1^2)/x_1^* e_1 \qquad (12)$$

A similar expression can be calculated for $DWL_2$. Now insert into the optimality requirements (2) and we obtain:

$$\frac{Z_1}{Z_2} = \frac{P_1 \Delta x_1^2 x_2^* e_2}{P_2 \Delta x_2^2 x_1^* e_1} = \frac{e_2}{e_1} \qquad (13)$$

This result, $Z_1/Z_2 = e_2/e_1$, the 'inverse elasticity formula', confirms the implication arrived at earlier, that the more inelastic the demand for the product, the greater should be the percentage deviation from marginal cost. To cite Baumol and Bradford (1970) the price of each product should be set so that 'its percentage deviation from marginal costs is inversely proportional to the item's price elasticity of demand'.

This socially optimal pricing rule would be difficult for any regulatory agency to follow. The informational requirements are too exacting, and the precise cost and demand schedules for all products cannot be known to the authorities. Without such information, attempts at imposing optimal pricing behaviour would be futile. Even if those data were available it is doubtful if any quasi-political pricing body with discretionary power would employ them in the optimal manner. High-demand elasticity generally means ready availability of substitutes. Low-demand elasticity, conversely, tends to mean that people who want a certain product have few alternatives available to them and/or regard the product as a 'necessity'. When this is the case they would be likely to raise considerable and vocal objections to a relatively high price for such a product. The political mechanism works in such a way that overt pressure group objections of this kind tend to be deferred to, irrespective of their overall social merits.

In short, where there is (and in reality there always is) market failure and government failure the issue crystallizes around which form of organization is the least bad.[6]

How does the (imperfect) market react to situations of the kind under discussion, namely the recovery of joint costs? An unregulated profit-maximizing firm will adopt a pricing scheme at least qualitatively similar to the socially optimal one. In the short run overhead costs will be regarded by the firm as sunk, and the firm will then set MR = MC for all products. Given that $MR_i = P_i(1 + 1/e_i)$ for any product i, where $P_i$ is selling price including mark-up and given that $Z_i = (P_i - MC_i)/MC_i$ then with profit-maximization:

$$MR = MC$$

So

$$P(1 + \frac{1}{e}) = \frac{P - MC}{Z} = \frac{P - MR}{Z}$$

and

$$\frac{P(1 + e)}{e} = \left[ \frac{P - P(1 + e)}{e} \right] / Z$$

cancelling and multiplying through by e we have

$$1 + e = -1/Z$$

Thus in a two-product profit-maximizing firm, prices are set so that for products 1 and 2:

$$\frac{1 + e_1}{1 + e_2} = \frac{Z_2}{Z_1} \tag{14}$$

which is certainly different from but not dissimilar to equation (13).

If one could assume that a central authority sets prices according to inverse elasticities, firms might still not behave in an optimal manner. The reason is that recoupment of common overhead costs would be guaranteed *ex post* by regulation and by the necessary price adjustment. Only if common overhead costs could be predicted in advance and so the constraint $\Sigma_{i=1}^{2} R_i$ predetermined by regulation before outlay would the social optimum be achieved.

Lack of market discipline would then result in a regulated industry incurring unnecessary organizational slack. Overhead costs or corporate perquisites for staff above those required for running the business in the consumer interest would appear. The lesson is not that direct price regulation should be coupled with regulation of the minutiae of management activities. The point is that, even if price regulation were enlightened enough to follow the socially optimal formula, it would create long-run misallocation of overhead expenditures. To the extent that regulation fails to take elasticities into account then the problem is enhanced.

A third policy option is that government should *invoke the rule of proportionality*. Perfect competition is allegedly 'efficient' because, in equilibrium, price equals marginal cost. Yet perfect competition may be undesirable or unattainable because of the need for some industries to be composed of a few firms large enough to reap the benefits of scale economies.

The prime attraction of perfect competition, however, is not its atomistic structure, but rather the P = MC condition. Price equals marginal cost is a condition which in principle could be legally enforced but which in practice would result in inefficiency and equity anomalies in declining cost industries and similar anomalies in industries (almost all?) where common, non-allocable costs are present. One other proposed route out of the theoretical morass and one which would still achieve a similar social optimum to marginal cost pricing is the rule of proportionality. This rule could enable industries or firms to charge a socially optimal price while still covering their costs. Thus for any two goods optimal pricing would require:

$$\frac{P_x}{MC_x} = \frac{P_y}{MC_y} \qquad (15)$$

That this represents a social optimum can be seen by considering actual numbers. Say the relationship is:

$$\frac{10}{5} = \frac{15}{7.5}$$

Then a shift of an insignificant amount of resources in a fully employed two-sector X and Y economy, such as £15 from Y to X will result in a gain of 3 units of X (selling at £10 each) and a loss of 2 units of Y (selling at £15 each). The position cannot be improved by resource reallocation.

Scherer gives two main reasons why this rule would be unworkable in practice. First, the world would have to be composed entirely of non-perfect markets otherwise P = MC would hold in the perfect markets. There is one fundamental market which cannot be rendered imperfect without at least some unacceptable degree of interference with individual liberty and that is the labour–leisure market. Second, the rule of proportionality only holds in an economy where all sales are made to final consumers not to intermediaries or reprocessors. In a complex economy this too is a virtually unattainable prerequisite.

Consider first the leisure market argument. The price of leisure is its opportunity cost. That is, it is the wage forgone in a perfect labour market, or it is that rate plus some premium in an imperfect market. For a situation where all markets are imperfect the price of leisure must be raised above its marginal cost to firms (i.e. the ruling wage rate) to that level where it has the same P:MC ratio as is ruling in all other markets. This could be done if the government gave each member of society a subsidy per wage unit worked in order to raise the opportunity cost (the price) of leisure *vis-à-vis* the wage paid. This is manifestly impractical. But unless it were done leisure's low price would result in too small a supply of labour in a society where the rule of proportionality holds in every other market. Allocative efficiency would not be achieved, GNP would be too small, and too much leisure would be consumed.

Now consider the second obstacle to enforcing the rule of proportionality. In an economy where some sales are not to final customers but are made to intermediaries, then output is not maximized if the P:MC ratio is identical in all markets. For example, say 100 kg of sugar can be produced from beet with

1 hour of labour costing £5. The sugar sells for £10, a P:MC ratio of 2:1. In the brewing industry 1000 litres of beer also require 1 hour of labour costing £5, and 100 kg of sugar to aid fermentation, costing £10. The P:MC rule suggests the beer should be sold for £30. But consumers buy both beer and sugar. Two hours of their labour can produce sugar valued at £20 or beer valued at £30. This suggests that labour should be reallocated away from sugar for final consumption towards beer (which will still require intermediate sugar). In this way the aggregate value of output will be raised, but the rule of proportionality will be violated.

Finally, another policy approach is to ignore market structure and allow pricing freedom but *require firms to maximize profitability subject to a constraint on rate of return*. One model (provided by Stein and Borts, 1971) assumes that the regulatory objective is to bring profits down to the competitive level as indicated by a zero margin above the long-run average costs.

How would a monopoly react if such a constraint were imposed by government? Four plausible alternatives suggest themselves. First, as a parallel to the natural monopoly situation with a subsidy at $P = MC$, the firm might simply raise costs above the minimum efficient level (x-inefficiency and/or some other form of managerial or organizational slack would arise). Second, if the firm operated in markets other than that in which it holds monopoly power, it might reduce its rate of return to near zero in the latter and if it possessed some market power in the former, price its products in such a way that cross-subsidization would enable monopoly rents to be reaped in the firm as a whole, albeit not (apparently) from the monopoly. Third, the firm might keep its return on capital down to the desired level, not by reducing prices and profits, but rather by raising its capital base by inefficiently and unnecessarily using excess or obsolete (and hence high-cost) capital equipment. Finally, and as a variant on this third point, the firm might even operate on its production possibility frontier (that is, at full technological efficiency on the product transformation curve) but be too capital-intensive to permit allocative (i.e. $P = MC$) efficiency.

This is illustrated in Figure 2.17. Consider a firm operating with a capital stock of $K_o$ at $Q_{monopoly}$ where $MR = SMC(K_o) = LMC$ and a cost of capital embodied in the short-run average cost curve SAC(i) equalling i *together with* the relevant gap between D and $SAC_1$. There is no incentive for the firm to expand output at price $P_1$ and profits are duly maximized. The social optimum of $P = MC$

*Figure 2.17*

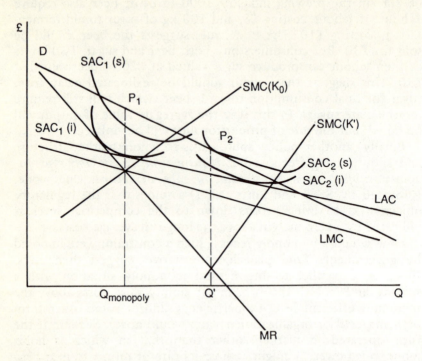

has not been obtained, however; expansion should take place for this to occur. Now impose a return on capital constraint of s per cent where s, although greater than i, must not be exceeded. This has the diagrammatic effect of raising $SAC_1$ to $SAC_1(s)$.

$P_1$ must be reduced since it permits abnormal profits. Abnormal profits only disappear when plant size is raised from $SAC_1$ to $SAC_2$, a capital stock of $K'$ against the original smaller stock of $K_o$. With plant size $SAC_2$, profit-maximizing behaviour results in $SMC(K')$ being equated with MR. Price is $P_2$, output is $Q'$, and the profitability constraint of s per cent is satisfied. Economically, the perceived cost of capital to the firm has been reduced. Originally it was i plus the relevant abnormal profit. After regulation the best available alternative yielded only s. The price of capital is apparently lower, consequently more capital is employed. But at $Q'$, SMC < LMC suggesting that the firm is over-invested in capital equipment. The labour:capital ratio is socially non-optimal. This is so since, if at $Q'$ LMC > SMC, then what is forgone by producing with one extra unit of capital (LMC) is greater than what is forgone by producing with one extra unit of labour (in the short run capital is a fixed input). Alternatively:

| The actual cost of capital divided by its marginal product | $>$ | the price or cost of labour divided by its marginal product |

or symbolically,

$$i/MP_k > W/MP_l$$

where W is the wage rate. Rearranging,

$$MP_k /i < MP_l/W$$

which implies that output could be raised by shifting one pound of resources from capital to labour. Control of the rate of return has resulted in a production technique which is too capital-intensive.

## 2.4 FROM ELEGANCE TO PRAGMATISM

Perfect competition may be undesirable because of the presence of scale economies. Marginal cost pricing appears to capture the benefits of perfect competition without incurring the cost of atomism. But the problems of decreasing cost industries and non-allocable common costs make universal marginal cost pricing an impractical and even an undesirable policy. Pricing in proportion to marginal costs provides results qualitatively similar to marginal cost pricing but this alternative is no less impractical given the presence of some markets which are and will always remain perfectly competitive, and of other markets which are for intermediate goods and not goods for final consumption. Finally we noted that controlling rates of return also resulted in resource misallocations.

Many of these problems were tackled by Lipsey and Lancaster in their theory of the second best. If the first best (P = MC) solutions are unobtainable for the reasons detailed above, then can the relevant function (say GNP) be maximized subject to these constraints? In principle they answer positively. But as Scherer indicates, their 'general solutions are so complex that it is impossible to deduce unambiguously even the direction in which particular controlled prices should be adjusted'.

What then should be the role of the industrial economist when faced with such a counsel of despair? He can abandon the fight and leave the ring to politicians and others with normative, often non-quantifiable goals of national prestige, technological progress, income distribution, more or less socialism, and/or the competing interests of sectional groups of society. Alternatively he can attempt to obtain ever more sophisticated methods of applying marginal cost pricing rules in public utilities, and regulated or nationalized industries. Or he can make a subjective decision based on an assessment of (inconclusive) arguments that either more or less atomism or more or less concentration in industrial structure is a 'good thing'. Or he could search for ways to make economic theory more meaningful to the policy makers, and if this implies some forfeiture of elegance this is a cost he should be prepared to bear. This however, is essentially a long-run solution. In the immediate situation he can possibly only argue that generalized inflexible rules cannot be laid down. Rather, the advice to be given perhaps should be that institutional alternatives be carefully examined on a pragmatic, case-by-case basis and with a modest degree of eclectic agnosticism.

## NOTES

1. John Rawls put this notion forward in *A Theory of Justice* (Harvard University Press, 1981). The underlying rationale is that any individual given Figure 2.1a as depicting possible income distribution levels between himself and the second person in a two-person economy would always select point G on the assumption that he might be person 2.
2. At first glance it may seem impossible to reconcile equations (4) and (7), since equation (7) equals unity, while equation (4) equals $P_X/P_Y$. The paradox is resolved when one recalls that *at the margin, for the last pound spent* on X and Y, $MU_X = MU_Y$.
3. The arguments of this section draw on those elaborated in the first five chapters of F.M. Scherer, *Industrial Structure and Economic Performance* (Rand-McNally, 1970).
4. In strict perfectly competitive theory firms are assumed to be of optimal size, thus the two LMC curves would not be unequal. However, in industries where firms are in fact of optimal size they may then be so few in number that oligopoly obtains and the firms no longer price at MC. To illustrate why or why not a statutory industrial concentration or deconcentration policy is desirable the assumption is made here that the cost curves do differ. In the next sub-section the converse assumption is

made: that firms are permitted to expand to optimal size but are then required to price at (optimal) LMC.
5.   This is so since if at P = SMC and SMC > LMC, then if price is reduced from $P_1$ to $P_2$ and output increased from $Q_1$ to $Q_2$, the marginal social benefits of expansion are equal to $\frac{1}{2}(P_2 + P_1)(Q_2 - Q_1)$ or $\frac{1}{2}(SMC_2 + SMC_1)(Q_2 - Q_1)$, i.e. the short-run marginal costs of expansion. The marginal social costs of expansion are k (incremental capital cost) plus r $(Q_2 - Q_1)$, where r is unit operating costs. The optimal expansion of an industry should continue until marginal social benefits (SMC) equal marginal social costs (LMC).
6.   See also the discussion 'Second best' in section 2.4.

# REFERENCES

Bator, F.M. (1957), 'The Simple Analytics of Welfare Maximisation', *American Economic Review*, 47.

Baumol, W.J. and Bradford, D.F. (1970), 'Optimal Departures from Marginal Cost Pricing', *American Economic Review*, 60.

McGee, J.S. (1971), *In Defence of Industrial Concentration* (New York: Praeger).

Stein, G.L. and Borts, J.H. (1972), 'The Behaviour of the Firm under Regulatory Constraint', *American Economic Review*, 62.

Williamson, O. (1968), 'Economies as an Anti-Trust Defence: The Welfare Trade-Off', *American Economic Review*, 58.

# 3. The SCP Rationale and Obstacles to its Application

## 3.1 THE SCP PARADIGM

Perfectly competitive equilibrium is a state where an apparent form of socially optimal behaviour by firms exists. The situation may in reality be undesirable or unattainable but it has the virtue of a tractable and readily comprehensible theoretical base. In diagrammatic form it implies the following:

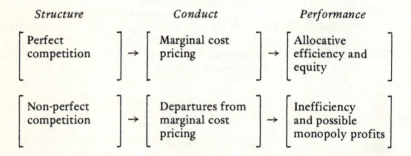

It is but a small step from a model of this kind to argue that monopoly profits will increase the more concentrated is the market. Bain (1951) was among the first to spell out this relationship explicitly. He argued that successful collusion between firms would approach or result in joint profit-maximization. The ability to collude would increase with concentration and so, other things being equal, monopoly profit rates could be expected to increase with concentration as collusion became progressively more successful.

In essence the SCP paradigm implies that the closer an industry is to a multi-firm structure, where firm demand is infinitely elastic and where firms cannot collude to mimic their presumed conduct in more concentrated oligopoly settings where some degree of control over price exists, then the 'better' is the social performance of the firm and industry in marginal cost/pricing terms. Conversely, as numbers of firms decrease, as collusion becomes more probable, and as demand becomes less elastic the less close will industry and firm behaviour be to the $P = MC$ ideal. The paradigm is not restricted to the polar extremes of monopoly and perfect competition.

What we have not yet done, except by implication, is formally to explain the linkages between the attributes of competition theory and the SCP paradigm.

To demonstrate this analytically we shall examine two cases:

1. The situation where number of competing firms alone is of crucial importance.
2. The situation where numbers are not relevant but where beliefs about the ease of collusion between alleged competitors is the matter at issue.

The first case originated with Cournot's theory of oligopoly where each firm (i) believes that others will *not* change their output (q) even if the original firm does alter its output.

Let the industry demand curve be:

$$P = a + bQ \tag{1}$$

where $Q = f(q)$.

Let the profits of firm i be:

$$\pi_i = Pq_i - cq_i \tag{2}$$

where c is constant average (and hence marginal) cost.

Now use the multiplication rule and differentiate

$$\frac{d\pi_i}{dq_i} = \frac{Pdq_i}{dq_i} + \frac{q_i dP}{dq_i} - c = P + q_i\frac{dP}{dq_i} - c = 0 \tag{4}$$

in the profit-maximizing situation.

Now similarly differentiate equation (1) and we have:

$$\frac{dP}{dq_i} = 0 + b\frac{dQ}{dq_i} \tag{5}$$

So by substitution (5) and (1) into (4) we have a profit-maximizing condition of:

$$\frac{d\pi_i}{dq_i} = a + bQ + bq_i\frac{dQ}{dq_i} - c = 0 \qquad (6)$$

Now given the Cournot assumption that i believes others will not change output if he does then any change in Q (i.e. dQ) = $dq_i$ so $dQ/dq_i = 1$. Thus:

$$\frac{d\pi_i}{dq_i} = a + bQ + bq_i - c = 0 \qquad (7)$$

for firm i in the profit-maximizing situation.

So for all n firms the industry's profit-maximizing situation can be established by multiplying equation (7) by n. Hence:

$$
\begin{aligned}
&\quad bQn + bQ = n(c - a)\\
\Rightarrow\;&\quad bQ(n + 1) = n(c - a)\\
\Rightarrow\;&\quad Q = n(c - a)/(n + 1)b \qquad (8)
\end{aligned}
$$

But recall $\qquad\qquad P = a + bQ \qquad (1)$

so by substitution of (8) into (1):

$$
\begin{aligned}
P &= a + n(c - a)/(n + 1)\\
&= a + (nc - an)/(n + 1)\\
&= (an + a + nc - an)/(n + 1)\\
&= (a + nc)/(n + 1)
\end{aligned}
$$

Now since $P = MC = c$ in perfect competition, and since $n = 1$ in monopoly, then in the former:

$$
\begin{aligned}
&\quad (P =) c = (a + nc)/(n + 1)\\
\Rightarrow\;&\quad cn + c = a + nc\\
\Rightarrow\;&\quad c = a(=P)
\end{aligned}
$$

While in monopoly:

$$
\begin{aligned}
P &= (a + 1.c)/(n + 1)\\
&= (a + c)/2
\end{aligned}
$$

So as n changes from 1 to infinity and market structures from monopoly to perfect competition price falls from $(a + c)/2$ to c where $(a + c)/2$ is the monopoly price.[1]

Thus on this view the number of firms in an industry (which is one aspect of structure) is clearly important. As numbers fall price rises from MC to the level where MR = MC. Numbers are not the *only* issue, however. The degree of inter-firm collusion and the firm's demand elasticity can also influence pricing behaviour.

If the Cournot assumption (that each firm assumes all other firms maintain output constant in the face of its own output changes) is dropped then the output of other firms, $Q_i$, will change as $q_i$ changes. The profit equation for firm i can then be written thus:

$$\pi_i = Pq_i - C(q_i) \qquad (9)$$

where $P = f(q_i, Q_i)$ and $C = g(q_i)$.

To find the profit-maximizing conditions equation (9) is differentiated with respect to $q_i$ and set equal to zero in the normal fashion. Thus:

$$P\frac{\delta\pi_i}{\delta q_i} = P\frac{\delta q_i}{\delta q_i} + q_i \times \left\{\begin{array}{l}\text{derivative of p} \\ \text{with respect to } q_i\end{array}\right\} - \frac{\delta C}{\delta q_i} = 0 \qquad (10)$$

Equation (10) was derived using the multiplication rule, but p, the industry price, is a function not only of $q_i$, but also of $Q_i$, which in its turn is a function of $q_i$. So from the chain or function of a function rule of differentiation

$$\frac{\delta\pi_i}{\delta q_i} = p + q_i\left(\frac{\delta p}{\delta q_i}\frac{\delta q_i}{\delta q_i} + \frac{\delta p}{\delta Q_i}\frac{\delta Q_i}{\delta q_i}\right) - \frac{\delta C}{\delta q_i} = 0 \qquad (11)$$

$$= p + q_i\left(\frac{\delta p}{\delta q_i} + \frac{\delta p}{\delta Q_i}\frac{\delta Q_i}{\delta q_i}\right) - \frac{\delta C}{\delta q_i} = 0 \qquad (12)$$

where $\delta Q_i/\delta q_i$ reflects dropping of Cournot assumptions and indicates i's beliefs about rivals' reactions.

$$\Rightarrow \frac{p - c_i}{p} = -\frac{q_i}{p}\left(\frac{\delta p}{\delta q_i} + \frac{\delta p}{\delta Q_i}\frac{\delta Q_i}{\delta q_i}\right) \qquad (13)$$

where $c = MC = \delta C/\delta q_i$

$$\Rightarrow \frac{p - c_i}{p} = -\frac{q_i}{Q}\left(\frac{Q}{p}\frac{\delta p}{\delta q_i} + \frac{Q}{p}\frac{\delta p}{\delta Q_i}\frac{\delta Q_i}{\delta q_i}\right)$$

$$= S_i(1/\eta + a_i/\eta)$$

$$= \frac{S_i}{\eta}(1 + a_i) \qquad (14)$$

where $S_i$ (= $q_i/Q$) is market share, $\eta$ is elasticity and $a_i$ is the perceived response of rivals. Equation (14) thus provides the firm's profit-maximizing mark-up and does so in terms of its market share, its demand elasticity and the degree to which it can forecast competitive reactions. The *average* industry mark up over marginal cost can be found by taking equation (14) for each firm, weighting it by the relevant market share and summing across firms. Thus for the industry:

$$\frac{p - c}{p} = \Sigma s_i^2 (1 + a_i)/\eta \qquad (15)$$

where $c = \Sigma S_i c_i$ and $\Sigma S_i = 1$ by definition.

$\Sigma S_i^2$ is known as the Herfindahl index (see p. 47) and is a commonly-used measure of market structure and industry concentration. $a_i$, the perception of competitors' responses will be high when there is collusive behaviour and low when collusive behaviour is absent. (If collusion is non-existent, $Q_i$ will not vary with $q_i$, the Cournot case.[2] If collusive behaviour is complete each firm will keep outputs perfectly in alignment proportionately $\delta Q_i$ will equal $\delta q_i$.)

Thus price will exceed marginal costs most when concentration is great, when collusive behaviour is likely and when elasticity is low. Price will equal MC (mark-up will be zero) if the Herfindahl index is zero (indicating an infinitely diffuse market structure as in perfect competition) and/or if elasticity is near infinity (again as in perfect competition). If collusive behaviour is non-existent ($a_i = 0$) as in perfect competition, then the excess of P over MC would be dependent on elasticity and structure alone (the 'numbers matter' case). If $a_i = 0$ and there is a monopoly, $(p - c)/p = 1/\eta$. While with perfect competition $\Sigma S_i^2 = 0$, $(p - c)/p = 0$ and so $p = c$.

The former result, $(p - c)/p = 1/\eta$, is not dependent on numbers, however. Consider any market structure with perfect collusion (each firm changes output in direct proportion to existing shares) then $a_i = Q_i/q_i$ (= $\delta Q_i/\delta q_i$). Thus for *any* market structure:

$$\begin{aligned}
\Sigma S_i^2 (1 + a_i) &= \Sigma S_i^2 (1 + Q_i/q_i) \\
&= \Sigma S_i^2 ([q_i + Q_i]/q_i) \\
&= \Sigma S_i^2 (Q/q_i) \text{ since } q_i + Q_i = Q \\
&= \Sigma S_i^2 (1/s_i) = \Sigma S_i = 1
\end{aligned}$$

so again by substitution in (15) we have $(p - c)/p = 1/\eta$, a situation of successful collusion, analogous to monopoly.

We have now established a conceptual link between firm mark-up, average industry mark-up, competitors' reactions and firm elasticity of demand. Indeed, between equations (14) and (15) we assumed that ith firm and the average firm had the same elasticity, $\eta$. This was not a misleading assumption but it could lead the unwary to equate average or ith firm demand elasticity, $\eta$, with industry demand elasticity, $\eta_m$. The two are different and related to each other by the three variables firm market share ($S_i = q_i/Q$), rivals' anticipated reactions as gauged by their elasticity of supply in response to a price change ($\eta_r = \%\Delta Q_i/\%\Delta P$) and rivals' market share ($S_r = Q_i/Q$).

Figure 3.1 shows intuitively how these variables are connected. A market demand curve and three alternative firm demand lines are shown. If the market and firm curves have the same slope, then rivals are presumed to hold output constant irrespective of price.

*Figure 3.1*

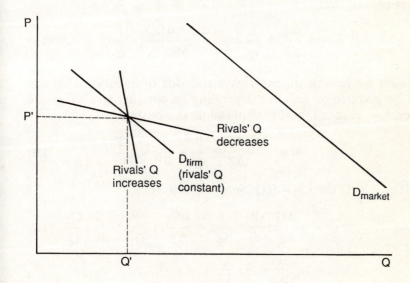

If the firm assumes rivals will expand output at a greater rate than it would in response to any price reduction it initiates then the firm demand curves will have a steeper slope than the market demand · curve. While if the rivals are expected to reduce their output, given a price cut, the firm's demand curve will have a smaller slope than the market demand. Since the reciprocal of slope is part of the elasticity formulae, this explains how $\eta$ and $\eta_m$ are interdependent. The formula for firm elasticity is not simply dependent on slope, however, it also depends on the values of P and Q. Thus the smaller is $S_i$, the greater is $S_r$, and so the further to the left would be $Q^1$ in Figure 3.1.

Formally we say that a firm will profit-maximize where:

$$\frac{P - C}{P} = \frac{1}{\eta} = \frac{S_i}{\eta_m + \eta_r S_r} \qquad (16)$$

That is, we are claiming that firm elasticity of demand

$$= \frac{\eta_m + \eta_r S_r}{S_i} \qquad (17)$$

This is proved thus:

$$\eta = -\frac{\Delta q_i}{\Delta P} \cdot \frac{P}{q_i} = -\frac{(\Delta Q - \Delta Q_i)}{\Delta P} \cdot \frac{P}{q_i} \qquad (18)$$

The first expression on the right-hand side of equation (18) can thus be positive or negative depending on whether rivals increase or decrease output by more than the total industry.

$$\Rightarrow \eta = -\frac{\Delta Q}{\Delta P} \cdot \frac{P}{q_i} + \frac{\Delta Q_i}{\Delta P} \cdot \frac{P}{q_i} \qquad (19)$$

But if $S_i = q_i/Q$ then $q_i = S_i Q$. So by substitution:

$$\eta = -\frac{\Delta Q}{\Delta P} \cdot \frac{P}{Q} \cdot \frac{1}{S_i} + \frac{\Delta Q_i}{\Delta P} \cdot \frac{P}{Q_i} \cdot \frac{1}{S_i} \frac{Q_i}{Q} \qquad (20)$$

$$= \eta_m \frac{1}{S_i} + \eta_r \frac{S_r}{S_i}$$

$$= \frac{\eta_m + \eta_r S_r}{S_i} \qquad \text{QED}$$

Equations (16) and (17) are clearly powerful tools. The first half of equation (16) shows the price:cost mark-up of the firm, but unless the observer has access to corporate accounts or internal market research data enabling him to compute firm elasticity of demand, he cannot make an assessment of the situation. The value of equation (17) is that an outsider can more readily gauge or estimate the variables used, and thus, by an alternative route, arrive at a measure of the gap between price and marginal cost for any given firm.

## 3.2  MEASURES OF STRUCTURE

We have already noted in passing that numbers of firms in an industry, market shares of the firms and other variables are structural variables which may influence conduct. In this section we formally itemize several methods of measuring market or industry structure, discuss their strengths and weaknesses and the problems or ease of operationalizing the concepts.

*Concentration indices* embody, to a greater or lesser extent, information on the numbers of firms operating in an industry or market. One of the commonest of such indices is the *concentration ratio* which measures the percentage of some index of industry size (e.g. sales, assets, employment) which is in the hands of the three (or other number) largest firms. The larger the ratio the more monopolistic is the industry. An alternative is to measure the number of the industry's largest firms which account for a given percentage of industry size. The smaller is this number the more concentrated is the industry.

Such measures fail to indicate the differences in industrial behaviour which can occur as a result of differences in the remaining number of firms in an industry. They do not indicate whether the 'tail' of firms is composed of a few medium-sized firms or a plethora of small ones. In like manner, they do not indicate whether the top firms themselves are of similar size or are composed of one giant and two small firms. These problems can be partially overcome with the use of more information, such as *cumulative share curves*.

Table 3.1 shows the approximate standards given by Bain for concentration in manufacturing industries. The zone of moderate concentration is shown in Figure 3.2, together with three hypothetical cumulative share curves. The curves enable comparisons to

*Table 3.1   Concentration standards for manufacturing industries*

| Percentage of market occupied by the first four firms | Percentage of market occupied by the first eight firms | Degree of concentration |
|---|---|---|
| 75% or more | 90% or more | Very high |
| 65–75% | 85–90% | High |
| 50–65% | 70–85% | Moderately high |
| 35–50% | 45–70% | Moderately low |
| under 35% | under 45% | Low |

*Source:* J.S. Bain, *Industrial Organisation* (John Wiley, 1967), pp. 137–44.

*Figure 3.2   Concentration: cumulative shares*

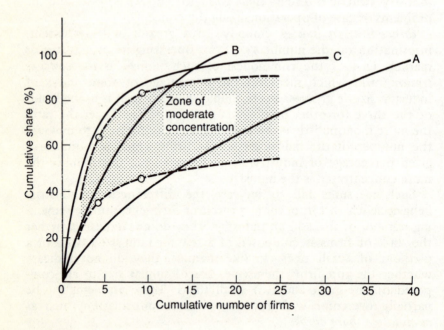

be made between industries (A, B or C) or between different points in time for one industry (where A, B and C are points in time). They show the concentration ratios firm by firm from one through to the total number of firms in the industry. The firms are ranked along the horizontal axis from the largest to the smallest, cumulatively, until the share of all firms (namely 100 per cent) is reached. Clearly B and C are more highly concentrated than A. C is more concentrated than B only at certain levels of numbers of firms (e.g. at the 5- or 10-firm concentration ratios). After 14 firms the situation is reversed; in B the smaller firms have a larger share than in C and there are fewer of them. A would not be regarded as a highly concentrated industry whereas C would; B is moderately concentrated, at least up to the 12-firm level.

An alternative measure of concentration which takes account of the total number of firms in an industry (and hence is called a summary concentration index) is the *Herfindahl concentration ratio*. It focuses on the inequality of firm sizes, or relative concentration, as opposed to the absolute concentration ratios we have looked at so far. It is equal to $(c^2 + 1)/n$, where c is the coefficient of variation of firm sizes and n the number of firms in the industry. When all firms in an industry are of equal size the standard deviation of firm sizes equals zero and so the index equals $1/n$. If there is only one firm in an industry, the standard deviation is again zero and the index reaches a maximum value of unity.

The same (numerical) result can be obtained for the Herfindahl index by summing the squares of the (decimal) values of the market shares of each firm. The Herfindahl index, however, although attempting to account for differences in firm size, is still heavily weighted towards larger firms. (The square of the market share of a firm with 1 per cent of the market is $0.01^2 = 0.0001$.) Adding this to the overall value of the index will make very little difference. In fact, because of this the Herfindahl index is often inverted to obtain the so-called *numbers equivalent index*: that is, the hypothetical number of firms of equal size which could produce the industry's output and have the same Herfindahl index as the actual number of firms. Thus if a Herfindahl index of 0.2 is calculated, the numbers equivalent is five, since five firms, with 20 per cent of the market each, would also result in a Herfindahl index of this value ($0.2^2 \times 5 = 0.04 \times 5 = 0.2$).

A more obvious way to obtain a relative measure of concentration (also graphical but less ambiguous than cumulative share

*Figure 3.3   Concentration: Lorenz curves*

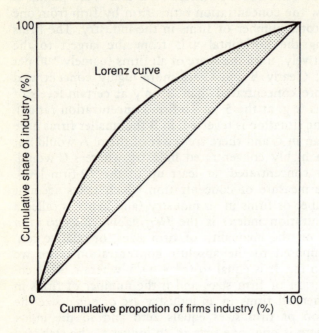

curves) is to use a *Lorenz curve* as in Figure 3.3. Unlike cumulative
share curves the Lorenz curve for one industry will not intersect
with that for another. This is because of the difference in method
of construction of the two curves. The vertical axis is identical,
but the horizontal axis is the cumulative proportion of firms in
the industry, not the absolute numbers. If all firms are of equal
size then the Lorenz curve is the straight diagonal running from
bottom left to top right in Figure 3.3. The greater the curvature
the greater the inequality in firm sizes. The shaded area can be
measured by the *Gini coefficient*; this ranges from zero in cases
of complete equality to unity when firms are completely unequal
in size (i.e. a single-seller monopoly with only one firm plotted in
the group in the extreme top left-hand corner). The Gini coefficient
is the ratio of the shaded area to the total triangle above the
diagonal. Clearly it takes no account of firm numbers. Thus two
firms of equal size and 100 firms of equal size could all be plotted
on the diagonal and the coefficient in both cases would be zero.

Hannah and Kay (1977) propose an index which satisfies four main criteria. Their suggested yardsticks are that the index should (a) not suggest one industry is more concentrated than another if the cumulative share curves intersect; (b) any sales shift from smaller to larger firms should increase the value of the index; (c) any addition of a small firm to the industry should decrease concentration — although this begs the question of what is 'small' since after a certain relative size a new entrant could increase concentration by any yardstick; and (d) any merger should increase concentration. Clarke (1986, p. 15) points out that the Herfindahl index does satisfy these yardsticks. However, Hannah and Kay's own index is more subjectively flexible since, instead of summing the squares of market shares, the power awarded to the decimal value of market share can be any figure, $a$, above zero. Clearly, if this value is below two then the Hannah and Kay index awards more weight to larger firms than does the Herfindahl index. The analogous Hannah and Kay numbers equivalent is their index to the power $1/(1 - a)$ provided $a \neq 1$.

How firms conduct themselves may not depend only on industrial structure at a point in time. It could also depend on structure over time. In short, while monopoly and perfect competition are regarded as opposites, the use of the words themselves is misleading. Moreover, since the measures of monopoly described earlier are imperfect, their use as predictors of rivalry (as opposed to perfect competition) will also be misleading, possibly more so. Two measures of firm rivalry are the *rank correlation coefficient* and the *Hymer–Pashigian index*. Again both of those have faults, but they do shed further light on industrial structure, particularly inter-firm rivalry from a dynamic viewpoint.

A measure of firm turnover (such as the rank correlation coefficient) looks at an industry at two points in time. All the firms in the industry are ranked by size in descending order (something like a sports league table) at the opening of the period and again at the close. They are awarded numbers 1, 2 and 3, and so on from the leader downwards. The rank correlation coefficient is then calculated.

If the ranking positions of the firms are unchanged a coefficient of +1.0 would be obtained (the implication is that the industry is uncompetitive). The more movement there is in the positioning of the firms the lower is the calculated coefficient and the more competitive the market is deemed to be (the possible values range from −1.0 to +1.0). However, while changes in the rank of a firm can be meaningful in economic terms, they need not be. Certainly, if a change in rank implies a substantial change in firm size or market share then it may well have meaning. But if there is any tendency for firms in a market to bunch together in size then rank change measures are meaningless. Alternatively, a market can undergo changes of great economic importance but experience no change in firm ranking. For example, a two-firm industry (a duopoly) composed of firms A and B, where A had 51 per cent of the market and B 49 per cent, would produce a rank correlation coefficient of unity even if A's share rose to 99 per cent and B's fell to 1 per cent. Another defect of the index is that it ignores differences in economic importance between the leading and lagging firms. The 'tail' of small firms may influence the calculated coefficient, but it is what is happening between the large firms (or to them if small ones are growing) which matters.

The Hymer–Pashigian (1962) or *instability index* takes account of all firms, even the smallest, but is only affected by them if they grow substantially. Equally it is only sensitive to the presence of large firms if they experience significant size changes. It is calculated between two points in time by subtracting each firm's share of the industry from its corresponding share at the later or earlier period (whichever is the larger). The differences are then summed. The higher the value of the index the more unstable and hence the more competitive is the market. To illustrate, consider again a duopoly where A and B exchanged ranking but simply moved from a 51:49 to a 49:51 relationship. The rank correlation coefficient would register unity (negatively) the most 'competitive' value. The instability index would register 4. Conversely, had the market shares changed instead from 51:49 to 99:1 the rank correlation coefficient would be +1.0, implying no ranking change, while the instability index would have a value of 96 (as against 4) implying a very high degree of economic change.

## 3.3  PROBLEMS OF STRUCTURAL MEASUREMENT

Irrespective of the measure of monopoly or competition other factors must be borne in mind when *selecting the variable to measure firm size*. Absolute concentration ratios measured by *fixed assets* are often higher than ratios measured by *sales*, for the same industries. This reflects the fact that larger firms tend to be more capital-intensive than smaller.

The ratio of assets (and *employment*) to sales will be higher the more vertically integrated is the firm examined. Thus, unless all firms in an industry are equally vertically integrated, asset, employment and *value-added* concentration ratios will differ from the sales concentration ratios, and will reflect vertical aspects of firm size as well as horizontal aspects. These two concepts of size are best kept separate. Similarly, when a firm is diversified, sales or value-added concentration ratios are preferable to employment or asset measures. The latter inputs would require to be arbitrarily allocated in some way between industries.

The degree to which an industry is *vertically integrated* can be measured in at least three ways. *Ratio of value added to sales* can be computed. Value added (i.e. sales less expenditure for raw materials, fuel and power) to sales will be higher the greater the number of productive stages carried out by the firm. However, input and output price changes will alter the value of the index. Second, other things being equal, a more profitable firm will have a higher ratio than a less profitable one. The index will also be lower, other things being equal, at later stages of production than at earlier since sales figures will be higher at each successive stage. It is mainly of value when comparing firms in the same industry, at the same stage of the productive process, facing the same input and output prices.

A second measure of vertical integration is the *ratio of inventory values to sales*. The rationale for this index is that the greater the number of successive stages performed by a firm the greater will be the value of stocks carried. This assumption is not altogether realistic if vertical integration permits economizing on stockholding. It is also dependent on the levels of both input and output prices.

Finally, *the degree of dependence on input and output markets* is a criterion of vertical integration. An example of this index as a measure of backward integration is the ratio of inter-firm purchases or transfers at a particular stage to total inputs used at that stage. To gauge forward integration total inter-firm transfers of output at a particular stage would be expressed as a proportion of total output at that stage. These ratios will be invariant with input and output price changes since both numerator and denominator involve the use of the same price. Alternatively, volume rather than value data could be used. The main problems will arise around the definition of a 'stage' in the productive process.

When corporate *diversification* is examined, two main methods are in common use. First, *ratio of non-primary output to total output* can be computed. The higher is this ratio the more diversified is the firm. The drawback with it as an index is that no indication is given as to whether non-primary output is divided between several industries or confined to only one. Second, a *straight count of industries in which the firm operates can be made*. This overcomes the objection to the previous measure but may give undue weight to many activities which account for only a small proportion of the firm's total business. An alternative or additional measure is to use a *composite index*, such as the arithmetic product of the non-primary output ratio and the straight count. The danger with composite indices, at least if used in isolation, is that they may conceal more than they reveal. For example, a composite index of 3 would be obtained for a firm with a ratio of non-primary to total output of 1:10 and a straight count of 30 industries, as well as for a firm with a ratio of 1:2 and a straight count of six industries.

These issues, of course, raise yet another practical problem. How should the analyst define the collection of products or firms to be studied? Clearly how the industry or market is defined will affect the nature of any statistical results. Industries can be defined from a *technological* stance or a *market* stance. They can be assessed at a high *level of aggregation* or a low. When the economist defines an industry technologically he does so by specifying a group of products between whom there is a high *cross-elasticity of supply*. That is, two firms would be deemed to be in the same industry if the resources of the one could be readily transferred to producing the products of the other. Thus firms in the footwear industry would be deemed to be competitors by this definition. Yet if the level of aggregation was changed to men's and women's footwear and the two firms were found to operate respectively in these submarkets, would supply cross-elasticity still be considered high? Alternatively, even at the same level of industry aggregation, is there really high cross-elasticity of supply between a Ford and a Chevrolet? To the customer they are alternative products, but to retool the Ford factory to produce Chevrolets would be prohibitively expensive.

Another alternative is to use *cross-elasticity of demand*. The more acceptable are substitutes to consumers in the market the higher is the index. The relevant market or industry to examine is that group of firms or products between which the cross-elasticity is high. Two brands of instant coffee are then competing in the same industry (even though one might be produced by a spray drying technique and the other by the very different freeze-drying technology). But is tea, or beer, or cola a substitute for coffee?

The problems are immense, and, as we discuss in Chapter 5, are not necessarily overcome by the statistics available from official government sources which tend traditionally to have been collected on a basis of 'what is practical' rather than 'what is desirable'. This is less true of commercial market research data which cater for fee-paying clients interested in direct competition and, more recently, the US Federal Trade Commission has introduced 'Line of Business' data to supplement the traditional Standard Industrial Classifications.

Asch (1983, pp. 168–9) illustrates the difficulty by emphasizing that consumer substitutability is the key for defining the market as it currently stands, but that since conduct depends not only on existing structures but also on potential entry, then producer substitutability must also be taken into account. These 'criteria can be extremely difficult to satisfy simultaneously'. If markets are defined too broadly, concentration measures may misleadingly understate the true situation. If they are defined too narrowly then concentration may be overstated. Table 3.2 illustrates aspects of these problems numerically.

*Table 3.2  Hypothetical concentration ratios for top three firms*

| | Per cent of sales in submarket | | | Per cent in total market | | |
|---|---|---|---|---|---|---|
| Firm | *1* | *2* | *3* | | | |
| A | 50 | 50 | 5 | 105 | = | 35% |
| B | 20 | 20 | 10 | 50 | = | 17% |
| C | 20 | 10 | 10 | 40 | = | 13% |
| D | 5 | 0 | 25 | 30 | = | 10% |
| E | 3 | 5 | 25 | 33 | = | 11% |
| F | 2 | 15 | 25 | 42 | = | 14% |
| | — | — | — | — | | — |
| | 100 | 100 | 100 | 200 | | |

Top 4 concentration ratio

| | | | | |
|---|---|---|---|---|
| 95 | 95 | 85 | | 55 |

Even that is not the end of the story, however. Part of the aggregation problem (i.e. deciding whether or not to aggregate sub-industries) is due to the understatement:overstatement difficulties illustrated in Table 3.2. These difficulties in part reflect the fact that different firms are more dominant in some submarkets than others. This may not always be so. Moreover, whether or not it is the case, different submarkets may differ widely in their unit or value size (in Table 3.2 they are all awarded equal weights). So standardization for size should be carried out before share of total market is computed. Such exercises could well alter the data in Table 3.2 in directions dependent only on the facts of the case.

## 3.4  MEASURES OF CONDUCT

So far we have assumed that the price:marginal cost ratio is the main conduct measure. Analytically it is highlighted by the perfectly competitive framework and by departures from that framework. It is consequently easy conceptually to include it in the SCP paradigm. Policy-makers, however, are interested in more than just one manifestation of market power. We shall now examine the P:MC ratio and alternatives in more detail.

The *Lerner index*, first put forward in 1934, equals zero in perfect competition. It is calculated as $(P - MC)/P$ (P is price, MC is marginal cost). In conditions of monopoly it is positive, and the larger the index, it is presumed, the larger is the firm's degree of monopoly power. However, the index depends partly on price elasticity which, although determined in turn partly by industry structure, is also dependent on the nature of the good sold. Second, the index also depends on the level of costs. High marginal costs could give a low index even if monopoly power was great. Third, the index ignores market size. The index might be low for Sainsbury and high for the corner grocer in a suburban housing estate, yet the market power of each is very different. Fourth, it depends on traditional perfect competition theory yet, if entry is free and if demand is downward-sloping, price can equal average cost and be well above marginal cost, and little monopoly power need be present.

Joe Bain (1941) used the existence of persistently high profit rates. Essentially this has now evolved into a computation of the *ratio of profit rates to interest rates*. This index rests on the assumption that, under perfectly competitive conditions, accounting profits are merely the normal return or interest rate on the capital employed in the business. In such circumstances the ratio would equal zero and would become increasingly large as the firm approached monopoly with larger and larger monopoly profits. It ignores the implications of X-inefficiency (that is, operating at less than lowest technological and managerial costs), and it ignores the possibility that supra-normal profits can arise for reasons, such as risk-bearing or innovation, other than monopoly. Further, a firm may well be conducting itself mono-polistically, but there is no reason why it must do so successfully. Monopoly profits will only be earned if sufficient consumers in the market place are prepared to pay the price for the firm's products. The Bain index could, therefore, be zero even in the presence of monopoly conduct, and alternatively, be positive in its absence.

The *Rothschild index* (1942) of monopoly pricing behaviour is highlighted in Figure 3.4. It is an *ex ante* measure of conduct rather than an *ex post* one as were the two previously discussed

*Figure 3.4*

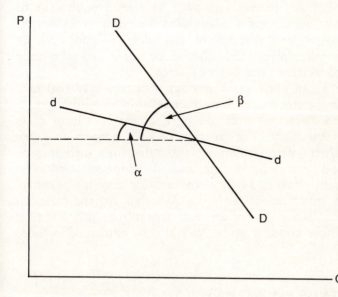

measures. It displays the potential conduct a firm could exercise and so arguably it should be seen as an index of structure not behaviour. The diagram shows two demand curves for one firm similar to that of Chamberlain's monopolistic competition analysis.[3] DD is drawn on the assumption that rivals change their price in line with the illustrated firm, dd on the other hand, is constructed on the assumption that rivals do not alter prices. In perfect competition the two coincide in a single horizontal line. In monopoly they also coincide but have some positive slope (ignoring the algebraic sign). Thus in perfect competition the ratio of the angles $a:\beta$ is zero, in monopoly it is 1. (Rothschild used the ratios of the respective demand curves.) The $\tan a:\tan \beta$ ratio does give an indication of the potential power of the firm within a given market. It does not, however, indicate whether market demand itself is elastic or inelastic, and that also affects firm conduct in the market place.

There are at least two other measures of conduct which we should note here although both will be discussed in detail below. First, if firms have market power but do not have a monopoly then there will be an incentive to engage in *collusive behaviour* in order to share the fruits of monopoly. Two or more firms, for example, can collude to maintain price at a level equivalent to what the market would pay a monopolist operating at an output level where MR = MC. Whether or not such collusion can be identified if it takes place, and whether or not it can take place successfully are issues we will defer till later.

Finally, firms can conduct themselves in such a way that new competition is deterred if existing competition is minimized. If successful, then discretion over pricing is increased and/or costs are raised non-optimally. The erection of such *barriers to entry* includes *product differentiation* through the medium of advertising and research, design and development. Whether product differentiation is a barrier to entry or a means of entry, however, is a much contested issue. Whether expenditures on product differentiation are or are not desirable is also a matter for dispute. These conduct issues will also be explained in more depth below.

## 3.5 CRITERIA OF PERFORMANCE

The SCP paradigm assumes that certain basic economic conditions such as supply, demand and state of technology lead to specific types of market structure, which in turn influence conduct and so firm or industry performance.

Apart from the Pareto optimal inferences of the benefits of marginal cost pricing what are seen by industrial economists to be yardsticks of good performance? One is *technical efficiency*, that is production at minimum possible average cost. In a situation of perfect competition there is no 'organizational slack' or 'X-inefficiency' (see Chapter 4). Another goal is *equity*. Although allocative and distributive efficiencies are subjective concepts and it is on these that notions of equity are based, firms are judged (or at least condemned or condoned) by some outsiders if their actions or results seem 'unfair' or 'wrong'. We shall examine such concepts and discuss how economists tackle them in Chapter 11.

Thirdly, firms are judged on their *technical progressiveness* or *innovative ability*. Again there are subjective elements involved here and further, there are conflicts between what innovativeness (in techniques or products) is a desirable performance outcome and what is an undesirable piece of entry deterring product differention. *Profitability* can be a yardstick of good performance, emanating from successful and efficient conduct. Or is it a measure of monopoly power? Ambiguity again exists. In situations of high unemployment some in society may argue that *employment growth* is a yardstick of good performance. Others might suggest that it indicates a poor, suboptimal capital:labour ratio. Further, growth (by any yardstick, sales, profits or market share) may be a measure of competitive success in meeting consumer demand. It therefore results in increased market concentration. Is this feedback loop to be condemned?

The SCP paradigm is clearly not a simple model. There are ambiguities and two-way interactions all through it. None the less it is the most developed of all industrial organization theories. Remaining chapters will continue to build on it but not to the exclusion of other approaches or insights.

## NOTES

1.   This is illustrated as:

   wy = ½ca since wz = cw
   wx = oc
   wy + wx = xy = oc + ½ ca

xy = monopoly P = (2oc + oa − od)/2 = (oc + oa)/2

$P_{monopoly}$ = (a + c)/2

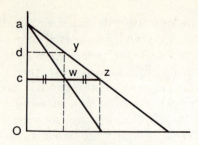

2.  $\delta Qi/\delta qi$ is consequently zero. This is the Cournot case, as was dQ/dqi = 1. Confusion can be avoided by noting the different numerators, Qi and Q respectively.

3.  They are not conceptually identical to Chamberlin's but are a more general case. We will assume there are no substantive differences, however.

## REFERENCES

Asch, P. (1983), *Industrial Organisation and Antitrust Policy* (Chichester: John Wiley).

Bain, J.S. (1941), 'The Profit Rate as a Measure of Monopoly Power', *Quarterly Journal of Economics*.

Bain, J.S. (1951), 'Relation of Profit Rate to Industry Concentration: American Manufacturing, 1936–40', *Quarterly Journal of Economics*.

Clarke, R. (1986), *Industrial Economics* (Oxford: Basil Blackwell).

Hannah, L. and Kay, J.A. (1977), *Concentration in Modern Industry* (London: Macmillan).

Hymer, S. and Pashigian, P. (1962), *Review of Economics and Statistics*.

Lerner, A.P. (1934), 'The Concept of Monopoly and the Measurement of Monopoly Power', *Review of Economic Studies*.

# 4.  Monopoly Gains and Losses

In this chapter we look at three broad measures of industrial performance and assess the theory and evidence surrounding some issues raised. The three measures are the deadweight social loss consequential on pricing above marginal cost levels, the technical inefficiency or X-inefficiency which arises if costs are above minimum feasible levels, and third, the degree to which technological progressiveness is fostered or discouraged by monopoly.

## 4.1  DEADWEIGHT SOCIAL LOSS

The monopoly 'loss' to society, as the discussion in Chapter 2 of Figures 2.13 and 2.14 highlighted, can be viewed as the deadweight loss (DWL) which occurs in the monopolized industry or industries in the economy. If the DWL can be identified and measured for each industry, then a straight aggregation will provide the cost to society of monopoly elements in the economy. Figure 4.1 shows an industry demand curve with monopoly and competitive prices and quantities $P_m$, $P_c$ and $Q_m$, $Q_c$ respectively. The area $\pi$ is not lost to society when monopolistic pricing behaviour occurs, it is simply transferred from consumers to producers. The area R represents resources which are transferred from this (monopolized) industry to producing marginally more valued output in other industries. No social gain or loss occurs. The triangle DWL, however, represents that part of consumers' surplus, previously obtained by society at $P_c$ which, due to a price of $P_m$ is now lost. This is the welfare loss due to industry monopolization.

To calculate the value of DWL is conceptually simple.

$$DWL = \tfrac{1}{2}\Delta P \Delta Q \tag{1}$$

where $\Delta P$ and $\Delta Q$ are respectively the change in price and quantity

*Figure 4.1*

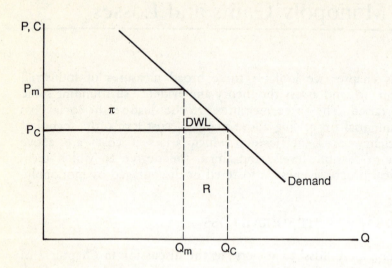

between the competitive and monopolistic levels. Of course, only the actual ('monopoly') price and quantities are known.

However, market price elasticity of demand is:

$$\eta = -(\Delta Q/\Delta P).\,(P_m/Q_m)$$

and the price:cost margin can be defined as $P_m - MC/P_m = \Delta P/P_m = M$. Thus $\Delta P = MP_m$ while $\Delta Q = \eta\Delta P(Q_m/P_m) = \eta MQ_m$. So by substitution in (1) we have:

$$DWL = \tfrac{1}{2}\,\eta M^2 P_m Q_m \qquad (2)$$

Thus to calculate DWL requires knowledge of market demand elasticity, mark-up and sales revenue ($P_m Q_m$).

The seminal worker in this field was Harberger (1954) who calculated that the monopoly DWL in the US economy over his study period (1924–28) was equivalent to 0.08 per cent of US national income. To arrive at his conclusions Harberger had to make certain assumptions. He did not have values for $\eta$ so he argued that for each industry $\eta$ should be assumed to equal unity.

For a pure monopoly this is clearly too low (it implies the firm is operating at MR = O not MR = MC). For concentrated industries it is still possible that $\eta = 1$ will provide an underestimate of DWL, that is $\eta$ should have been assumed to be higher than unity. This is not so unambiguous as in the pure monopoly case, however, since if the 'rivals' price constant' assumption holds industry or market demand elasticity will generally be much lower than firm demand elasticity as customers switch to or from the price changing firm (only when price changes are expected to be matched will the two be equal). Thus an industry value of $\eta = 1$ may not be quite such an underestimate as some of Harberger's critics have suggested. It is nevertheless erring on the low side.

Harberger's study applied only to the manufacturing sector of the economy. If we assume that monopoly is as big or as small a problem in other sectors then his figure should be increased accordingly. (In 1924–28 manufacturing accounted for approximately 25 per cent of GNP. Thus a multiple of 4 should arguably be applied to his estimates.)

Third, Harberger used the average return on capital as a proxy for the competitive return. Deviations from the average were then expressed in dollars by industry and, with industry sales known, the mark-up by industry was calculated. This proxy would downward bias the estimate of DWL since the average return on capital must (given the existence of monopoly power in at least some industries) be above the true competitive rate. Computed mark-ups would, therefore, be correspondingly lower than the 'true' monopoly mark-up.

Fourth, Stigler (1956), on a related point, argued that the Harberger DWL was also downward-biased because accounting rates of return would tend to equality across industries, thus minimizing the value of any monopoly mark-ups eventually computed. This for two reasons, one relating to the numerator, the other to the denominator of the return on capital ratio. To the extent that monopoly rents are capitalized in balance sheets under headings such as 'goodwill' then the denominator will be larger and hence the ROC smaller than it otherwise would be. Conversely, to the extent that managers, workers or licence-holders receive monopoly payments for their inputs included in their salaries, wages, or royalties then these costs of monopoly, which are deducted from the profits or numerator of the RO ratio, would not have been included in Harberger's DWL estimate.

Fifth, to the extent that manufacturing industry is more or less monopolistic than the remainder of the economy then the DWL figure would have exaggerated the importance or unimportance of monopoly.

Over the years since Harberger's study several industrial economists have tried to overcome these difficulties and refine and hone the method of approach. Schwartzman (1960) re-estimated the DWL triangle for the US for 1954. He either avoided some of the original Harberger pitfalls or relaxed the assumptions. Thus demand elasticity was allowed to double to 2, not 1. Many of the rates of return issues were removed by direct use of price:cost margins. Harberger's result proved robust. Schwartzman arrived at a monopoly loss of 0.13 per cent of 1954 GNP.

Worcester (1973) used a disaggregated approach by examining the largest 500 US industrial firms. This overcame the criticism that industry mark-up figures include both high (monopoly) profits and the offsetting low profits (or losses) of failing firms. His study period of 1959–69 uncovered welfare losses ranging from 0.2 to 0.7 per cent of GNP. None of these studies, therefore, produced high estimates of welfare losses (albeit they did vary by a multiple of nearly tenfold). There would seem little cause for concern. As Stigler (1956) remarked, economists might be better employed fighting 'termites' rather than monopoly. None of the studies, of course, denies that welfare losses might still be large in a given industry, even if not great in the overall economy.

Posner (1975) adopted a different philosophical approach to the writers so far discussed. He argued that the welfare loss from monopoly in Figure 4.1 should not be restricted to DWL but should also include $\pi$, monopoly profits. Posner, following Tullock (1967), argues that people are rent (or profit)-seekers. When the potential of monopoly profits exists these resources will be attracted towards ways of acquiring these profits. If the resources are expended on activities which would not occur in competitive conditions then they are socially wasteful. Such expenditures could include anything from advertising through to the costs of negotiating with (or downright bribing) government officials and regulatory authorities in general. Posner assumes first, perfectly elastic supply of inputs for obtaining monopolies; and second, 'no socially useful by-products' from expenditures on the inputs. Given these assumptions, firms will expend resources on obtaining monopoly profits until their marginal benefits equal their (constant) marginal costs. The benefits obtainable are monopoly profits in pounds. Consequently, total monopoly profits are an accurate indicator of the total rent-seeking outlays which have been made and which are totally wasted. (Are monopoly profits from innovative expenditures waste?) Clearly this is an unrealistically strong assumption but the point is taken. Compliance with regulations, for example, is costly, and as Stigler (1971) pointed out, under certain conditions 'the regulatory process benefits primarily (the) industry'. Similarly advertising expenditures may be socially valuable but on the other hand, they may be excessive.

Posner's approach has other implications than simply adding $\pi$ to DWL. It also increases the numerical precision, if not the economic accuracy, with which both can be measured. Thus if $\pi$, monopoly profits are indeed being maximized, then for any given firm with constant costs and a linear demand curve DWL = $0.5\,\pi$ (since $Q_m$ would equal $\frac{1}{2}\,Q_c$ in Figure 4.1 under such conditions given that an MR curve bisects any horizontal from the vertical axis).

Cowling and Mueller (1978) build on this in their approach to measuring monopoly welfare loss. Like Worcester they tackle the problem at the firm level and do so for both the UK and USA. The DWL for each is then $0.5\,\pi$. At the firm level given profit-maximization, $(P - C)/P = 1/\eta$ for each firm. This assertion can be used to modify equation (2) to arrive at the same result.

$$
\begin{aligned}
\text{Thus if DWL} &= 0.5\,\eta M^2\,P_m Q_m = -0.5\,MP_m Q_m \\
&\qquad \text{(given that } \eta \text{ is negative)} \\
&= -0.5\,(\Delta P/P_m)\,P_m Q_m \\
&= 0.5\Delta P\Delta Q = 0.5\pi \qquad\qquad \text{QED}
\end{aligned}
$$

(since $\Delta Q$, the reduction on competitive Q, is negative and $Q_m = 0.5\,Q_c$).

The Posner/Cowling and Mueller approaches to measuring social losses from monopoly are clearly going to increase the estimates arrived at. First, dropping the arbitrary assumption $\eta$ equal to unity will raise the value. Second, the increase in the relevant (geometric) area is a substantial conceptual difference. Third, by dropping the decimal fraction, $M^2$, for the mark-up the estimates must increase. To the extent that M was underestimated in earlier studies such as Harberger's then the squaring of that underestimate would further downward bias the calculations.

Cowling and Mueller then proceeded to estimate the social loss from monopoly for 734 large US firms in 1963–66 and for the 103 largest UK firms for 1968–69. They obtained values many,

many times higher than earlier studies (7.2 per cent of gross corporate product in the UK and up to 13.1 per cent of gross corporate product in the USA). It is worth commenting, before appraising their approach that they did not only add DWL to declared $\pi$. This would have been conservative by Posner's argument. Rather they added advertising expenditures to profits (post-tax) in order to obtain the equivalent of $\pi$ (above $P_c$) in Figure 4.1 and then to this added a further 50 per cent to obtain Figure 4.1's equivalent of DWL plus $\pi$. These adjustments had to be made since profits pre-tax are not received in full by monopolists (taxes must be paid) and furthermore the advertising expenditures have to be incurred over and above competitive costs in order to generate the monopoly profits arising subsequent to such expenditures.

This may appear conservative by Posner's standards since he argued that any expenditures incurred to obtain monopoly profits should be included. Surely such profits are not dependent only on advertising but also on other activities such as resources expended on negotiations with regulators, some packaging materials, research and development and the like. Alternatively, it could be argued that to add advertising (or any of the other expenditures) to post-tax monopoly is to engage in double counting. After all Posner's case is that the profits equal the resources so expended. That is the profits are socially wasteful, but the expenditures made to obtain them are merely diverted from one sector of the economy to another.

Further, the profits themselves generate economic activity elsewhere as they are either ploughed back into the firm or spent elsewhere by dividend recipients. They are no more a social cost than are the taxes ignored by Cowling and Mueller which are redistributed by government.

These criticisms are, of course, inherent in all the partial equilibrium approaches to measuring social costs from Harberger onwards. Cowling and Mueller were indeed aware of such deficiencies and computed DWL as $0.5\,\pi$ for their US sample and their social loss estimate dropped from 13.14 per cent to 3.96 per cent. Using the Harberger measure (with $\eta = 1$) for the same sample they came up with a figure of only 0.4 per cent. Thus while Harberger estimates seem to be understating any costs, the maximum Cowling and Mueller estimate may be highly exaggerated.

A more fundamental criticism was levelled at the whole concept of measuring DWL using this methodology by Littlechild (1981).

Littlechild argues from the Austrian, 'competition is a process' stance. Competition is not an equilibrium situation (general or partial). Profits are not to be viewed as the outcome of departures from a perfectly competitive state but are rather the outcomes of successful grasping of opportunities by innovation (technological, marketing, organizational, or whatever) by alert entrepreneurs. In such a framework the demand curve observed is only present because entrepreneurs have, through advertising or whatever means, drawn consumers' attention to the possibility of obtaining (in Figure 4.1 terms) $Q_m$ at $P_m$. The relevant alternative is not $Q_c$ at $P_c$, says Littlechild. Rather perfect competitors would not have noticed the opportunities for producing the good. The alternative comparison is for the good not to have been supplied at all. Thus the very fact of production and sale implies a net social gain equal to $\pi$ plus the consumers' surplus to which production and consumption gave rise. However measured, DWL then becomes an irrelevancy.

## 4.2 X-INEFFICIENCY

In 1966 Liebenstein developed the concept of X-inefficiency. His argument was that inputs are not used as technically efficiently in monopolistic as in competitive markets. Competition, he argued, disciplines firms to hold costs down to the most technically efficient level. When this discipline is absent costs may tend to rise due to X-inefficiency. (Liebenstein is here ignoring the scale effects we discussed on pp. 24–6.) First, competition eliminates high-cost producers, while its absence may result in higher price:cost margins by low cost firms so allowing high cost firms to remain in business under the pricing 'umbrella' of their more efficient rivals. Second, the pressure placed on profits in competition tends to discipline both managers and employees. They will tend to work more energetically given a higher probability of job loss and what Cyert and March (1967) called organizational slack will be minimized.

Figure 4.2 draws on Comanor and Liebenstein (1969). The area X has no allocative effect since $Q_m$ is now (merely) produced with higher costs than would be the case in the absence of X-inefficiency. (We use the word 'merely' given the partial equilibrium nature of our analysis.) In reality, in a general equilibrium framework these resources could well have been used to

*Figure 4.2*

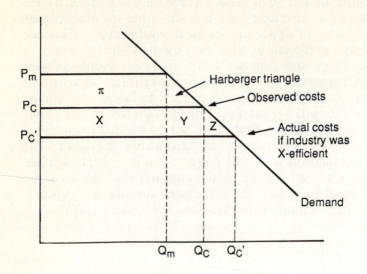

produce other goods and services which might just, at the margin, have been worth more than $P_m$ (the reader is referred back to Figure 2.13 for a fuller discussion of how the presence or absence of X has allocative impact). The increase in DWL, however, is unambiguous. Output has not fallen from a hypothetical competitive level of $Q_c$ to $Q_m$ as it did in Figure 4.1. Rather, if a competitive industry does have lower costs than a monopolistically organized one (due to the presence of X-inefficiency in the latter) then the output reduction is from $Q^1{}_c$ and the price increase from $P^1{}_c$ (not from $P_c$) to $P_m$. The triangle computed by Harberger and others to estimate DWL must be expanded by Y and Z. The magnitude of Y and Z relative to the Harberger triangle will, of course, vary industry by industry depending on the degree of X-inefficiency, elasticity of industry demand and the price:cost mark-up, $P_m$ over $P_c$. Indeed, other things equal, the smaller is the observed price:cost mark-up the greater will be the unmeasured loss, Y plus Z, relative to the Harberger triangle.

X-inefficiency, of course, is nothing more nor less than what laymen and managers call inefficiency in everyday life. The technical terms allocative and distributive efficiency are to most people just that, jargon. It was possibly with this in mind that Stigler (1976) called X-inefficiency an 'awful name'. Stigler was particularly concerned that Liebenstein's statements that the social losses due to X-inefficiency under monopoly were large, indeed even larger than misallocations due to recognized standard imperfections such as tariffs or pricing above marginal cost levels.

Liebenstein's main argument, of course, was that firms were not operating on, but within their production possibility frontier due to motivational deficiencies at either management or worker level. Stigler challenged this assertion arguing that it had no validity in theory. Everyone (or every firm) argues Stigler, is on his (or its) frontier. The only issue is what combination of outputs do they choose to maximize. Utility maximization can include profits (due to cost minimization) but not necessarily to the exclusion of all else. (This is in line with some revisionist theories of the firm such as those discussed in Chapters 9 and 12.) Furthermore, people or firms may be motivated to increase one of their outputs (say profits, given revenues) but may be unable to do so because the managerial or other technology available to them is not the least cost available. Firms (as represented by shareholders), managers and workers all contract with each other to perform certain tasks. These tasks lead to profits, but the drawing-up, execution, and monitoring of these contracts is not costless. Stigler, drawing on Alchian and Demsetz (1972) and in a precursor of Williamson's (1985) arguments, emphasizes that not all firms have equal access to least cost contracting mechanisms, and this inequality of access is not necessarily anything whatever to do with monopoly or competition. There is no theoretical or empirical evidence to suggest it has, and if not, then the whole Liebenstein case for X-inefficiency losses (X + Y + Z in Figure 4.2) *due to monopoly* breaks down.

Stigler laments that Liebenstein, like many others before, and since, have abandoned Marshall's notion of the Representative Firm and substituted for it what Reid (1987) calls Viner's (1964) misinterpretation of Marshall where in stable competitive equilibrium all firms are assumed to be operating at minimum feasible cost. According to Marshall (1948, p. 317), however, the representative firm is not

some new producer just struggling to get into business . . . content for a time with little or no profits . . . nor . . . a firm which by exceptionally long-sustained ability and good fortune has got together a vast, . . . huge

[and] well-ordered . . . superiority over almost all of its rivals. But [it] must be one which has had a fairly long life, and fair success, which is managed with normal ability, and which has normal access to the economies, external and internal, which belong to that aggregate volume of production . . . .

By this argument not only is Liebenstein chasing a hare, but the attack on Harberger's use of the *average* rate of return as a proxy for the competitive rate is misplaced (at least in a Marshallian context).

Stigler, having questioned Liebenstein's motivational doubts on grounds of varying contractual creation and enforcement technologies then queries whether competition, as opposed to monopoly, need spur firms to acquire the least cost technology. Competitive selection assumes that inflows and outflows of entrepreneurs occur and that (p. 216) 'entrepreneurs of various qualities will converge on a high efficiency equilibrium in each competitive industry'. But, says Stigler, this assumes the absence of error by entrepreneurs, and 'waste can arise *ex post* because *ex ante* plans rested upon erroneous prediction'. High costs, therefore, may arise not simply because of the inability (or still higher net incremental cost) of obtaining the least cost transactions technology but because even with minimum anticipated costs outcomes differ from expectations. Neither of these X-inefficiencies needs have anything to do with monopoly or market power.

Indeed, Kirzner (1979, p. 127) takes the discussion one stage further, by defining error even more strictly than Stigler, and simultaneously restating the validity of the X-inefficiency concept. Stigler's critique, says Kirzner, is valid given an equilibrium framework. Firms can have differing input qualities (associated for example with motivational variations). They can have differing output levels (because, for example, they choose to take decisions based on greater or lesser amounts of costly-to-acquire information). These do not however (to Kirzner) amount to examples of 'erroneous prediction'. For Kirzner errors *have* occurred if the individuals concerned would have reproached themselves *at the time* (not *ex post*) for taking the courses of action they did in the light of the knowledge then available but not perceived. In short, X-inefficiency can exist with firms operating within their production possibility functions because of disequilibrium in markets. Given equilibrium, however, Kirzner would accept the Stigler critique that the phenomenon can be explained as merely one of deliberate choice as to where on the production possibility frontier a firm chooses to operate. What causes X-inefficiency in a Kirznerian framework (the failure to be alert to a price spread presenting arbitrage opportunities) is something we tackle in Chapters 8 and 9.

At this juncture we content ourselves with noting that it obviously has nothing to do with monopoly or market power in the normal equilibrium SCP framework.

## 4.3 MONOPOLY AND COST-REDUCTION

Some writers have argued that monopoly power does have an effect on the incentive to reduce costs. The literature we refer to here relates less to the desire to achieve best practice technology (i.e the removal of X-inefficiency) and more to the improvement of that technology (what is sometimes called process innovation). This literature is theoretically-based and so avoids some of Stigler's complaints about Liebenstein's argument from self-determined definition instead of by *a priori* reasoning from either axioms or empirical evidence.

There have been two main contributions to this debate, one by Arrow (1962) and a counter-argument by Demsetz (1969). Figure 4.3 highlights the differences in their approaches. Arrow argues that the incentives for a monopoly to make use of an invention which would lower production costs from C to $C^1$ are given by the additional profits generated at the new MR = MC output of $Q^1_m$, price $P^1_m$, relative to the profits previously obtained at $Q_m$ with price $P_m$. Revenues increase by W + Z under this scenario (recall that total revenue is the area under the MR curve) while costs fall by V but increase by Z (the former due to lower cost production techniques, the latter due to a rise in output). W + V is therefore the net incentive per period which is available to the monopolist who adopts an invention (assuming no costs of producing the invention or payment of royalties to the inventor). The monopolist would therefore pay a lump-sum of anything up to W + V to obtain access to such a cost reducing process. A perfectly competitive industry would, however, have an even greater incentive to obtain the same invention.

If one perfect competitor in the industry produces or discovers the innovation, licenses all other firms in the industry and can successfully protect that patent position then it can extract

V + W + X + Y in licence fees. The industry continues to sell at $P_c Q_c$. When we leave the single-period situation and move into patent expiry the attractiveness of perfect competition socially becomes even greater. Not only has it provided a greater incentive to technical progressiveness but in the longer term the benefits will be diffused more widely as prices are pushed down to $P^1_c$ and output up to $Q^1_c$.

Demsetz, however, challenges this conclusion on the grounds that Arrow is not comparing like with like. $Q_m < Q_c$ because of the presence of monopoly prior to the innovation, therefore Arrow's conclusions are simple geometric tautologies. The relevant comparison, says Demsetz is between a monopoly and a competitive industry of the same initial size. Thus, in Figure 4.3, $Q_m$ and $Q''_c$ are equal at $P_m$ and the monopolist's demand curve is $D_m$. The competitive industry's demand curve, however, is $D_c$ (= $MR_m$). Neither industry now has a greater incentive to invent than the other (in both cases it is V + W).

Demsetz goes one stage further. Assume the inventor is *outside* the industry. Assume also that royalties are paid to the inventor on a per unit basis and that the inventor need not charge the differing industries the same royalties. The best the inventor can do over time is to charge a unit royalty of $c - c^1$ obtaining total royalties of V per period.

If the inventor is outside the monopoly industry, however, the most he can extract from the monopolist in royalties is the difference between pre- and post-invention profits. This is U (pre-invention profits) and (U + V + W) (post-invention profits). Consequently, the outside inventor can charge royalties of up to V + W, a greater amount than he could extract from the competitive industry. Thus an inventor or new patent-holder supplying a monopolized industry will have a greater incentive to invent than one supplying a competitive industry, other things equal.

Demsetz's argument is analytically correct. The only counter is that when one is examining any given industry then demand is consumer-determined and therefore comparing two alternative demand schedules is misleading. For a given case the question is what would be the impact of a greater or lesser degree of monopoly concentration? The alternative situations then become amenable to abstraction by the Arrow model. But the question is then begged that given its theoretical deficiencies, what practical cost will be involved in misleading implications? Should one apply

*Figure 4.3*

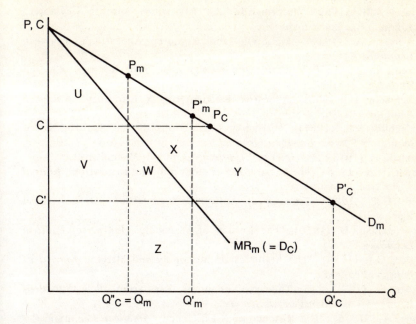

incorrect theory to a practical situation or valid theory which is inapplicable?

Clearly the relationships between efficiency, technical change and the measures of losses and gains therefrom are complex and their analysis is fraught with pitfalls. Such lack of definitiveness is yet another argument for an eclectic, case-by-case pragmatic approach to industrial economics policy.

## REFERENCES

Alchian A. and Demsetz, D. (1972), 'Production Information Costs and Economic Organisation', *American Economic Review*, 62.

Arrow, K.J. (1962), 'Economic Welfare and the Allocation of Resources for Invention' in Nelson, R.R. (ed.), *The Rate and Direction of Inventive Activity* (National Bureau for Economic Research).

Comanor, W.S. and Liebenstein, H. (1969), 'Allocative Efficiency, X-Efficiency and the Measurement of Welfare Losses', *Economica*.

Cowling, K. and Mueller, D.C. (1978), 'The Social Costs of Monopoly Power', *Economic Journal*.

Cyert, R.M. and March, J.G. (1963), *A Behavioural Theory of the Firm* (New York: Prentice-Hall).

Demsetz, H. (1969), 'Information and Efficiency: another viewpoint', *Journal of Law and Economics*.

Harberger, A. (1954), 'Monopoly and Resource Allocation', *American Economic Review*.

Kirzner, I. (1979), *Perception, Opportunity and Profit* (Chicago: Chicago University Press).

Liebenstein, H. (1966), 'Allocative Efficiency vs X Efficiency', *American Economic Review*.

Littlechild, S.C. (1981), 'Misleading Calculations of the Social Costs of Monopoly Power', *Economic Journal*.

Marshall, A. (1948), *Principles of Economics* (London: Macmillan).

Posner, R.A. (1975), 'The Social Costs of Monopoly and Regulation', *Journal of Political Economy*.

Reid, G.C. (1987), *Theories of Industrial Organisation* (Oxford: Basil Blackwell).

Schwartzman, D. (1960), 'The Burden of Monopoly', *Journal of Political Economy*.

Stigler, G.J. (1956), 'The Statistics of Monopoly and Merger', *Journal of Political Economy*.

Stigler, G. (1971), 'The Theory of Economic Regulation', *Bell Journal of Economics and Management Science*.

Stigler, G. (1976), 'The Xistence of X-Efficiency', *American Economic Review*.

Tullock, G. (1967), 'The Welfare Costs of Tariffs, Monopolies and Theft', *Western Economic Journal*.

Williamson, O.E. (1985), *The Economic Institutions of Capitalism* (New York: Free Press).

# 5. Business and its Organization

This chapter examines the structure of modern industry as it is, as it has developed and as it is evolving. Study of industrial structure is interesting not only for its own sake, but because the linkages between perfect competition and price, and monopoly and price, are often assumed to be reflected in reality in company behaviour. As a consequence, public policy recommendations are sometimes made to government, to nationalized industries or to regulatory agencies which are based on inferences drawn about industrial behaviour, which in turn depend on the view that market structure affects behaviour. The first section of this chapter examines the role of business in the overall economy. The second examines trends and organizations in industry. Finally, the implications of size of firms are studied.

## 5.1 THE MIXED ECONOMY

The United Kingdom, the USA and most Western European states are often called 'mixed economies'. They are neither wholly dirigiste and centrally planned, nor are they totally free markets. Actually, the name is somewhat misleading since all countries are mixed economies, only the degree of the mixture varies. Thus the USSR has a substantial private sector in taxicabs, marketplaces and agriculture. The USA has significant governmental interests in health, welfare and social security, as well as the more obvious expenditures on defence and policing and less obvious ones on particular industries such as long-distance passenger trains. In Britain, total government expenditure as a percentage of the Gross National Product (GNP) has risen irregularly over the century. The impact of the two world wars is obvious. Less so is the failure of the expenditure to decline in peacetime. And although various welfare measures over the century have been responsible for increasing social (e.g. pensions, sickness and unemployment benefits) and educational expenditures, the rise between 1960 and 1970 is less understandable. This is particularly so when one remembers that the percentages are growing shares of a generally increasing GNP (Table 5.1).

Figure 5.1 provides a similar picture for the USA.

*Figure 5.1    US Federal and State expenditure
            as per cent of GNP*

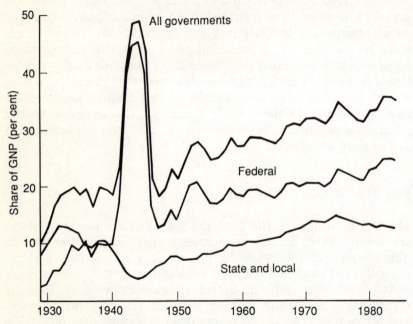

Source: US Department of Commerce.  Reproduced for P.A. Samuelson and W.D. Nordhous, Economics (1985) New York: Prentice-Hall, (12th edition).

Table 5.1   Government (central and local) expenditure
as a percentage of total Gross National Product

| 1900 | 14.3 | 1950 | 39.1 |
|------|------|------|------|
| 1910 | 12.2 | 1960 | 39.2 |
| 1920 | 26.2 | 1970 | 47.1 |
| 1930 | 25.0 | 1984 | 53.9 |

Source:   Barclays Bank Review (1980); Economic Trends, annual supplement (1986).

Tables 5.2 and 5.3 illustrate how government expenditure is broken down. Social security payments (plus, of course, their administration) account for over one-quarter. The National Health and associated services, together with education, account for a similar proportion. The defence budget is the next largest recipient of money from government. The remainder are absolutely large but relatively small. The government sector is, of course, an important ultimate customer of business or industry, through one or other of its programmes (e.g. agriculture, fisheries and food; parts of the defence, housing, industry and road budgets, etc.). Even government programmes such as health and education pay not insignificant sums to (for example) the construction, medicine instrumentation and publishing industries. In the USA the picture is not dissimilar although defence plays a larger role, and health and education account for smaller proportions. These differences, however, are only partly accounted for by the larger private sectors in US health and education. The main reason is that Table 5.3 is not strictly comparable with Table 5.2 due to its exclusion of state relative to federal funding. Average state expenditures on education exceed federal by a multiple of more than two.

The mixed economy, that hybrid of paternalism and free enterprise which exists in practice, is neither ruthless (as autocratic economies can and have been) nor devoid of concern for others (as totally free enterprise economies theoretically could be). Rather, it combines some of the best of both worlds. However, debate can and does exist as to whether the 'mix' is correct. Is a 'caring bureaucracy' not a contradiction in terms? Would not voluntary charity be more effective? Is government participation too weak? Or too strong? These are legitimate matters of debate, but will be left to texts other than this one.

*Table 5.2   UK central and local government expenditure*

| Major headings | 1986 (£m) | % |
|---|---|---|
| Defence | 18.6 | 11.5 |
| Overseas aid and other overseas services | 2.2 | 1.4 |
| Agriculture, fisheries, food and forestry | 2.4 | 1.5 |
| Industry, energy, trade and employment | 11.6 | 7.2 |
| Roads and transport | 3.7 | 2.3 |
| Housing | 8.0 | 4.9 |
| Law, order and protective services | 6.7 | 4.1 |
| Education and science, arts and libraries | 19.5 | 12.0 |
| Health and personal social services | 19.4 | 12.0 |
| Social security | 50.2 | 31.0 |
| Debt servicing | 17.0 | 10.5 |
| Total | 162.0 | 100.0 |

*Source:*   *UK National Accounts* (1987) (BlueBook) (London: HMSO).

*Table 5.3   US Federal expenditure, 1985*

| | Estimate (billions $) | % of total |
|---|---|---|
| National defence, veterans, and international affairs | 316 | 34 |
| Social security | 191 | 21 |
| Interest on public debt | 116 | 13 |
| Income security | 114 | 12 |
| Health | 103 | 11 |
| Transportation, commerce, development | 36 | 3 |
| Education, training, employment | 28 | 3 |
| Agriculture | 14 | 2 |
| Energy, natural resources, environment | 14 | 2 |
| General government, justice | 12 | 1 |
| Science, space, technology | 9 | 1 |
| Miscellaneous and offsetting receipts | −28 | −3 |
| | $925 | 100 |

*Source:*   Office of Management and Budget, *Budget of the US Government, Fiscal Year 1985.*

## 5.2  BUSINESS IN THE ECONOMY

For our purposes the degree to which the economy is or is not 'mixed' is not of primary importance. Rather, we are interested in modern business *per se*, which is to a greater or lesser extent influenced by the state (from ownership and regulation at one extreme, to taxation of profits or even occasional subsidizing of losses at the other). State influence on industry will be examined in detail later. Here we simply take a snapshot view of industry in the United Kingdom, the United States and elsewhere.

The broadest subdivision of industries is into primary (generally meaning agriculture, mining, quarrying and oil production), secondary (energy production such as gas, electricity, and water, construction and manufacturing industries) and the tertiary sector (government, distributive trades, finance and services generally).

Table 5.4 does not precisely follow these subdivisions but shows none the less that for all countries the tertiary sector is now the dominant employer of labour. The UK, where the Industrial Revolution was inaugurated, led in the rapid fall in agricultural employment. (France, in 1960, still had proportionally as many employed in agriculture as the UK had in 1870.) Since 1960, on

*Table 5.4  Employment structure, 1870–1984 (percentages of total employment)*

|             |      | France | Germany | Japan | Netherlands | UK   | US   | Average |
|-------------|------|--------|---------|-------|-------------|------|------|---------|
| Agriculture | 1870 | 49.2   | 49.5    | 67.5  | 37.0        | 22.7 | 50.0 | 46.0    |
|             | 1913 | 37.4   | 34.6    | 64.3  | 26.5        | 11.0 | 32.3 | 34.4    |
|             | 1950 | 28.5   | 22.2    | 48.3  | 13.9        | 5.1  | 13.0 | 21.8    |
|             | 1960 | 21.9   | 13.8    | 30.2  | 9.5         | 4.6  | 8.2  | 14.7    |
|             | 1973 | 11.0   | 7.2     | 13.4  | 5.7         | 2.9  | 4.1  | 7.4     |
|             | 1984 | 7.6    | 5.5     | 8.9   | 4.9         | 2.6  | 3.3  | 5.5     |
| Industry    | 1870 | 27.8   | 28.7    | 13.8  | 29.0        | 42.3 | 24.4 | 27.7    |
|             | 1913 | 33.8   | 37.8    | 13.9  | 33.8        | 44.8 | 29.3 | 32.2    |
|             | 1950 | 34.8   | 43.0    | 22.6  | 40.2        | 46.5 | 33.3 | 36.7    |
|             | 1960 | 36.3   | 48.2    | 28.5  | 39.2        | 46.7 | 34.3 | 38.9    |
|             | 1973 | 38.4   | 46.6    | 37.2  | 35.7        | 41.8 | 32.5 | 38.7    |
|             | 1984 | 32.0   | 40.5    | 34.8  | 26.4        | 32.4 | 28.0 | 32.4    |
| Services    | 1870 | 23.0   | 21.8    | 18.7  | 34.0        | 35.0 | 25.6 | 26.4    |
|             | 1913 | 28.8   | 27.6    | 21.8  | 39.7        | 44.2 | 38.4 | 33.4    |
|             | 1950 | 36.7   | 34.8    | 29.1  | 45.9        | 48.4 | 53.7 | 41.4    |
|             | 1960 | 41.8   | 38.0    | 41.3  | 51.3        | 48.7 | 57.5 | 46.4    |
|             | 1973 | 50.6   | 46.2    | 49.4  | 58.6        | 55.3 | 63.4 | 53.9    |
|             | 1984 | 60.4   | 54.0    | 56.3  | 68.7        | 65.0 | 68.7 | 62.2    |

*Source:*  A. Maddison (1987), 'Growth and Slowdown Advanced in Capitalist Economies', *Journal of Economic Literature*, p. 689.

average, it has been the turn of the secondary sector to decline as more people moved into service provision. Here the USA was the pacemaker as far back as 1950, but unlike the shift from primary to secondary production, other countries are rapidly approaching or have exceeded the US proportion of labour in services. Given modern technology, communications and the rapid spread of knowledge of opportunities for employment alternatives this relatively swifter shift is possibly not too surprising.

At a narrower level countries subdivide industries by Standard Industrial Classification (SIC) systems. These are not comparable across countries although the European states are beginning to move towards uniformity since the UK changed its system in 1980. Furthermore, for reasons already stated, they probably do not identify exactly with what economists define as an industry for purposes of study. Moreover the SICs often need to be re-defined to attempt to bring them into line with students' requirements. This is laudable and is due to changing tastes and technologies as well as to data improvements. It does render comparisons over time that much more difficult. Table 5.5 con-trasts the US and UK SIC systems. The terminology differs between the countries, and the US goes to a much finer level of disaggregation (7) than the UK (4). Direct international com-parability is thus not possible. Concentration ratios are provided in both sets of data. In the USA four and eight firm ratios are given as far down as the Six-Digit Level. While in the UK the five firm ratio is provided at the Three-Digit level. Inspection of the digits can show which of the Activities, Groups, Classes and Divisions (for the UK), a Census industry is in. Thus, from Table 5.5 Tractors (3212), the first digit (3) indicates membership of the Division, the second digit (2) the Class, the third digit (1) the Group and the final digit (2) the Activity. Clearly the number of subdivisions any more highly aggregated industry may have varies case by case in both countries depending on the facility with which a statistical breakdown is possible.

It is quite clear from the data available that the primary sector has suffered a decline in employment. Agriculture's share of GDP has also fallen but, owing to improved agricultural labour pro-ductivity, output has increased almost inversely with employment decrease. In the UK the category energy and water supply (see Table 5.6) has maintained its share of GDP, mainly (although this would only be shown by going to the appropriate digit level) owing to the advent of North Sea oil and gas, which have offset

*Table 5.5  Standard Industrial Classification systems*

| USA (examples) | UK (examples) |
|---|---|

*One-Digit Sectors*

    0  Agriculture, Forestry and Fishing
    2  Manufacturing

    4  Transportation, communications, electric, gas and sanitary services
    6  Finance, Insurance and Real Estate

*One-Digit Divisions*

    0  Agriculture, Forestry and Fishing
    3  Metal goods, engineering and vehicle industries
    5  Construction

    7  Transport and communication

*Two-Digit Major Groups*
(one-digit industries are broken down into several two-digit categories)

    08  Forestry
    28  Chemicals and Allied Products
    45  Transportation by Air
    61  Credit agencies other than Banks

*Two-Digit Classes*

    01  Agriculture and Horticulture
    32  Mechanical engineering
    75  Air transportation

*Three-Digit Fields*

    284  Cleaning and Toilet Products

*Three-Digit Groups*

    321  Agriculture machinery and tractors
    326  Mechanical power transmission equipment
    327  Machinery for the printing, paper and wood industries; laundry and dry cleaning equipment

*Four-Digit Industries*

    2834  Pharmaceutical Preparations
    2844  Toilet Preparations

*Four-Digit Activities*

    3211  Agricultural machinery
    3212  Tractors
    3276  Printing, bookbinding and paper goods machinery

*Five-Digit Product Classes*

    28445  Other Cosmetics and Toilet Preparations

*Six-Digit Commodity Levels*

    284451  Sun Tan Oils, Lipsticks, Cleansing creams, etc.

*Seven-Digit Product Lines*

    2844515  Sun Tan Oils

*Sources:* F.M. Scherer (1980), *Industrial Market Structure and Economic Performance* (New York: Rand-McNally, 2nd edition); W.G. Shepherd (1986), *The Economics of Industrial Organisation* (New York: Prentice-Hall, 2nd edition); *Business Monitor* (1987), *Report of the Census of Production* (London: HMSO).

*Table 5.6    Employment and changes in employment,
            and GDP and changes in GDP, UK industry 1981–85*

| SIC | | 1981 | 1985 | % Change | 1981 | 1985 | % Change |
|---|---|---|---|---|---|---|---|
| | | ('000s Employees) | | | (GDP %) | | |
| 0 | Agriculture, forestry, fishing | 353 | 339 | – 4.0 | 2.1 | 1.7 | –19.0 |
| 1 | Energy and water supply | 709 | 614 | –13.4 | 10.6 | 10.6 | 0 |
| 2 | Other mineral and ore extraction, etc. | 934 | 800 | –14.3 | | | |
| 3 | Metal goods, engineering and vehicles | 2919 | 2612 | –10.5 | 24.2 | 23.8 | – 1.7 |
| 4 | Other manufacturing industries | 2367 | 2122 | –10.4 | | | |
| 5 | Construction | 1139 | 970 | –14.8 | 5.7 | 5.8 | + 1.8 |
| 6 | Distribution, hotels, catering, repairs | 4167 | 4471 | + 7.3 | 11.8 | 12.5 | + 5.9 |
| 7 | Transport and communication | 1423 | 1304 | – 8.4 | 6.9 | 6.5 | – 5.8 |
| 8 | Banking, finance, insurance, etc. | 1740 | 1971 | +13.3 | 11.3 | 13.2 | +16.8 |
| 9 | Other services | 6121 | 6266 | + 2.4 | 21.2 | 20.4 | – 3.8 |
| | Total | 21 872 | 21 466 | – 1.9 | | | |

*Source:    Annual Abstract of Statistics.*

*Table 5.7    Relative growth rates of selected sectors (%)*

| Group heading | | Production (1980–1984) | Employment (1981–1984) |
|---|---|---|---|
| 221 | Iron and steel manufacture | + 4.3 | –17.4 |
| 222 | Steel tubes | +47.6 | –21.2 |
| 247 | Glass | – 4.6 | –11.3 |
| 251 | Basic industrial chemicals | +15.8 | –13.0 |
| 257 | Pharmaceutical products | +18.5 | 0 |
| 312 | Forgings, pressings and stampings | –22.7 | –12.5 |
| 322 | Machine tools and engineers' tools | –27.8 | –11.0 |
| 330 | Computers and office machinery | +107.0 | + 1.9 |
| 344 | Telecommunication equipment | +21.0 | + 1.0 |
| 351 | Motor vehicles and engines | –25.2 | –10.4 |
| 419 | Bread, biscuits and flour confectionery | – 2.5 | – 2.8 |
| 422 | Animal feeding stuffs | + 3.0 | – 4.3 |
| 453 | Clothing, hats and gloves | + 3.3 | – 8.6 |

*Source:    Annual Abstract of Statistics (London: HMSO, 1987).*

the decline in the coal industry. Secondary industries (Divisions 2–5) have also remained fairly steady in their contribution to GDP but like Division 1 they have also seen a substantial reduction in their contribution to employment. Manufacturing (Divisions 2–4) as a whole has seen a fall in both output and employment (a trend which has continued from the 1970s). Within the SIC classes and groups themselves, however, considerable differences would be evident. Annual output growth rates (see Table 5.7) have been high in steel tubes (222), chemicals (251 and 257) and computers and office machinery (330) and telecommunications equipment (344) while machine tools (322) and motor vehicles (351) have shown dramatic drops. Overall employment in Divisions 2–4 fell by 10 per cent. Conversely, employment and output in the tertiary industries (broadly the government and the distributive and service industries) have both risen (Divisions 8 and 9 in Table 5.6).

Table 5.6 does emphasize one point. All employees are at work in some 'industry'. Sometimes that industry is state-owned, sometimes not. According to some economists this is not of prime importance to an examination of the 'mixed economy'. Rather than the size of the state-owned or controlled sector *per se*,

> it is the public sector activities which do not provide marketed outputs that put particular pressure on the resources of the remainder of the economy . . . [as these rose] from 41.4 per cent of market output in 1961 to 60.3 per cent in 1974 . . . [they reduced] by nearly one-third the proportion of output that market-sector producers (state or privately owned) could themselves invest and consume. (Bacon and Eltis, 1976, p. 4)

In the remainder of this book we shall be concerned with markets and buyers and sellers, whether state, government, private firms, cooperatives or individuals. We shall not be examining the effect of state activities outside the marketplace except as they impinge directly on voluntary trading behaviour.

## 5.3 INDUSTRIAL STRUCTURE AND MORPHOLOGY

When considering changes in employment, output and contribution to GDP by Standard Industrial Classification care should be exercised for at least six reasons:

1.  The output growth figures are measured by a range of incompatible indices varying largely with data availability (e.g. sales, volume and employment may be used as proxies for net output).
2.  The aggregated SIC Divisions may disguise contrary movements within the Activities which go to make up the Groups and Classes.
3.  Output variations are not traced within any two points in time studied. Thus while mining has been in almost continuous decline for over three decades, in the UK oil has only rapidly risen since 1975.
4.  Quality changes are largely (if not totally) ignored by the indices.
5.  Employment data do not allow for changes in labour type or in quantity of hours worked.
6.  Interdependencies between Divisions and/or Classes are ignored. Thus if vehicles (Division 3) change, one would expect Transport (Division 7) to alter in a similar direction since transportation requires quantities of input from Division 3.

Table 5.6 summarizes the industrial structure of the UK by net output and by employment in 1980. Again this emphasizes the importance of the secondary and tertiary sectors of the economy.

Table 5.7 highlights even more clearly than do the highly aggregated figures of Table 5.6 that production growth and decline are not necessarily linked to employment changes. Technology can improve, thus dramatically changing labour productivity for the better. Alternatively, industries may be contracting; firms may wish to avoid declaring workers redundant (itself costly in the short run, given statutory redundancy payments only partially subsidized by government) to minimize the risk that if any trading downturn is temporary then costly labour upheavals, sackings and subsequent recruitment and retraining can be avoided. If this decision is taken then, of course, labour productivity falls and employment declines less rapidly than production. In the period covered by the Table, however, factors such as these seem to have been less important than the shedding of labour which, by inference, was surplus to requirements.

Recall Table 5.4 which related to a much longer timespan (1870–1984), and which showed how dramatic has been the broad employment shift in the last 100 years. Manufacturing has remained relatively static as an employer of labour (albeit there have been significant movements within that sector). But the major shift has been from agriculture, mining and other primary industries (1 in 10 of the employed labour force in 1913 to 1 in 40 in 1984) towards the service sector.

This is not necessarily a matter for condemnation. It is a typical pattern in most advanced economies that the tertiary sector should grow in relative importance. Sometimes it is bewailed that this is 'eroding the country's industrial base' but services can be just as important as tangible goods. Without the intangibles of distribution and insurance, many tangible manufactures would never reach the consumer. Without the intangible of advertising many consumers would never learn of new technologies in consumer hardware such as microwave ovens or video cassette recorders. As material wealth rises people often tend to prefer the intangible satisfaction of a holiday abroad, a symphony concert, better health care, a football match, or even pop music. From the viewpoint of the consumer, social value lies in what the consumer believes the goods or the services are worth. A singer may produce a sound which vanishes the instant it is produced, but if the consumer values it sufficiently highly to pay to listen to that sound then the tertiary sector increases and is valued as productive by those members of society who pay for its use.

Not only has British industry changed significantly over the years in terms of sectoral or sub-sectoral importance, but so also has its organization and structure. Table 5.8 shows how in manufacturing industry the share of net output accounted for by the 100 largest firms has increased from 22 per cent after World War II to around 40 per cent in the 1980s with the main rise occurring in the late 1950s and 1960s.

*Table 5.8  Share of 100 largest non-nationalized firms in manufacturing net output*

|  | % |  | % |
| --- | --- | --- | --- |
| 1949 | 22 | 1963 | 37 |
| 1953 | 27 | 1975 | 42 |
| 1958 | 32 | 1981 | 41 |
|  |  | 1984 | 39 |

*Source:*  S.J. Prais (1976), *The Evolution of Giant Firms in Britain* (Cambridge: Cambridge University Press); and *Business Monitor, Reports of the Census of Production* (London: HMSO).

It would appear that this increase in the importance of the top 100 firms is not due to growth in the average size of plant or manufacturing establishment, however. Plants, on average, are bigger than they were, but this is not the causal feature underlying Table 5.8. In Table 5.9 the first column, using a method derived by Sargent Florence, shows that the median worker was employed in a plant of 480 people in 1968 (i.e. 50 per cent of all workers were in plants smaller than the 480 employee size, and 50 per cent in larger plants). The second column, using a measure evolved by S.J. Prais, indicates that 25 per cent of all workers were employed in plants of under 130 persons in 1968, and 25 per cent in plants of over 1600 employees.

Prais points out that despite this (admittedly non-spectacular) plant size increase the share of the 100 largest plants in net output did rise but only from 9 per cent in 1948 to 10.8 per cent in 1968. Thus the increase in net output attributed to the largest firms in Table 5.8 probably owes far more to an increase in multi-plant ownership by individual firms than to an increase in establishment size as such.

Measures of aggregate concentration must, of course, be treated with care. First, they do not necessarily reflect what is happening at the level of the individual industry. Second, the yardstick used may alter the picture somewhat (e.g. net output, employees and capital assets could all be chosen and each could give different implications as to the level of concentration). Third, the number 100 is arbitrary. The top 50 or the top 200 firms, say, may or may not have changed in importance as did the top 100. Further, no indication is given, no matter what the number chosen, to what extent the firms examined are the same firms. Some of the top 100 firms in earlier years may now be extinct as a consequence of

Table 5.9   Plant size changes in manufacturing
                  measured by employees

| 1948 | Florence median | Prais central range |
|------|-----------------|---------------------|
| 1948 | 340 | 100–1220 |
| 1958 | 440 | 120–1650 |
| 1968 | 480 | 130–1600 |

Source:   Prais (1976), The Evolution of Giant Firms in Britain, Table 3.2.

bankruptcy or takeover, others may have shrunk and so fallen in ranking out of the top 100. Some of today's top 100, however, may not even have been in existence in earlier years or, if they were, may have been tiny. The effect such corporate mobility has for aggregate concentration is concealed, its implications are unclear and the inferences which could or should be drawn are indefinite. And, of course, no attempt is made here to ascertain which industries are or are not subject to overseas import competition or ownership.

Tables 5.10 and 5.11 attempt to shed some more light on British industrial organization, albeit they also introduce yet additional difficulties. They show the five-firm concentration ratios for employment and net output for a range of Two-Digit and Three-Digit manufacturing industries respectively.

*Table 5.10   Average five firm Three-Digit industry concentration levels analysed by Two-Digit divisions*

| Division | | No. of classes | Concentration ratios | |
|---|---|---|---|---|
| | | | Employment | Net output |
| 21 | Extraction and preparation of metalliferous ore | 1 | 99.0 | 99.0 |
| 22 | Metal manufacture | 4 | 58.0 | 63.8 |
| 23 | Extraction of minerals not elsewhere specified | 2 | 49.0 | 54.4 |
| 24 | Non-metallic mineral products | 8 | 42.0 | 48.1 |
| 25 | Chemical industry | 6 | 40.2 | 42.5 |
| 26 | Manmade fibres | 1 | 91.0 | 92.0 |
| 31 | Metal goods not elsewhere specified | 5 | 15.4 | 17.5 |
| 32 | Mechanical engineering | 10 | 20.5 | 21.9 |
| 33 | Office machinery and data processing equipment | 1 | 44.0 | 61.0 |
| 34 | Electrical and electronic engineering | 7 | 43.9 | 46.7 |
| 35 | Motor vehicles and parts thereof | 3 | 64.4 | 70.0 |
| 36 | Other transport equipment | 5 | 71.0 | 67.8 |
| 37 | Instrument engineering | 4 | 27.3 | 29.3 |
| 41/42 | Food, drink and tobacco* | 15 | 52.8 | 52.8 |
| 43 | Textile industry | 9 | 39.2 | 31.8 |
| 44 | Leather and leather goods | 2 | 21.5 | 24.1 |
| 45 | Footwear and clothing | 4 | 17.2 | 19.6 |
| 46 | Timber and wooden furniture | 7 | 14.3 | 16.3 |
| 47 | Paper, paper products, printing and publishing | 3 | 20.7 | 23.2 |
| 48 | Processing of rubber and plastics | 2 | 21.8 | 21.9 |
| 49 | Other manufacturing industries | 5 | 20.4 | 23.4 |

*Excludes 'sugar and sugar by-products' where only six enterprises compete.
*Source:   Business Monitor* (1987).

*Table 5.11*    *Five firm concentration ratios: UK*
                *manufacturing industries (SIC Divisions*
                *2-4), Three-Digit level, 1984*

| Concentration ratio (range) | Number of industries | % employment | Number of industries | % of net output |
|---|---|---|---|---|
| 0–19 | 19 | 28.1 | 16 | 20.0 |
| 20–39 | 36 | 38.0 | 35 | 36.0 |
| 40–59 | 28 | 19.1 | 28 | 24.3 |
| 60–79 | 12 | 9.0 | 14 | 10.8 |
| 80–100 | 9 | 5.7 | 11 | 8.9 |
| | 104* | 100.0 | 104 | 100.0 |

*Only 'sugar and sugar by-products' is omitted from all 105 industries since the number of major firms there is so small that commercial confidentiality would be breached if the Census takers published the information.

*Source:*   *Business Monitor* (1987), *Report of the Census of Production* (London: HMSO).

Concentration ratios show the percentage of whatever variable is being measured which is controlled by the top few firms (in this instance five). The number of firms chosen will itself obviously influence the results.

Table 5.10 shows that neither net output nor employment is heavily concentrated in those 11 and 9 industries respectively where the top five firms control more than 80 per cent of net output and employment. Rather both net output and employment are fairly evenly spread across the lower groupings of industries, peaking where the top five firms control between 20 and 39 per cent of the relevant variables. In these industries (36 and 35) the percentage of total employment provided and of net output emanating is 38.0 and 36.0 respectively. Interestingly, the groups of industries with the lowest levels of concentration have both substantially higher employment and higher net output figures than the most concentrated groupings. Although Table 5.10 shows that something like 34 per cent of all employees and 44 per cent of all net output is produced in industries with five-firm concentration ratios of 40 per cent and above, it does not guide us as to which industries these are. Table 5.10 provides this information, and although this is much more aggregated than Table 5.11 it does show the very few industries which have only low concentration levels.

Only a minority of the SIC classes have five-firm concentration ratios above 50 per cent. The average figures in Table 5.10 have been adjusted or weighted for the relative importance of each class. The results are little different from the crude data. The industries with low levels of concentration are those particularly suited to small-scale production (e.g. divisions 45 and 46); conversely, where mass production and heavy capital equipment are likely to favour scale economies, high concentration levels appear (e.g. divisions 21 and 35). In other cases, high concentration is apparent where, at least at first glance, scale economies would not appear to be vitally important (e.g. divisions 41 and 42).

Several comments should be made about all of these data on industrial structure. First, international statistics suggest that the UK has a more highly concentrated structure than most other countries (Table 5.12 refers to comparably sized economies; comparison with a large country like the USA would be even more extreme). Second, Table 5.13 shows 30 individual industries in descending importance of market share represented by their minimum optimum or efficient scale (the MES, or where the long-run average cost curve bottoms out in relation to the quantity axis as a percentage of total market). The 'market' in the MES column is the UK home and export market except where indicated. A number, but by no means all, of the industries have appreciable economies of scale. However the penalty for operating at half MES is also small in many cases.

In short, in a number of cases firms may be larger, or as we saw earlier, have more plants than are apparently required to reap the

*Table 5.12   Four-firm employment concentration ratios in EEC countries*

|  | Weighted average concentration ratio (%) | | | |
|  | UK | West Germany | France | Italy |
| --- | --- | --- | --- | --- |
| 40 industries | 30 | 19 | 22 | 19 |
| All manufacturing industries | 32 | 22 | 24 | 20 |

*Source:*   K.D. George and T.S. Ward (1975), *The Structure of Industry in the EEC* (Cambridge: Cambridge University Press), Table 3.2.

*Table 5.13   MES as percentage of UK market, in relation
to percentage increase in total cost per unit
at 50 per cent MES*

| Product, etc.[a] | MES as % of market | % increase in total costs at 50% MES |
|---|---|---|
| Aircraft | > 100 | > 20 |
| Diesel engine | > 100 | > 4 |
| Machine tools | > 100 | 5 |
| Newspapers | 100 | 20 |
| Dyes | 100 | 22 |
| Turbogenerators | 100 | 5 |
| Computers, etc. | 100 | 8 |
| Steel rolling: plant | 80 | 8 |
| Polymer manufacture | 66 | 5 |
| Electric motors | 60 | 15 |
| Cars | 50 | 6 |
| Refrigerators, etc. | 50 | 8 |
| Oil refineries: plant | 40 | 5 |
| Cement: plant[b] | 40 | 9 |
| Bulk steel production: plant | 33 | 5–10 |
| Bread: plant[b] | 33 | 15 |
| Polymer extrusion: plant | 33 | 7 |
| Sulphuric acid: plant | 30 | 1 |
| Cylinder blocks: plant | 30 | 10 |
| Ethylene: plant | 25 | 9 |
| Detergents: plant | 20 | 2.5 |
| Bicycles | 10 | (small) |
| Beer: plant[b] | 6 | 9 |
| Bricks: plant[b] | 5 | 25 |
| Warp knitting: plant | 3 | (small) |
| Cotton textile: plant | 2 | (small) |
| Book printing: plant | 2 | (small) |
| Plastics: plant | 1 | (small) |
| Engineering castings: plant | 0.2 | 5 |
| Footwear: plant | 0.2 | 2 |

[a]Unless a plant is specified, 'product' refers to one type, model or range of models.
[b]Serving regional submarket.

*Source:*   A. Silberston (1972), 'Economies of scale in theory and practice', *Economic Journal*, 82, pp. 369–91.

benefits of scale economies (or conversely be possibly unnecessarily large to avoid the often small costs of failing to operate at
MES). This emphasizes a third point: the continuing importance
of small firms in the economy.

Table 5.14 shows that although compared to pre-World War II
figures small firms are becoming less important, this decline ceased
in the 1960s and 1970s.

*Table 5.14   Small firms in manufacturing**

| Year | Number (% of total) | Net output (% of total) | Employment (% of total) |
|------|---------------------|-------------------------|-------------------------|
| 1935 | 97 | 35 | 38 |
| 1958 | 94 | 20 | 24 |
| 1963 | 94 | 16 | 20 |
| 1968 | 94 | 16 | 19 |
| 1970 | 95.1 | 21.2 | 18.4 |
| 1971 | 95.3 | 20.9 | 17.8 |
| 1972 | 95.3 | 21.5 | 18.7 |

*The figures above and below the dashed line are not computed on comparable bases.
A 'small firm' is defined as one employing under 200 people.

Source:   P.S. Johnson (1978), 'Policies towards small firms: time for caution', *Lloyds
Bank Review*, pp. 1–11.

Table 5.15 stresses even more than do Tables 5.9–5.13 just how
important the small plant (if not the small firm) continues to be in
UK industry. In ten industries out of 17, small establishments are
responsible for over 40 per cent of total employment (on average
the figure is 44.9 per cent). In some industries, where technical
scale economies are obviously unimportant, the figure exceeds
60 per cent. Conversely, in only two of the industries do large
units account for more than 50 per cent of total employment, and
in only one (other transport equipment) do the large units account
for more than 60 per cent of industry employment. Thus again
our initial view that British industry appears to be concentrated at
the firm rather than the plant level is substantiated. When large
plants exist they appear to do so in industries where technical
scale economies would be important. Large firms, therefore, must
exist either to facilitate reconciliation of the optima of the five

*Table 5.15   Small establishments in manufacturing 1983.*
*Employees as % total employment*

|  | Total | Employees in small units (under 200) | Employees in large units (1000 or more) |
|---|---|---|---|
| All manufacturing industries | 100.0 | 44.9 (36.5)* | 21.5 (29.0)* |
| Metal manufacture, etc. | 3.2 | 31.1 | 28.4 |
| Extraction of minerals n.e.s., etc. | 4.2 | 52.7 | 8.4 |
| Chemical industry and manmade fibres | 6.1 | 28.9 | 30.6 |
| Manufacture of metal goods n.e.s. | 6.7 | 64.8 | 3.5 |
| Mechanical engineering | 12.9 | 50.9 | 16.5 |
| Office machinery & data processing equipment | 0.9 | 29.2 | 32.4 |
| Electrical and electronic engineering | 11.3 | 29.0 | 30.6 |
| Motor vehicles and parts | 5.6 | 18.8 | 57.3 |
| Other transport equipment | 5.8 | 14.1 | 71.6 |
| Instrument engineering | 1.6 | 58.1 | 5.4 |
| Food, drink and tobacco | 11.5 | 35.2 | 22.0 |
| Textiles | 4.6 | 56.2 | 4.6 |
| Leather and leather goods | 0.5 | 84.8 | 0.0 |
| Footwear and clothing | 6.2 | 66.0 | 1.2 |
| Timber and wooden furniture | 3.9 | 79.2 | 0.0 |
| Paper, printing and publishing | 9.4 | 53.6 | 14.7 |
| Processing of rubber and plastics | 3.9 | 53.7 | 14.2 |
| Other | 1.6 | 77.4 | 1.9 |

*Figures in brackets are for 1976.

*Source:   Annual Abstract of Statistics (1987).*

Robinsonian criteria[1] or for the wish to acquire monopoly power, or to obtain as yet unrealized scale economy benefits at plant level. Given international comparisons, such as those of Table 5.12 and the evidence of Table 5.13 the last reason may be less likely than variants of the other two.

Comparisons with the United States are not easy to make directly because the sizes of the two markets differ. One would expect, therefore, given scale and technology and other things equal that the larger US market would be subject to less industrial concentration than the UK.

Table 5.16 provides evidence supporting this view. The share of the 100 largest firms in manufacturing net output is below the British equivalent levels (see Table 5.8 for similar although not directly comparable figures). Table 5.16 shows a similar pattern to the UK in that aggregate concentration has risen since pre-World War II levels but has not increased significantly in the post-war years.

*Table 5.16   Share of 100 largest US firms (%) of net output*

| 1909 | 22 | 1958 | 20 |
|------|----|------|----|
| 1975 | 26 | 1967 | 33 |
| 1947 | 23 | 1976 | 34 |
| 1954 | 30 | | |

*Source:*   M.C. Sawyer (1986), *Economics of Industries and Firms* (London: Croom Helm, 2nd edition), p. 39.

Table 5.17, relating to Four-Digit US industries, also shows there has been little if any substantive concentration ratio change in post-war years. Table 5.17 must not, of course, be compared directly with Table 5.10 or 5.11 for the UK since the aggregation levels are not identical, nor is the measure of concentration itself.

*Table 5.17   Average concentration ratios (4 firm) by*
*values of shipments (US)*
*(166 Four-Digit industries)*

| | Weighted | Unweighted |
|------|----------|------------|
| 1947 | 40.9 | 38.7 |
| 1954 | 40.6 | 43.0 |
| 1958 | 40.3 | 42.1 |
| 1963 | 41.3 | 42.9 |
| 1968 | 41.4 | 42.3 |
| 1970 | 42.2 | 42.6 |

*Source:*   Sawyer, op.cit., p. 39.

## 5.4   COST IMPLICATIONS OF COMPANY SIZE

In the discussion above we inferred that an industry's minimum efficient scale (MES) was important. Figure 5.2 illustrates how, even if unit costs are the same, the level of MES and the way in which it is achieved can have considerable impact on an industry or firm. Minimum unit costs in each of industries X, Y and Z are

$C_1$, but whereas eight firms could operate in X after achieving full scale economies, only two could in Y and Z. If the firms in Y and Z were only large enough to produce output $Q_1$, those in Y would operate at a unit cost of $C_2$, only slightly above $C_1$; yet the firms in Z would incur a much greater cost penalty in having to operate at $C_3$.

*Figure 5.2    Costs and minimum efficient scale*

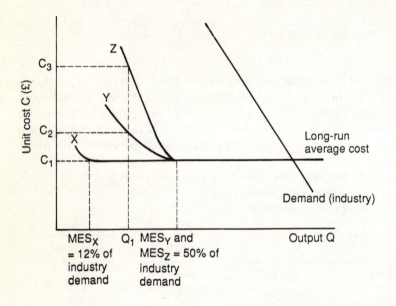

Clearly, bodies such as the Monopolies and Mergers Commission and the Anti-trust authorities are interested in how estimates of MES can be arrived at. There are three main methods of arriving at the data underlying a firm's or industry's long-run average cost (LRAC) curve.

First, there is statistical cost analysis whereby differing sizes of plants are compared at any one time. A number of problems must be overcome, however, if the results are to have credibility. The financial accounts of the firms to be compared must be uniform. Depreciation policies, for example, must be similar. Factor prices should be identical, a difficult requirement if a plant in Scotland is being compared with one in the South-East. Labour costs in Scotland may be lower but fuel prices may be higher. Each firm should be operating with the most efficient known methods. Perhaps most important of all, each firm should be operating in an equilibrium position on its short-run average cost curve, not on its long-run one. Short-run costs will be confused with long-run costs in the analysis. The statistician cannot even assume that, given a sufficiently large sample, at any one output level short-run costs will be evenly distributed round the long-run and so the error will be averaged out. Short-run costs can exceed, but cannot possibly be less than, long-run average costs at any one output level (since the LRAC curve is an 'envelope' curve).

Second, long-run costs can be estimated by the engineering technique. This is based on hypothetical estimations made by those with a knowledge of the production technology involved. Optimal input combinations are estimated for given quantities and the cost curve is found by applying the relevant input prices to these data. The technique is none the worse for being based on hypothetical data. Its accuracy may be questioned, however. Often, scale economies (or diseconomies) cannot be envisaged until a given scale of operations is operated in practice. The subsequent 'scaling-up' problems chemical engineers have when moving from pilot plant to full-scale factory operation are well known. Both of these techniques are further complicated by the presence of multi-product firms. The problems of apportioning joint costs must too often be solved in an arbitrary fashion.

Finally, there is the survivor technique developed by George Stigler. In essence this involves classifying the firms in an industry by size and calculating the share of industry output or capacity provided by each class over time. Size classes whose share increases over time are deemed to be more efficient and to have lower average costs, and vice versa. This technique does not give the precise level of money costs, it shows only the shape of the long-run average cost curve. It presupposes that all size classes of firms face the same economic environment; that they have the same objectives; and, unless technology has been constant over time, that they have been equally adept at introducing and assimilating new techniques. Since the survivor technique is used over time the LRAC as inferred does comply with the unchanging technology assumption of cost theory.

## 5.5 MORE NOTES OF CAUTION

The discussion in this chapter should have left the alert reader
with several more reservations about drawing dogmatic conclusions from either apparently logical paradigms or seemingly
unambiguous statistics. For example, most of the data related to
manufacturing industry. What are concentration levels like in the
primary and tertiary sectors? If the secondary sector is contracting
in relative terms what implications does that have for expected
concentration levels in that sector (or sub-sectors therein)? If
concentration levels are an adequate measure of structure how
should they be adjusted to take account of the facts that the
structure of competition in an industry should embrace also other
sources of competition in the marketplace? Imports, for example,
compete with domestic manufactures. Innovative products or
processes also compete with the manufactures in a given SIC
sector but may arise from a totally different SIC grouping. Within
SIC groupings new entrant firms themselves only really make an
impact on the census statistics after they have grown beyond some
minimum size, but their influence on existing firm's behaviour, as
well as that of extra-national or extra-SIC group competition can
easily be overlooked. We have also looked at scale economies, and
suggested, possibly rashly, that MES is often quite small relative to
market size. Yet again the data used tend to be based on manufacturing scale economies. Are there not possibly scale economies in
advertising, R & D activity, corporate financing and the practice
of international trading which make the MES for the firm much
larger than that for the plant? These caveats are very easy to over-
look by students who scan census data with the hope of readily
applying the often deceptively attractive SCP paradigm. They do
not necessarily negate the model. They do suggest, at the very
least, that care be taken in its application.

## NOTE

1.  Austin Robinson in his classic book from the 1930s, *The Structure of
    Competitive Industry*, suggested that scale economies are present in
    manufacturing, marketing, finance, risk, staffing and management. Given
    the principle of multiples, firms of optimal scale must be large enough
    not only to achieve minimum unit cost in each of these, but do so at
    such a size (the least common multiple) that no unexhausted scale

economies exist in any. Alternatively, optimal firm size is that size level where economies from one or more of the five Robinsonian functions outweigh any diseconomies which might be arising in one or more of the other four. This is the 'reconciliation of the optima'.

# REFERENCE

Bacon, W. and Eltis, R. (1976), *Too Few Producers?* (Oxford: Oxford University Press).

# 6. The Issue of International Business

This chapter focuses on two main issues. First and briefly, the fact that ignoring imports and exports when defining the supply and demand sides of markets can be misleading. Second, and in more detail, the subsequent issue that not only is foreign trade a factor which should not be omitted in any discussion of industrial economics, but that foreign direct investment (FDI) must influence the discussion also. Multinational companies (parents or subsidiaries) cannot simply be regarded as 'just another firm' in the national industrial sector under study. They are vertically integrated organizations which, to a greater or lesser extent, perform earlier or later stages in the chain of production in other national economies. This affects observed structure in any given economy and misleading inferences about conduct and performance may then follow.

## 6.1  FOREIGN TRADE

The dangers of omitting imports and exports from empirical industrial economics are obvious, although it is only relatively recently that workers in the field have explicitly acknowledged their importance in econometric studies. One reason for the omission is that early tests of the SCP paradigm originated in the USA where, with its large domestic market, foreign trade is relatively less important. Even there, however, this importance varies sector by sector and the long-term trend overall is up (exports as a share of US GDP approximately doubled in the 1970s). Table 6.1 shows the ratio of exports to GDP for selected non-communist countries. In general, the smaller the economy, the larger is the ratio.

International trade, of course, should not have been overlooked even in early work by industrial economists. Adam Smith argued for it on the basis of the advantages of division of labour and absolute cost differences. David Ricardo took the argument one stage further and showed that, even if a country was absolutely disadvantaged in the output of two commodities, specialization and trade were still worthwhile because of the principle of *comparative* advantage. The Ricardian comparative advantage was due to differential labour productivities between two countries (due in turn to varying national technologies and production functions). The latter was not explained by Ricardo, but his basic model still helps explain the pattern of trade flows. Hood and Young (1979, p. 137) explain that it was because of this deficiency that the Heckscher–Ohlin theory (H–O) was developed.

Heckscher and Ohlin were Swedes who attempted to explain the pattern of international trade as being consequential on a country's endowments of inputs, in particular the labour and capital factors of production. A nation will have a comparative advantage in these products in which its most abundant factor is used relatively intensively (and hence will export that product). Conversely, it will import those products which tend to require factor inputs with which the country is relatively poorly endowed.

Thus a country which is capital-rich but short of labour (relative to its trading partners) will have a comparative advantage in products which require a high capital:labour input ratio. Such goods will be exported, and products which require a high labour:capital input ratio will be imported. The rationale, of course, is that capital abundance will be reflected in a low (relative to other countries) price of capital and a high (relative) price of labour. Capital intensive goods will thus have a relatively low price. H–O theory obviously assumes international factor immobility, but, unlike Richardian theory, uniform production functions across nations and hence free flows of information.

Table 6.1  *Exports as percentage of GDP, 1982*

| Country | % | Country | % |
|---|---|---|---|
| Australia | 13.5 | Belgium | 60.7 |
| Canada | 23.0 | France | 17.1 |
| W. Germany | 26.7 | Indonesia* | 26.2 |
| Italy | 21.1 | Japan | 13.0 |
| Korea* | 32.3 | Netherlands | 48.1 |
| Singapore | 139.2 | UK | 20.3 |
| USA | 7.0 | Spain | 11.3 |

*1981.

Source:  S. Globermann (1986), *Fundamentals of International Business Management* (New York: Prentice-Hall), p. 5.

Despite the factor immobility constraint in H–O theory, factor prices still tend towards equality because of international trade. Thus, for example, a labour-rich country will export labour-intensive goods. This will increase demand for labour in the exporting country thus raising wages in that country (and depressing them in the importing country). In 1954 the H–O theory was subject to a major shock when in an empirical study Leontief produced evidence contradicting its predictions. His results are now known as the 'Leontief Paradox' and it will be seen below that the Paradox is (at least partly) due to the factor immobility constraint imposed in H–O theory. Relaxation of that constraint is, of course, necessary if we are to examine the phenomenon of the multinational enterprise (MNE) and foreign direct investment (FDI). For the moment let us examine the paradox in more detail and list explanations put forward for its existence.

Leontief applied Input–Output analysis to the US economy for 1947. He attempted to ascertain how much capital and how much labour was required to produce a given value of US exports on the one hand, and of US home-produced goods which competed with US imports on the other. Intuitively the US is a capital-rich/labour-poor country, and so, by H–O theory, it should specialize in and hence export capital-intensive products and import labour-intensive goods. Leontief's results, however, showed that US exports required a greater ratio of labour:capital than did production of import-competing goods. The US was apparently a capital-short country specializing in labour-intensive production.

Hood and Young (p. 138) summarize several explanations put forward to resolve the paradox. For example, H–O theory assumes similar consumption patterns at different income levels. But the US is a high-income country with a strong demand for capital-intensive goods resulting in a higher price in the US for such goods despite relative capital abundance. Second Input–Output analysis itself has deficiencies. There are fixed technological coefficients. That is, for a given type of product, irrespective of output level, the ratio of capital:labour is invariant. This flaw is magnified if (as Leontief did) US exports are compared not with US imports from other countries but with US produced import substitutes. The capital:labour ratios of actual imports in their countries of origin might have produced a different picture. Third, labour is not homogeneous, although it is assumed to be in both H–O and Input–Output analysis. Leontief himself argued that US labour may in fact be plentiful and hence cheap (in productivity wage terms) because of differences in skills, training, scale economies or superior technology.

In short, international trade theory as developed through to the H–O level has proved deficient as a satisfactory description of reality. The Leontief Paradox has highlighted some of the deficiencies. H–O was too abstract from reality, particularly in allowing for factor mobility, while Input–Output analysis, albeit spotlighting deficiencies, has weaknesses in handling the richness, diversity and heterogeneity of real-life business inputs and outputs, and this may be especially so when we turn away from international flows of trade towards international flows of (equity or risk) capital through the MNE.

## 6.2 FOREIGN DIRECT INVESTMENT

The sheer scale and importance of multinational enterprises (MNE) and of FDI are such that the failure of H–O trade theory to be consistently upheld by the data given exclusion of factor mobility is probably unsurprising. Table 6.2 provides one measure of the importance of FDI in several economies. The table relates to the mid-1970s and early 1980s, and the data shown relate to the share of total domestic employment which is accounted for (in manufacturing) by foreign affiliates (inward significance) and the equivalent percentage if foreign employees of domestic MNEs are expressed as the numerator over total home country employees (outward significance).

The UK is an active participant in FDI both inwards and outwards. Sweden (with its relatively large number of giant MNEs

*Table 6.2 Significance of MNE activity*

|  | Inward | Outward |
| --- | --- | --- |
| UK | 15.6 | 21.9 |
| US | 4.6 | 28.2 |
| Japan | 1.6 | 14.1 |
| Belgium | 38.0 | 15.0 |
| Sweden | 5.7 | 26.1 |
| India | 10.0 | 5.0 |

*Source:* J. Dunning (1985), *Multinational Enterprises, Economic Structure and International Competitiveness* (Chichester: John Wiley), p. 412.

given its small economy) is predominantly outward-oriented. However, Table 6.2 is very static. Table 6.3 shows that the picture is actually very fluid. Japan, for example, over the period of the table has swung from a situation where inward and outward investment flows were exactly equal to one where inward investment has shrunk to a relative trickle. The USA conversely (partly due to the depreciating dollar in the 1980s) has seen inward flows as a small percentage of outward flow expand to a multiple of over five). Of course, part of the reason for the swing is the relatively simple one that once a nation's existing stock of major firms have 'gone multinational' then the wave is past and only new firms or expanding existing firms will appear in each year's data on outward flows (and vice versa, once the major firms are established in a given foreign market only new growth or additional firms can keep the flow high). This is true but it still does not explain why FDI occurs in the first place as opposed to, for example, export and import trading.

*Table 6.3   Inward as % outward FDI flows*

|  | 1963–65 | 1969–71 | 1975–77 | 1981–82 |
|---|---|---|---|---|
| UK | 64.4 | 63.2 | 52.4 | 26.1 |
| US | 7.9 | 14.8 | 28.7 | 528.0 |
| France | 178.5 | 149.8 | 111.1 | 54.6 |
| W. Germany | 281.3 | 85.8 | 38.6 | 26.5 |
| Japan | 100.0 | 40.8 | 7.0 | 6.8 |
| Canada | 305.6 | 278.5 | 46.8 | 95.2 |
| Sweden | 82.7 | 55.2 | 9.3 | 20.6 |
| Belgium/Luxembourg | 895.0 | 296.8 | 294.7 | 6013.6 |
| S. Korea | – | 339.5 | 757.7 | 87.6 |
| Portugal | 1446.3 | 591.1 | 1523.1 | 720.0 |

*Source:*   Dunning (1985), op.cit., p. 410.

Three main types of MNE predominate. First, the European-based firms (e.g. Shell, Dunlop, Unilever) which undertook backwards integration into agriculture and minerals in colonial territories in the early decades of the century. Second, the US-based MNEs which were a phenomena of the 1950s and 1960s and which undertook import-substituting investments (most obviously in Europe) and third, Japanese firms which emerged in the 1970s and 1980s using low wage, 'Pacific Rim' countries as export sources. These categories are, of course, drastically simplified and caricature reality but they are conceptually helpful. Tables 6.4 and 6.5 show respectively the 25 largest US MNEs, and the 25 largest non-US MNEs, operating in the US.

We have seen that international trade theory is not comprehensively helpful in explaining trade patterns. Nor did it allow for the movement of equity capital between nations which is so commonplace. What are the economic reasons for the existence of FDI? Several reasons have been put forward which we shall examine in turn. These are the need for supply security (backward integration), the product-cycle approach, the proprietary knowledge model, and the integrative or 'eclectic' theory.

Backward integration to secure supply sources is a common feature of industrial structure not just international industrial

*Table 6.4   The twenty-five largest US multinationals, 1983*

| | Company | Industry | Foreign Revenue ($ millions) | Total Revenue ($ millions) |
|---|---|---|---|---|
| 1 | Exxon | Petroleum | 61 815 | 88 651 |
| 2 | Mobil | Petroleum | 32 629 | 55 609 |
| 3 | Texaco | Petroleum | 25 157 | 40 068 |
| 4 | Phibro–Salomon | Financial services | 20 100 | 29 757 |
| 5 | IBM | Computers | 17 058 | 40 180 |
| 6 | Ford Motor | Motor vehicles | 16 080 | 44 455 |
| 7 | General Motors | Motor vehicles | 14 913 | 74 582 |
| 8 | Gulf | Petroleum | 11 535 | 26 581 |
| 9 | Standard Oil Calif. | Petroleum | 10 952 | 27 342 |
| 10 | Du Pont | Chemicals | 10 816 | 35 173 |
| 11 | Citicorp | Financial services | 9 650 | 17 037 |
| 12 | ITT | Conglomerate | 7 808 | 20 249 |
| 13 | BankAmerica | Financial services | 5 943 | 13 299 |
| 14 | Dow Chemical | Chemicals | 5 726 | 10 951 |
| 15 | Standard Oil Indiana | Petroleum | 5 363 | 27 937 |
| 16 | Chase Manhattan | Financial services | 4 943 | 8 523 |
| 17 | General Electric | Aircraft engines/ generating equipment | 4 758 | 27 681 |
| 18 | Occidental Petroleum | Petroleum | 4 544 | 19 709 |
| 19 | Safeway Stores | Retailing | 4 528 | 18 585 |
| 20 | Sun Co. | Petroleum | 4 282 | 14 928 |
| 21 | Proctor and Gamble | Consumer goods | 3 685 | 12 452 |
| 22 | J.P. Morgan | Financial services | 3 446 | 5 764 |
| 23 | Xerox | Copy/office equipment | 3 393 | 8 464 |
| 24 | Eastman Kodak | Photo equipment | 3 270 | 10 170 |
| 25 | Sears Roebuck | Retailing | 3 246 | 35 883 |

*Source:*   *Forbes*, 2 July 1984, pp. 114–15.

*Table 6.5  The twenty-five largest foreign investors in the US, 1983*

| | Foreign investor | Home country | US company | Industry | Revenue ($ millions) |
|---|---|---|---|---|---|
| 1 | Seagram Co. Ltd | Canada | J.E. Seagram, Du Pont | Spirits/chemicals | 36 653 |
| 2 | Anglo American of S. Africa | South Africa | Numerous | Metals/financial services | 32 417 |
| 3 | Royal Dutch/Shell | Netherlands/UK | Shell Oil | Petroleum | 20 978 |
| 4 | British Petroleum | UK | Standard Oil of Ohio | Petroleum | 11 599 |
| 5 | Mitsui & Co. | Japan | Mitsui | Conglomerate | 9 545 |
| 6 | BAT Industries | UK/Canada | BATUS | Paper/retailing | 7 122 |
| 7 | Flick Group | Germany | W. R. Grace | Conglomerate | 6 219 |
| 8 | Tengelmann Group | Germany | Great A & P Tea | Retailing | 5 222 |
| 9 | Régie Nationale des Usines Renault | France | American Motors | Motor vehicles | 4 489 |
| 10 | Brascan Ltd | Canada | Scott Paper, Noranda | Paper/metals | 4 251 |
| 11 | Beneficiaries of US Philips Trust | Netherlands | North American Philips | Electronics | 4 250 |
| 12 | Generale Occidentale | France | Grand Union | Retailing | 3 519 |
| 13 | Volkswagenwerk | Germany | Volkswagen of America | Motor vehicles | 3 492 |
| 14 | Bayer A.G. | Germany | Numerous | Chemicals | 3 445 |
| 15 | Mitsubishi | Japan | Mitsubishi International Corp. | Trading company | 3 165 |
| 16 | Unilever | Netherlands | Lever Brothers/Thomas J. Lipton | Household products/food | 3 119 |
| 17 | Nestlé | Switzerland | Numerous | Household products/food | 2 700 |
| 18 | Midland Bank | UK | Crocker National | Banking | 2 560 |
| 19 | Hanson Trust | UK | Numerous | Conglomerate | 2 361 |
| 20 | Bell Canada Enterprises | Canada | Northern Telecom | Telecommunications | 2 195 |
| 21 | Hongkong and Shanghai Banking Corp. | Hong Kong | Marine Midland Bank | Banking | 2 156 |
| 22 | CIBA-GEIGY | Switzerland | CIBA-GEIGY Corp. | Chemicals/drugs | 2 104 |
| 23 | Petrofina SA | Belgium | American Petrofina | Petroleum | 2 069 |
| 24 | Française des Pétroles | France/Canada | Total Petroleum | Petroleum | 2 034 |
| 25 | George Weston | Canada | Numerous | Food products | 2 033 |

*Source:  Forbes, 2 July 1984, pp. 101–3.*

structure. Why does it occur in some industries and not in others? Clearly there are additional costs involved in international as opposed to domestic backward integration (e.g. the costs of learning about operating in an alien commercial and political environment, the costs of communication which to some extent even with modern communications increase with distance, and so on). These transactions costs must, in certain instances, be perceived as lower than the benefits to be obtained by inter-nationalization. Casson (1987, pp. 3, 30) points out that only in some industries is backward FDI deemed worthwhile. Thus it is common in aluminium, copper, oil and bananas. It is rarer with metals such as tin, minerals such as coal, or agricultural industries such as grain or cotton. The benefits which outweigh the trans-actions costs of FDI in the minerals case are due not to the presence or absence of scale economies in smelting. (These are present in all three examples.) But rather to the greater degree of uncertainty present in securing supplies at the desired price in the case of aluminium and copper. Sources of these metals are concentrated while those of tin are diffuse. Bilateral monopoly uncertainty is best overcome by backward FDI in the case of aluminium and copper. Tin industry smelters do not perceive such a requirement. Similarly there are economies in the continuous and guaranteed flow of oil through pipelines (or ship) to the oil refineries which operate on a 24-hour day basis (which do not exist with coal). With coal, storage is perceived to be a lower-cost method of industrial organization to minimize uncertainty than internalizing transactions in order to obtain the benefits of centralized monitoring (as with multinational oil companies). Again security of supply is paramount. In the agriculture areas the security (this time of quality) is the spur. Casson (p. 30) points out that unlike grain or cotton, bananas pose serious problems of quality control which can best be resolved through skilled plantation management and the integration of growing, ripening and shipping. The much more homogeneous grains, which are readily storable, relatively non-perishable and have many alternative supply sources do not pose such a quality control security problem to millers who consequently perceive market transactions to be less costly than in-firm integrated operations.

Vernon's (1966) life-cycle explanation for the existence of the MNE moved attention away from the European-originating, backward-integrating MNE to the post-war US-originating pheno-mena. Simultaneously, he put forward reasons why his views might help resolve the 'Leontief Paradox'.

Vernon's argument commences with the axioms that the US is a high-income country characterized by high wages and plentiful capital. These facts impact on the demand for both consumer and industrial products. There will be a demand for innovations which are labour-saving in the workplace (as producers try to economize on high-cost labour) and also for income-elastic consumer goods (due to high-consumer incomes). There are, therefore, incentives to invest in product developments in such areas in the USA. The initial manufacturing of the resulting innovations will also take place in the USA, even if a superficial examination of the comparative cost suggests otherwise. This will be so, argues Vernon, because innovations are generally non-standardized, either in their process of manufacture or as products *per se*. (For example, early motor cars were petrol-driven, steam-driven, electrically-driven, had cam-shafts or chain drives, and so on.) Unit production costs will consequently be high until the optimum product and process in terms of market demand is arrived at. In turn this requires close coordination with the market itself. The benefits of this will outweigh any costs involved in initial non-optimal production technologies. Second, demand for innovations is generally price-inelastic in the early stages of marketing. Consequently, any such cost differentials will be relatively unimportant to the innovators. However, as the product matures, standardization of design, production technology, and the like set in. Prices fall as the market widens and scale economies appear. Exports may begin. Demand will appear next in high income-elastic countries such as Western Europe. Simultaneously the high labour costs involved in US production will come to play an increasingly important role in corporate decisions (as they form an ever-increasing proportion of declining selling prices). Overseas manufacture will come to be seen as an attractive possibility. (Partly due to the shift in location of the market, partly due to the decrease in importance of immediate market liaison, and partly due to the rising importance of labour costs.) FDI will thus come about with eventual exports from the overseas subsidiaries back into the USA provided only that labour cost savings exceed the transportation cost differential.

Vernon sees this scenario as at least partially resolving the Leontief Paradox. In the early stages of the above process high value-added items with an unusually high labour cost component were being produced in the USA. This was not because US labour was necessarily more skilled as suggested on pp. 98-9 but rather simply because at that stage in the product lifecycle production is labour-intensive and it is economically more efficient to produce in the innovating and high income US market. As the cycle progresses, the demand for the product becomes more price-elastic, and capital-intensive mass production methods set in, the cheaper location becomes, non-US and imports from subsidiaries arise. Again (and naturally) this is also at odds with H–O trade theory which suggests that the exports of labour-rich countries would be of labour-intensive products. The Vernon view is that at advanced stages of standardization less developed countries may offer a comparative advantage as production locations. Certainly the Vernon view also fits in with Japan's use of Pacific Rim nations as 'export platforms'.

Vernon's view is certainly plausible but it leaves unanswered the question of why this international relocation of production is done through the means of FDI (or close variants such as joint ventures or licensing) rather than by straight imitation by entrepreneurs in the other nations. Caves (1971) was one of the first to provide a convincing answer to this question. He answered the question by first eliminating a series of alternative but unsatisfactory answers. FDI might be explained by equity (or risk) capital flowing from low-return countries to high-return countries. (Rather like labour migrating from Turkey to West Germany, from Mozambique to South Africa, or Mexico to the USA as workers seek higher wages in foreign markets.) However, equity capital does not appear to flow systematically in such directions. Indeed, even a casual glance at MNEs shows a network of equity capital flowing to and from virtually the same nations. The capital-exporting nations are not obviously low-profit ones and indeed are often capital-importing and exporting simultaneously. Likewise, the desire to get under tariff barriers is a plausible but far from universal or even prime empirical reason for FDI. Moreover FDI is not selected by firms because it is a low-cost alternative to exporting. It may be on occasion, but there are high costs involved in establishing and operating a foreign subsidiary. Indeed, other things being equal, it would be cheaper and easier for a firm to expand domestically since it would not have to incur the costs of learning about a new and alien socio-economic culture. This suggests that MNEs will tend already to be large in their own domestic markets and so have reached the stage where diminishing returns have set in to expansion in their home country. Otherwise the cheaper, local expansion option would be selected. Nor is it likely, argues Caves, that MNEs come into being because they have low-cost access to a particular input such as organizational skills or finance. If that were so then in the former case MNEs would tend to be consultants and not exist, as they do, in a multiplicity of industries; while in the latter instance if low-cost finance were the key, then conglomerate expansion domestically (in a known milieu) would be preferable to horizontal foreign expansion (in a strange and costly environment).

Rather, Caves suggests equity capital is transferred between countries as part of a package of capital plus proprietary knowledge. Both words are required. 'Knowledge' is costless to transfer (whether that knowledge is due to R & D expenditures, patenting, marketing skills, advertising expertise, or whatever) and so can be shifted with equity to another market at no cost to the owner of the equity. The word 'proprietary' is also required, however, if FDI is to be explained under Caves' scheme. The asset of knowledge can provide a return to the firm, but that return can only be maximized if the firm goes multinational. For that to be so implies that either the knowledge is difficult for foreigners to use (because they lack the technological or marketing expertise), or if they can use it then the original owner would find it difficult to capture maximum returns unless an equity stake was also held. These conditions are more likely to hold in industries typified domestically by product differentiation, whether that differentiation is due to high levels of R & D expenditures, brand-image advertising, marketing expenditures adjusting the product to consumers' needs, or whatever. In such industries local skills and expertise will either be inadequate or, the other side of the coin, be all too adequate from the viewpoint of the firm wishing to profit-maximize by selling a readily copiable product.

Sometimes, of course, proprietary knowledge can be capitalized on without FDI but by exporting or licensing. A classic example is syrup for soft drinks. Provided the originating company is satisfied with the quality control arrangements of its importer or licensee who adds carbonated water to the syrup, it can capture the rents from the transfer of its proprietary knowledge in a 'syrup plus brand name' package rather than a 'capital plus brand' package.

Caves' model goes a long way to explaining the existence of FDI and thus why MNEs will tend to be large firms with an oligopolistic home market operating with large R & D and/ or advertising and other product differentiation expenditures. In his more recent work (1982) he adds to this transactions cost framework by explaining in more detail the role of tariffs.

## 6.3  TARIFFS AND FDI

Firms engage in FDI to secure markets and supply sources (vertical integration) and to maximize rent capture from proprietary knowledge (horizontal integration) given that FDI provides the lowest transactions cost integration method. Firms also opt for FDI to get under host government-imposed tariffs. Conversely, governments may impose such tariffs to encourage domestic production. Caves (1982, pp. 36–43) examined both the theory and evidence of this issue. Thus Canada and Australia were early adopters of tariffs (in the nineteenth century) for this purpose, while the creation of the European Economic Community is a more recent example of a large internal market which can provide scale economies for in-Europe production by foreign firms while discouraging imports from such firms by means of tariff protection. Figure 6.1 analyses how a firm would allocate its production activities in such circumstances.

Production for the foreign market can occur at home, in the host market or in both, depending on the relevant cost and demand schedules and tariffs levied. Thus consider the firm initially operating at home only. Output of $Q_1$ is being sold at the appropriate price on $D_H$. If exporting becomes possible at the given price of M it would be worthwhile to expand output to $Q_2$, selling $Q_3$ at home (at a higher price than domestic consumers were originally paying) and exporting $Q_2 - Q_3$. $C_x$ is the marginal cost of exporting schedule (panel b) and shows for each price such as M, the quantity the firm will export. (Thus $X = Q_2 - Q_3$ while $C_x$ intersects the price axis where $MR_H = MC_H$.) Panel c shows the firm's subsidiary in the foreign market. With complete independence of operation it would produce $Q_4$ for local sale with a corresponding price on $D_F$. Now assume the ability to import at price $M_t$. Local sales would be increased by the subsidiary management to $Q_5$ and local production reduced to $Q_6$. Price in the foreign market would be reduced accordingly to clear the increased output, $Q_5$. $R_m$ in panel b is the firm's marginal revenue from importing and is constructed from panel c analogously to the way $C_x$ was constructed from panel a. It shows for each price such as $M_t$, the quantity the firm will import. (Thus $X = Q_5 - Q_6$, while $R_m$ intersects the price axis where $MR_F = MC_F$.)

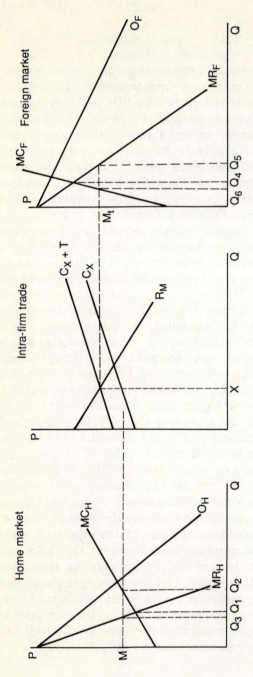

*Figure 6.1*

The diagram has shown so far the normal result of foreign trade, that prices of the traded good fall in the importing country, and rise in the exporting country. Production and, other things equal, jobs rise in the exporting country and decline in the importing nation. In addition panel b enables us to examine the impact of tariffs on the MNE's production location decision. The lower is $M_t$ the larger are imports, and vice versa. However, as it stands, the three panels are not reconciled. The intersection of $R_m$ and $C_x$ is the equilibrium level of imports/exports. This does not comply with the situations in panels a and b (for expository reasons only). Now assume the foreign government imposes a tariff on the imported good equal to t. The marginal cost of exporting rises to $C_{x+t}$ and the model is in equilibrium (and less will be exported than would have been in panel a's original construction). Indeed if the tariff was sufficiently high (so that $C_{x+t}$ intersected the vertical axis where $R_m$ does, which is where $MC_F = MR_F$) then only foreign production would be undertaken and home production would be restricted for sale to the domestic market. If there are unexhausted scale economies in production, Caves (p. 39) indicates that $MC_F$ and $MC_H$ would then slope downwards. The answer is less determinate. Certainly the firm would never produce in one market and also import into it. In the absence of tariffs it would either prefer to concentrate production in one location or in both, and market size and national absolute cost differences would play important roles. (The above arguments, of course, have assumed also no transfer price distortions.)

## 6.4 FDI TRADE-OFFS AND INDUSTRIAL ORGANIZATION

Hood and Young (1979, p. 182) using a model originally developed by MacDougall show the simplest case of how FDI impacts on both host and home countries' industrial conduct and performance. Figure 6.2 plots the host country's marginal productivity schedule against its capital stock before and after new increments of FDI. (Readers of managerial economics texts will see an analogy between the y and x axes of corporate Internal Rate of Return and capital budgeting diagrams.)

In panel a the existing capital stock is AC, of which BC is already foreign-owned, AB is domestically-owned and profits are

AFDC attributable to domestic and foreign owners of capital as indicated by the AB:BC split. The total product of the economy is the area GDCA of which GFD is wages to local employees (there are assumed to be no other factors of production such as land, and technology is constant). When FDI rises to BM profits attributable to foreigners change from CBDE to MBJL, a gain of KLCM to incoming foreign capital, but a loss of JKDE to existing foreign capital. That is, as the capital stock increases, given the labour force, the return on capital falls. Domestic capitalists lose HFEJ. This latter loss, however, and the loss JKDE, represent a redistribution of income to wage-earners in the host country whose total wage income rises from GFD to GHL (which includes the productivity gain of DKL resulting from the increased capital available to the labour force). Thus the host country (capital or labour) makes a net gain of DEJL. Moreover, this gain can be further increased by imposing a profits tax of t such that a gain of $(1 - t)$ (KLMC + JKBC) is appropriated.

Conversely the capital-exporting country would see an increase in its rate of return of capital and a reduction in wages, and a loss of potential tax revenue should the host government impose a profits tax.

MacDougall's framework is useful but it assumes a straight one-for-one transfer of capital from home to host country, perfectly competitive equilibrium and full employment in both countries. Payment balances are assumed to be in equilibrium and to remain that way, and scale economies do not exist. Once we drop these assumptions the analysis is more complex and a listing of costs and benefits may have to be resorted to on a case-by-case basis.

However, as we have already noted, it is not simply capital which is transferred but 'proprietary knowledge'. The host country therefore gains access to technology and management skills which by definition are not freely available locally. On the other hand, the capital investment (such as BC) might not be a new capital inflow but merely represent local borrowing by the MNE for domestic application, thus diverting it from other uses (or for that matter diverting it from less productive local users or even idle balances). Similarly the indigent manpower employed may be diverted from other more or less productive uses domestically (or from unemployment). To the extent that local labour or capital is diverted from less productive uses there seems little cause for concern. Those who worry when it has been diverted from more productive local uses must rest their case on either

*Figure 6.2*

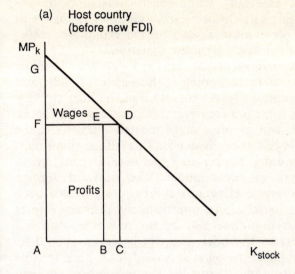

(a)  Host country
     (before new FDI)

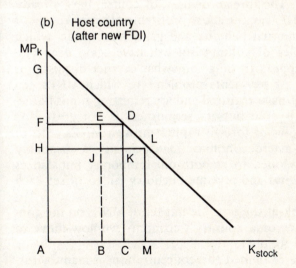

(b)  Host country
     (after new FDI)

chauvinistic arguments or on very long-term arguments in the local economy (a difficult logical task but a relatively easy propaganda exercise, especially when specific instances of disinvestment and branch plant closures can be cited). The answer to such propagandistic pleas must always be the economic query: 'What is (or was) the next best alternative situation?'

There are other externalities not obvious in Figure 6.2. The host country will gain access to technologies, management skills and other practices as manpower leaves the MNE in the host country and moves into other firms (no firm ever has a static labour force). The MNE, of course, will at some stage repatriate profits in the form of licence fees, royalties or dividends. This will, at that point, result in the host country having to experience a reduction in domestic expenditures to accommodate the outward foreign currency flows. (The reverse effects have, of course, already been felt at the time of the initial capital injection, and the same effects will have been felt at that time also by the investing country.) There are net benefits to the host country, however, even if its GNP must fall (as opposed to what it would have been at time with no repatriation of funds) provided the increase in national economic productivity has exceeded the return to the foreign owners of the MNE. The foreign owners, of course, have already also decided that FDI was the most profitable alternative use of their funds so the 'mutual benefits and gains from trade' which underlie the principles of voluntarism will have again been vindicated. This may appear to be a somewhat cavalier dismissal of the genuine balance of payments problems to which MNEs can contribute once they have matured and are remitting funds homewards. This charge is true but its seriousness is not great. (As already indicated, flows of foreign capital through MNEs tend to be bilateral and macroeconomic management is probably sufficiently well developed to smooth out temporary imbalances arising if capital inflows and revenue outflows fail to offset each other exactly.)

With this brief look at the possible impact of MNEs on the conduct and performance of a country's economy we now move to look at structure and conduct.

In earlier pages we examined the concentration of manufacturing in an economy on the SCP assumption that this would impact on competition. Any such concern should be modified by noting that on the demand side of the market consumers are faced not only with domestic producers but also with choice of supply from imports. Thus a domestic employment concentration ratio of 90 per cent for the top five firms may have very little meaning if, say, 80 per cent of sales are of imports. The top five firms by domestic employment should then only be seen as having 18 per cent of the market (by employment). Thus international trade increases the complexity of industrial economics studies. So too does the existence of MNEs.

Domestic firms may export much of their output. Domestic firms may themselves operate internationally, and the MNEs, locally or foreign-owned, in a given country may not be directly comparable in any given economy. Their degrees of vertical and horizontal integration will differ, as will their access to central corporate services (or proprietary knowledge) and so their market power (either in their ability to compete with each other or in their revealed price:cost margins) will not be directly comparable. If comparisons are made then misleading inferences will follow.

Tables 6.6 and 6.7 show respectively, for UK SIC Divisions 2–4 the nationality of ownership of UK private sector enterprises and the industrial classes in which they are located.

The tables relate only to foreign MNEs operating in the UK, and do not separate out British MNEs. Moreover they do not relate to sectors other than manufacturing and so may be unrepresentative of the economy as a whole. However, we can see that 13 per cent of total manufacturing employment is engaged in foreign-owned enterprises operating within the UK, and these enterprises are predominantly non-EEC-based, and indeed 670 of them are USA-owned. In terms of enterprise size, the MNEs are well above the average size of operating firm by employment. They account for 1.1 per cent of all enterprises and 14.9 per cent of employment. Their level of beneficiation per head is also higher, with 14.9 per cent of employment producing 20.3 per cent of net output. This, of course, is in line with what one would expect given the quasi-rents which can be reaped from proprietary knowledge.

Table 6.7 shows that MNE employment is concentrated in four industry groups (chemicals, mechanical engineering, electrical and electronic engineering and motor vehicles and parts) which account for well over half of total MNE employees. The second column in Table 6.7 shows those sectors where MNE employment is important (even if the sector is small by total employment standards). To the four sectors already mentioned can be added office machinery and data processing equipment, instrument engineering and rubber and plastics processing.

*Table 6.6   Foreign ownership of UK private
              sector enterprises (1984)*

| Country of ownership | Enterprises (No.) | Total employment (000s) | Net output (£m) |
|---|---|---|---|
| Belgium/Luxembourg | 11 | 2.4 | 39.6 |
| Denmark | 38 | 6.9 | 195.2 |
| France | 50 | 29.2 | 503.0 |
| W. Germany | 12 | 18.4 | 476.3 |
| Ireland | 60 | 10.7 | 165.9 |
| Italy | 8 | 1.1 | 45.0 |
| Holland | 53 | 30.4 | 643.2 |
| Total EEC | 342 (0.3%) | 99.0 (2.1%) | 2 068.3 (2.5%) |
| Australia | 31 | 18.3 | 488.2 |
| Canada | 67 | 55.2 | 1 268.0 |
| Hong Kong | 3 | 0.3 | 5.6 |
| Japan | 23 | 5.3 | 78.6 |
| Leichtenstein | 8 | 16.5 | 384.8 |
| Norway | 16 | 5.1 | 114.9 |
| S. Africa | 3 | 1.8 | 26.1 |
| Sweden | 52 | 16.8 | 318.0 |
| Switzerland | 57 | 32.0 | 584.6 |
| USA | 670 | 446.6 | 11 214.2 |
| Other | 58 | 19.5 | 569.0 |
| Total rest of the world | 988 (0.8%) | 617.3 (12.8%) | 15 025.1 (17.8%) |
| Total all UK (domestic and foreign) | 119 172 (100%) | 4 827.8 (100%) | 84 321.0 (100%) |

*Source:   Business Monitor (1987).*

*Table 6.7   Foreign ownership importance in
              UK manufacturing, 1984*

| SIC class | % of total foreign employees in this group | % of total UK employees in foreign enterprises |
|---|---|---|
| Metal manufacturing | 3.1 | 13.6 |
| Extraction of minerals m.e.s. | 0.01 | 0.9 |
| Manufacture of non-metallic mineral products | 1.6 | 5.6 |
| Chemicals | 12.7 | 31.6 |
| Man-made fibres | 0.1 | 8.7 |
| Metal goods m.e.s. | 4.0 | 8.5 |
| Mechanical engineering | 15.4 | 17.1 |
| Office machinery & data processing equipment | 2.0 | 33.3 |
| Electrical/electronic engineering | 14.5 | 18.5 |
| Motor vehicles and parts | 13.8 | 34.2 |
| Other transport equipment | 0.7 | 1.6 |
| Instrument engineering | 2.2 | 19.7 |
| Food, drink and tobacco | 10.0 | 11.7 |
| Textiles | 0.9 | 2.6 |
| Leather | 0.04 | 1.4 |
| Footwear/clothing | 1.1 | 2.4 |
| Timber and wooden furniture | 0.8 | 2.8 |
| Paper, printing and publishing | 9.8 | 15.3 |
| Processing of rubber and plastics | 5.9 | 20.8 |
| Other manufacturing | 1.4 | 12.4 |

*Source:   Business Monitor (1987).*

# REFERENCES

Casson, M. (1987), *The Firm and the Market* (Oxford: Blackwell).

Caves, R.E. (1982), *Multinational Enterprise and Economic Analysis* (Cambridge: Cambridge University Press).

Hood, N. and Young, S. (1979), *The Economics of Multinational Enterprise* (Harlow: Longmans).

Leontief, W. (1954), 'Domestic Production and Foreign Trade: The American Capital Position Re-examined', *Economica Internazionale*.

MacDougall, G.D.A. (1960), 'The Benefits and Costs of Private Investment from Abroad', *Economic Record*.

Vernon, R. (1966), 'International Investment and International Trade in the Product Cycle', *Quarterly Journal of Economics*.

# 7.  Costs and Market Structure

It has long been appreciated that technological factors affect the nature of industrial structure. We have already discussed aspects of traditional cost theory and the influence of minimum efficient scale (MES) in Chapters 2 and 5. More recent literature has built on these foundations and understanding of the linkages between costs and structure has immensely improved. Here we look in particular at the contributions in the field of multi-product costs (Baumol, 1982) multiplant costs (Scherer, 1980), industry life-cycle costs (Stigler, 1968), product lifecycle costs (Alchian, 1963) and transactions costs (Williamson, 1985).

## 7.1  MULTIPRODUCT COSTS

Baumol's (1982) paper on multiproduct costs begins with the normal logic of establishing the MES on the long-run average-cost curve. Thus if two large firms in a given industry produce at, say, 20 per cent less costs per unit than 1000 small ones then the latter is not an equilibrium structure. Entry by a more efficient larger firm would occur and the industry structure would evolve towards a natural duopoly. The two main differences in the multi-product case are that the minimum cost for 'output bundles' must be determined and the proportion of each product in the bundle must somehow be selected. How does the optimal structure emerge given these constraints?

Baumol uses a diagram like Figure 7.1 to explain his argument. The firm can choose between producing combinations of boots and/or shoes as in panel a. The ray OR assumes a given proportion has been selected already. Thus points A, C and B are points of greater output bundle size but the ratio of boots:shoes is unchanged. The average cost of each bundle could be plotted on panel a's three-dimensional figure, vertically above OR; or as has been done here, the average-cost axis and ray OR could be

*Figure 7.1*

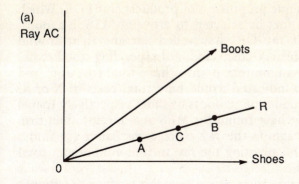

(a)
Ray AC

(b)
Ray AC

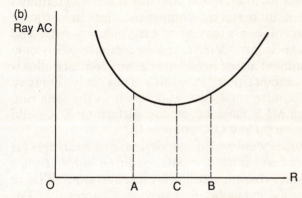

(c)
Firm's TC

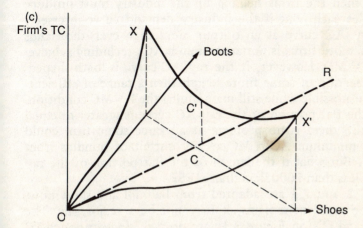

examined alone, as in panel b. Clearly, bundle size C is the one with the lowest average cost of production, but that is true only in relation to that unique proportion of products along OR. Which proportion should in fact be selected to arrive at MES in a multi-product situation? If ray OR is swivelled left and right around point O different average-cost (and corresponding total cost) curves will emerge. Assume that point C has a total cost of C' and that the plant size so indicated would have total costs of X or X' if it specialized its production in boots or shoes respectively (panel c). In other words, we have found the MES of a multiproduct firm by simultaneously scanning the ray average cost curve (to find a minimum average) and pivoting the ray to find a minimum total cost surface (O X X').

Baumol then attempts to ascertain how this analysis determines market structure not in perfectly competitive, but in perfectly contestable conditions (i.e. a situation of easy industry entry and exit where firm size is not determined by contestability conditions). For the moment all we need know about contestability is that, like perfect competition, P = MC. Thus only industry structures which minimize total costs can persist in the long run. Hence multiproduct MES must be on the surface O X X', and more specifically above the ray OR, at point C'.

There are, of course, problems in cost-determined structures (as in the single-product case) if the P = MC condition holds. Thus a price equal to marginal cost may still not cover average cost (as in the natural monopoly example discussed in Chapter 2). For example, if the ray average cost curve is minimized at C = 1000 in panel b then the firms making up the industry must produce 1000 bundles each. But if the industry demand curve intersects the industry AC curve at an output more than even thousands then one or more firms is not at minimum AC precluding achievement of P = MC. However, if the ray AC curve is 'bath-shaped' with a flat section of some finite length then a range of efficient-sized firms is possible while still maintaining the P = MC condition. In fact, if the flat portion of the ray AC curve is greater or equal to twice MES there is no problem at all since some firm could produce at minimum AC = MC at any output of bundles from 1001–1999. But what if the length of the flat portion of the ray AC curve is less than 1000, less than MES?

Figures 7.2 and 7.3 are adapted from Baumol and show how, although the problem remains, it may not be a major one. The curves OX and OX' in Figure 7.1c are normal, single-product TC

*Figure 7.2*

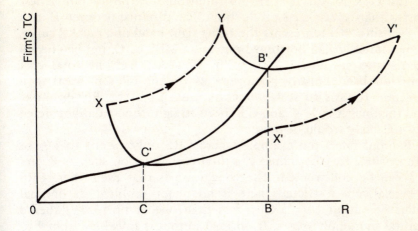

*Figure 7.3*

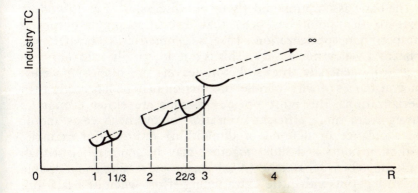

curves. The curve OD′ in Figure 7.2, however, is taken from Figure 7.1c (vertically above OR) and is the bottom of the valley of the O X X′ surface. That is, multiproduct production is less costly than specialized production. The distance between C′ and B′ (a rising TC) represents the rising right hand of a ray AC curve, which initially had bottomed out at an MES of C, but had begun to rise, as in Figure 7.1b to B. However, had the total cost function been linearly homogeneous (in the relevant area) then constant returns to scale would have been present. For example, had the lines XY, X′Y′ and C′B′ been straight then a flat-bottomed ray AC curve would be present.

Baumol takes the example where CRS only extend to $1^1/_3$ of MES. Then for the industry a total cost function such as Figure 7.3 can be constructed. The conclusion is that even where CRS are relatively restricted there is no major problem. If optimal industry output (P = MC) is less than one or up to $1^1/_3$ then a natural monopoly exists. If optimal output is anywhere from 2 to $2^2/_3$ then duopoly is the least-cost structure. While with an output of 3, or any level above 3, 3 firms or more can achieve minimum and constant AC. Only the gaps $1^1/_3$–2 and $2^2/_3$–3 pose problems, relatively narrow regions where no equilibrium is possible. And, as Baumol points out, with changing prices, tastes and technologies, such small gaps may have little practical relevance in industrial organization studies.

The basic assumption underlying our discussion of multiproduct costs to this point has been that diversification of output is cheaper than specialization. That is, geometrically, ray OR was beneath a valley not a ridge. This is not universally true (nor even necessarily generally true) so before leaving this discussion we list some instances of why 'bundle' production may be less costly than specialization. The most obvious reasons are either economies arising from more efficient utilization of overhead costs and/or the avoidance or deferral of diminishing returns. For example, marketing boots and shoes together may be more efficient than marketing them separately. (A salesman or a retailer could double his throughput with little extra selling effort when he has a 'full line' to offer customers than if he was a specialist shoe or boot-seller.) The point may be clearer if one considers the multiple thousands of products sold by a supermarket. Retailing costs would be much higher if each high street had a specialist tea store, soap powder store, dairy, and so on. Similar research and development overheads may operate in a less costly way in diversified firm. Thus chemical research into human and animal medicines can be carried on side by side, with many common operations conducted only once, not twice as they would be in specialized single-product firms. Drucker (1985, p. 55) has given examples of where such high-cost 'unbundled' research has occurred illustrating how OR is under a valley not a ridge. At the level of production processes the reasons for this may be less the ability to spread overhead costs more thinly and more the existence of joint costs of manufacture as such. Thus a refinery produces many types of and product from the same crude oil. A pottery plant produces cups and teapots from the same kiln. Specializing in only the production of petrol (or of teapots) would be technologically stupid and economically more costly than multi-product production.

## 7.2  MULTIPLANT COSTS

Why should a firm operate several rather than a single plant? Even if diseconomies of scale set in after a point surely they can be avoided by replication of the most efficient plant size? These two questions raise a number of subsidiary issues which we must tackle in turn. The simplest reason for multiplant operations is to be physically close to the marketplace or raw material sources if transportation costs are high.

For example, consider Figure 7.4. Long-run average manufacturing cost indicates an optimal least cost plant size of $Q_1$. However, when transportation costs (inwards and outwards) are added to manufacturing costs optimal size shrinks to $Q_2$. Had transportation costs been even higher (because of, say, the bulk, weight or fragility of raw materials or the end product) then manufacturing costs would play an even smaller role in determining optimal plant size which would shrink (given transport costs of $T^1$) to $Q_3$.

Long-run average cost curves, however, are affected by more than just transportation costs. Once MES has been achieved, the conventional view has been that either diseconomies of scale to manufacturing set in (in which case replication of optimal plant size should take place, giving an L-shaped LAC curve) or that such diseconomies can be avoided by replication but that the costs of management and coordination would ultimately rise resulting in a U-shaped, or at least a bath tub-shaped LAC curve for the firm.

*Figure 7.4*

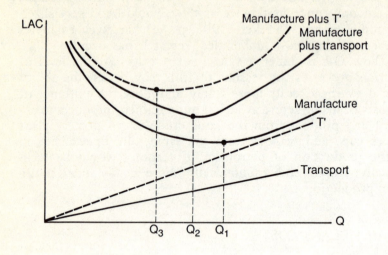

*Figure 7.5*

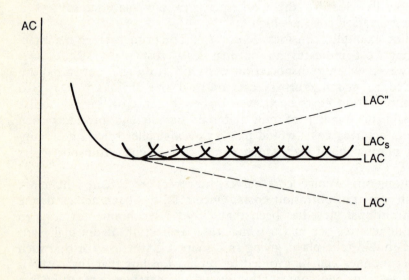

More recently, however, detailed studies of multiplant dis-economies *and* economies have been carried out by Scherer (1980) and others enhancing our understanding of the multiplant firm. Diagrammatically the alternatives are given in Figure 7.5. LAC, LAC" and LAC' represent respectively envelope long-run average cost curves displaying no multiplant economies, multiplant dis-economies, and less conventionally, multiplant economies.

Management and coordination costs are the ones most frequently cited as causing multiplant diseconomies. Special functions can be centralized at a head office or other central point for all plants. This would avoid duplication and hence permit a declining LMC. Such services might include purchasing, market research, personnel, advertising and R & D. Conversely, such centralization could increase costs, for example, if the personnel function lost touch with industrial relations at 'shop floor' level, if research and development became ossified, bureaucratic and out of touch with processes and production problems encountered at plant level, and so on. The questions become empirical and the answers vary instance by instance.

One less ambiguous multiplant economy is the pooling of risks. If the risks are not systematically related then individual plants may require to hold less slack capacity or inventories to guard against contingencies than would individual, single-plant firms. This in turn may result in lower costs of raising capital or finance (as lending to such firms is perceived to be less risky) while simultaneously (because of size of financial issue) flotation and other fixed financing costs might be lower for the very large multiplant firm.

(In parentheses we must note that we have all along been speaking of real resource-saving scale economies (or diseconomies). Multiplant firms, because they are large, may also reap the benefits of pecuniary as opposed to real economies. For example, lower input costs for raw materials, advertising space or finance because of the firm's bargaining power, as opposed to the real cost savings due to economies arising from the size of the trade are pecuniary only. The firm gains, but socially this is merely a transfer from one resource owner to another.)

## 7.3 INDUSTRY LIFECYCLE COSTS

Stigler (1951), like Adam Smith, accepted that division of labour is limited by the extent of the market. He found it paradoxical, therefore, that all industries should not be monopolized. He resolved the paradox in a different way from much of the orthodox writing of the time. A paraphrase of the contemporary position might have read: 'Division of labour is limited by the extent of the market except for the function of coordination, which is a special case, and which is indivisible and to which there are some kind of decreasing returns resulting in an optimum firm size.' Stigler saw all functions as being divisible, not excluding co-ordination. The reason some industries are organized differently from others, he argued, is due to the stage of the industry's life-cycle.

He put forward the following theory and illustrated it with reference to Figure 7.6. Vertical integration will be extensive in young industries; disintegration will be observed as an industry grows; and reintegration will take place as an industry passes into decline. These lifecycle effects are illustrated by reference to a multi-process product, each process having its own distinct cost function. Some of these processes display individually falling cost curves, others rise continuously, and still others have U-shaped cost curves.

*Figure 7.6*

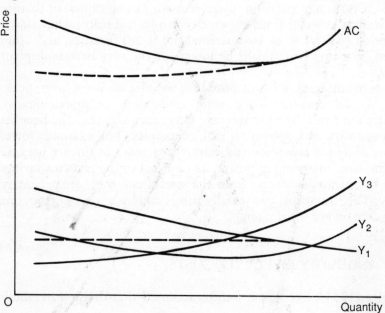

Why then does the firm not exploit decreasing cost activities (such as process $Y_1$) and expand there to become a monopoly? Because, says Stigler, at any given time in the lifecycle of an industry, 'these functions may be too small to support a specialised firm'. As an industry grows, however, the magnitude of the process $Y_1$ may become sufficient to support a specialist firm. Existing firms will abandon $Y_1$ and a new firm will take it over. This abandonment of $Y_1$ will alter the cost curves of the original firms. $Y_1$ will be replaced by a horizontal line (the purchase price which equals the previous average cost of the process to the firms abandoning $Y_1$) and so the final product's total average cost curve (the vertical summation of $Y_1$, $Y_2$ and $Y_3$) will also change shape and position. The new industry, in its turn, may come to abandon parts of the process $Y_1$ to a new set of specialists.

As the industry contracts and the market is no longer available to support a specialist firm in process $Y_1$ the reverse procedure postulated by Stigler of reintegration will occur.

Processes such as $Y_2$ and $Y_3$ which are subject to increasing costs can be handled in the conventional manner. There is no need for a firm to restrict its scale of operation in these functions. Stigler argues that part of the required amount can be made within the firm and the remainder purchased from outside suppliers. 'Outside' suppliers could, of course, include replicated optimal-sized plants within the same firm.

This view of why firms integrate vertically and disintegrate into specialist entities is technological in its underpinnings. It complements the alternative 'transactional' approach discussed in section 7.5 and Chapters 8 and 9. We shall discover that the two are not competing theories and it is useful to retain both perspectives. Thus in transactions costs language, as process $Y_1$ grows sufficiently to support a specialized firm, then the knowledge required to produce and monitor $Y_1$ will have become increasingly widespread and well known. Information asymmetry between potential buyers and sellers will be minimized, bounded rationality will thus be relaxed, and so the scope for opportunistic behaviour by buyers and sellers at each other's expense will be less. Market transactions can economically replace hierarchically-related ones.

## 7.4 PRODUCT LIFECYCLE COSTS

Firm costs not only vary by stages of the industrial lifecycle, thus impacting on structure and integration level, they also vary by stage of the product lifecycle. This phenomenon has long been articulated but one of the first to formulate the notion was Alchian (1963). Figure 7.7 shows the well-known product lifecycle S-shaped curve, with sales rising slowly at first, then accelerating as markets become familiar with the product and prices reduced, then levelling off as the product matures and markets become saturated. Variant I shows product sales going into decline as trades change or a new product superseded the old. Variant II in Figure 7.7 shows static sales on maturity as the product matures but does not decline, while Variant III shows that the producers of the product have discovered and exploited previously untapped market segments for the product (for example, two-car or two-TV set households after each household has purchased one and the market had 'settled' to simply a replacement level) or had discovered new uses for the product (for example, nylon, after having been heavily used in the clothing industry, was taken by its innovator, du Pont, and successfully introduced to tyre manufacturers as a product which could be successfully combined with rubber in the manufacture of tyres).

The lifecycle curve has its characteristic shape, as can be inferred from the above discussion, both because of consumer and producer changes in tastes, costs, technologies and prices (and other myriad factors) over time. When producers introduce a new product not only are they aware of the S-shaped lifecycle curve they are also aware that one of the main factors underlying its position and shape (actual and potential) are the costs of production. But costs of production themselves are not simply a matter of mechanistically forecasting average cost curves and making allowances for varying volumes over time and hence distinguishing between short- and long-run curves, diminishing returns to scale and diseconomies of scale as in conventional analysis. Such forecasts are prediction of a static point in time only. When the dynamics are taken account of what is known as the 'learning' or 'experience' curve comes into play. Examples of the shapes such a curve can take are given in Figure 7.8.

The crucial difference to note between the conventional AC curve and the unit costs indicated by a learning curve is that the quantity axis in the former relates to a given period of time (albeit that period is typically unspecified except for the 'short'-run and 'long'-run distinctions where some costs are 'fixed' in the short run, and all costs are 'variable' in the long run). Even then,

*Figure* 7.7

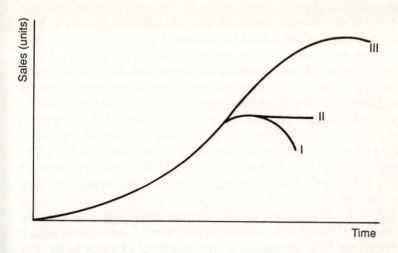

*Figure* 7.8

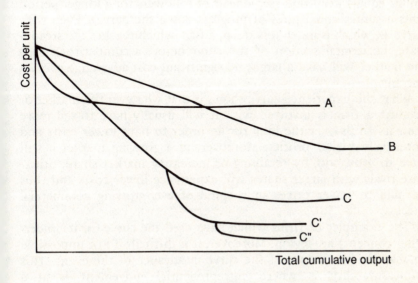

however, the quantity axis still relates to the same time period, it is only the inputs *within* the diagram which are or are not allowed to vary. The learning or experience curve, however, is not concerned with these disparities, nor even with time as such but rather with the impact on costs as experience is gained as production accumulates at some optimal rate.

When a new product or process is initiated by a firm a learning process commences and, by trial and error and the accumulation of expertise, as more and more units are produced the firm and its labour force learn the least-cost ways of carrying out the manufacturing or production process. People gain dexterity, machinery is adapted to be more appropriate for its tasks, faulty or stupid (in the light of events) habits or machine processes are removed. 'Debugging' takes place. Other things equal, the first firm into an industry will have a cost advantage over later entrants for as long as the curve is declining.

Figure 7.8 shows examples of three different kinds of learning or experience curve. The nature of the curve is one factor which will determine how successful later entrants can expect to be. For example, curve A is very steep and innovators will quickly reach minimum unit costs, but because it levels off rapidly that advantage will be short-lived relative to a firm in an industry with a learning curve shaped like C, where the 'first comer' can (other things equal) keep one step ahead of followers for a longer period (this assumes equal rates of progress down the curve). Even with curve B, which is much less steep, a firm which reaches the steady-state, horizontal section of the curve before a competitor enters the market will have a large and significant cost advantage over an entrant.

What the experience curve shows is that whatever the market or product a firm is involved with it will usually have to sell more than its rivals over the long run in order to have lower costs and potentially higher profits. Moreover, in a growing market it will have to grow too, by retaining or increasing market share, otherwise rivals with larger shares will experience lower costs and thus be able to lower prices in a spiral of ever-growing commercial success.

The examples of firms which have used the curve (or its underlying concept) are legion. Moreover, it is difficult if not impossible to measure the nature of the curve in advance of the event. This immeasurability is where entrepreneurial judgement is at a premium. Gilder (1984, p. 159) gives several examples. He quotes

Henry Ford's autobiography: 'Our policy is to reduce the price, extend the operations, and improve the article. You will note that the reduction in price comes first . . . . Then we go ahead and try to make the prices. We do not bother about costs. The new price forces the costs down . . . so one knows what a cost ought to be. One of the ways of discovering [it] . . . is to make a price so low as to force everybody in the place to the highest point of efficiency.'

Texas Instruments followed the same strategy (Gilder, p. 154) of 'aggressive pricing' and 'extending capacity ahead of demand' in the semi-conductor industry. It rapidly descended the experience curve. The examples are endless. And just as firms (as in Figure 7.7) must either innovate into a totally new area or find new uses or users for their product (curves II and III) to avoid the decline in the product lifecycle, so they must be alert to the fact that the 'steady state' on the learning curve is probably more apparent than real. New processes will suddenly appear, or the product will have to be modified to meet changing consumer tastes and a whole new family of experience curves can emerge (Figure 7.8) as, for example, curves $C'$ and $C''$ enabling later entrants to overtake the first comer and/or providing the innovator with continuous challenges.

The experience curve and the need for entrepreneurial judgement in advance, of course, poses a problem for policy-makers. Predatory pricing or dumping are two business activities which are often condemned as anti-competitive. The definitional problems of when pricing at a low level is non-competitive are difficult at the best of times (is it when prices are below marginal costs, below average total costs, below average variable costs, or below the costs of competitors?). But when, as with the entrepreneurial use of the experience curve, pricing is in anticipation of some immeasurable cost reduction in the future to enable the firm to move rapidly down what Gilder called 'the curve of growth' then policy-makers can only wait till after the event. (By which time the price-reducing firm will either have successfully captured a large market share or unsuccessfully made an error of judgement resulting in rivals increasing *their* market shares.)

## 7.5  TRANSACTION COSTS

Traditional cost analyses, then, take a static view of costs. It disregards the fact that over time they can fall dramatically as firms move down the experience curve. Another aspect of cost which is also often ignored is that of transactions costs (Williamson, 1985). Here, the objective of economic actors is not assumed to be that of optimizing the allocation of scarce resources to obtain a particular output of a good or service, rather it is another perspective of economic analysis which takes centre stage. The objective is to ascertain the costs involved in trade and to set up transactions in such a way that the gains of trade are maximized.

The two underlying assumptions of transactions cost analyses are first that traders, buyers and sellers enter into contracts with each other subject to bounded rationality constraints. That is, information is incomplete, is costly to acquire, and while all participants think full information would be 'nice to have' they perceive that it is more economical (less costly) to initiate and monitor trading relationships with each other under some governance structure which departs from the classical, market contracting mode.

Second, transaction cost economics assumes that traders are opportunistic. This is a stronger assumption than the normal classical belief that individuals are self-seeking. Here 'self-seeking with guile' is admitted. That is, individuals entering into a trade with each other not only do not have complete information but each will be motivated to a greater or lesser degree to conceal from the other information which he does have which would otherwise make the terms of trade finally agreed upon less favourable to the information-holder. *Ex ante* opportunism is known in the insurance literature as adverse selection. That is, insurance companies are unable, before the event, to distinguish perfectly between risks, and poor risks are unwilling candidly to disclose their true risk situation. *Ex post* opportunism is known as moral hazard. The insured may fail to behave in the most responsible risk-mitigating manner.

As Williamson points out (p. 67), where opportunism and bounded rationality are both absent a 'state of bliss' can exist. Perfect classical market contracting can take place and there are no transactions costs. Admit opportunism and long-term 'comprehensive contracts' between traders would be required if the problems arising from opportunistic behaviour are to be eliminated. The drawing-up and monitoring of such contracts or alternative governance structures involves incurring transactions costs. Admit bounded rationality without opportunism and the comprehensiveness of the contracting procedure can be replaced with 'general clause contracts' where the traders agree freely to divulge all pertinent information to each other and to behave co-operatively during contract execution and at contract renewal. Allow both opportunism and bounded rationality to be present and the transactional problems or costs become very high.

The transactions costs problem then becomes one of devising a governance structure other than a perfectly classical trading market which economizes on bounded rationality whilst simultaneously safeguarding transactions against opportunistic hazards. As always in economics, even transactions cost economics, a key issue is still choice among alternatives. Given non-zero transactions costs, *which* governance structure (including standard perfect market classical contracting) will maximize the net gains from trade (given that trading involves planning and adapting contracts, executing and monitoring them through to completion, and contract renewal)? The reader will have perceived that the passage of time is again seen as important (as with experience and learning curves, but unlike conventional cost theory).

The reason that time is crucial in transactions cost analysis is due to what Williamson calls the 'fundamental transformation' (p. 61). When contracts or trades are initiated there are typically large numbers of bidders. The terms of the trade will depend on the degree to which collusion exists or could exist between the varying suppliers (or demanders). This much is part of mainstream theory, and reaches its ultimate in monopoly or monopsony theory. Transactions costs analysis, however, goes beyond the day on which the contract of trade is drawn up to the periods beyond, namely contract execution, and indeed renewal. The fundamental transformation (not taken account of in conventional analyses) is that the large numbers, or relatively large numbers of bidders at the date of contract agreement could well become a small number (or relatively small number) during the execution and renewal stages. The reason (which will not always be present) is that in some instances once a trade has been entered into suppliers will be supported by transaction-specific human or physical assets. (Human assets include know-how but also know-who. Thus familiarity and trust are opportunism-attenuating assets.) Once such assets are in place (the asset-specificity condition), existing market participants are more likely to continue meeting with each other than with outsiders. (On the supply side the asset will have a much higher value in use in contract renewal than in alternative uses; on the demand side the buyer presumably will be unable to find a supplier with such a transaction-specific asset, or if he can find one who is willing to create it, it is presumably unlikely that it would be available on terms as favourable as those provided by existing suppliers.)

Thus the presence of bounded rationality and opportunism both encourage the emergence of the fundamental transformation when asset specificity is present. Before leaving this issue with its rather forbidding jargon we shall list some of the complications or alternative institutions which Williamson has suggested as examples of governance structures providing maximum net gains from trade and minimization of transactions costs.

Economics, and most especially industrial economics, then may well reduce to more of what Buchanan called a 'science of contracts' than a 'science of choice' (cited in Williamson, p. 29). The contracting process can be one of centralized planning, mutual cooperation, conventional competition or governance structure selection. Planning requires full information. Cooperation (promise) requires the absence of opportunism while competition is infeasible over time given asset specificity. Table 7.1 summarizes the reasons given by Williamson why economizing on bounded rationality while safeguarding against opportunism requires a non-competitive contracting process in the presence of asset specificity.

*Table 7.1   Attributes of the contracting process*

| Behavioural assumptions | | | |
| --- | --- | --- | --- |
| Bounded rationality | Opportunism | Asset specificity | Implied contracting process |
| No | Yes | Yes | Planning |
| Yes | No | Yes | Promise |
| Yes | Yes | No | Competition |
| Yes | Yes | Yes | Governance |

*Source:*   Williamson, op. cit., p. 31.

Transactions costs are 'the economic equivalent of friction in physical systems' (Williamson, p. 19), therefore what might be regarded *prima facie* as a market or monopolistic imperfection in a no-transactions costs framework, might well simply be observation of a governance structure created to gain the benefits of trade at least cost. For example:

1. Vertical market restrictions are presumed to be anti-competitive in traditional analysis (e.g. franchising). Under transactions cost analysis the possibility must be addressed that the contract exists to safeguard transactions. For example, franchisees cannot free ride on franchisor promotion, nor can they shift costs of lower quality onto the whole franchise network since strict quality controls are implemented, for example, by purchase inputs agreement as well as by inspection (see Williamson, p. 40).

2. Price discrimination may not be so immediately indictable as under some regulatory regimes (e.g. the Robinson–Patman Act in the USA prohibits the charging of differing prices to differing purchasers of the same good if the effect is 'substantially to lessen competition or tend to create a monopoly'). Scherer (1980, pp. 319–23) has given a listing of the conventional defences for breach of this prohibition: the need to monetize consumer surplus to provide the funds to cover total costs where markets are too small fully to provide for overheads when pricing is carried out at a uniform $MR = MC$ level; by extension this argument could be valid in situations of natural monopoly where marginal cost pricing is practised but where some blocks of output must be more highly priced to cover the resulting deficit. To these defences Williamson adds that of transactions costs between buyer and seller. Diagrammatically or verbally his thesis is easy to exposit. The difficulty is operationalizing his argument, which suggests again that competition policy will continue to be exercised on a case-by-case basis until (if ever) the theory is sufficiently developed to be universally applicable. Figure 7.9 shows the basic Williamson argument. If P is the profit-maximizing price and CS consumers' surplus prior to price discrimination then first degree discrimination is worthwhile if $\Delta \pi > CS + V - T > 0$, where V is additional (but appropriated) consumers' surplus due to the lower price $P^1$ being charged for the last unit of the increase in quantity and T the transactions costs necessary to enable price discrimination successfully to take place (e.g. partitioning and sealing the market segments off from each other). To ascertain if the discrimination is socially (as opposed to privately) worthwhile the condition $\Delta \omega > V - T > 0$ must be satisfied where $\Delta\omega$ is the addition to social welfare. In the earlier expression CS, of course, had simply been a transfer from consumer to producer, neither a social gain nor loss.

*Figure 7.9*

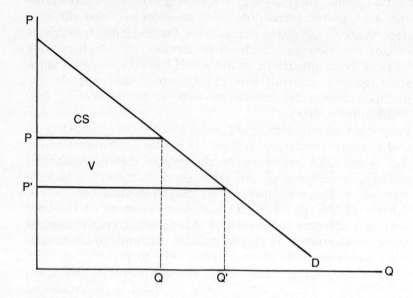

*Figure 7.10*

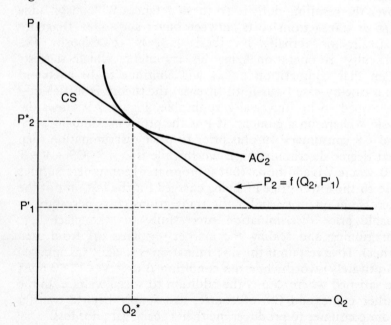

Price discriminatory practices such as 'loyalty rebates' (where the buyer gets a lower price not because of order size but because of cumulative purchase volume to date) may be seen (traditionally) as anti-competitive on a pre-contractual basis, or less conventionally, they may be a means of lowering transactions costs over both pre- and post-contractual periods. The seller has to expend less resources in marketing and the buyer gains by having his search costs lowered and has the incentive of a lower price to participate.

3.  Resale price maintenance by individual sellers is even explicable on a transactions cost basis. A practice which for several decades has traditionally been frowned upon by legislators may in fact be justifiable provided, as always, that the arrangement is what consumers ultimately want. The abolition of RPM in the UK in 1964 when the practice was declared illegal may simply have been ratifying a state of affairs which businesses and consumers no longer found advantageous. Vertical agreements between buyer and seller relating to resale price were rapidly disappearing in many trades in the 1950s and 1960s in any event. But was there a case for declaring them illegal across the board? Williamson, using transactions cost analysis, thinks not (pp. 183–9). Consider Figure 7.10 for a differentiated product sold through a retailer in competition with other products. This product has a contractually maintained resale price of $P_2^*$, substitute products sell for $P_1^1$. The retailer is obliged to provide associated services with the product (these could include after-sales service, stocks of spares, repairs, guaranteed display or shelf space for the product in the retail outlet, and so on) while the manufacturer will only sell to a limited number of nominated retailers, and will refuse to supply if the contract is not fulfilled. The traditional view is that if the product is 'really superior' it will sell at the premium price without the need for legal restraints, or, if the price falls, some of the associated services will be supplied elsewhere as separate 'packages'.

An alternative view (not necessarily universally applicable but certainly worthy of consideration by those who otherwise would argue for blanket regulation) against the *voluntary* practice of resale price maintenance, that is who would argue *for* the imposition of so-called 'fair trade laws' is expounded by Williamson (pp. 185–9) and also by Telser (1960, 1965). It runs as follows. For *some* customers the opportunity cost of search is high, and so is that of repair, maintenance and/or complaint if the product is faulty, hence buying a product with a known and reliable brand name, easy returns and repair policy will minimize the total costs of such customers (opportunity and unit cost). Those consumers who are inept at post-sales repair or have a high opportunity cost of time will prefer to pay $P^{2*}$.

But why can this credible market demand not be satisfied by competing distribution channels offering the required product packages rather than by restrictive contractual relationships between manufacturer and retailer? The answers again lie in transaction cost analyses. The manufacturer's brand image on which the buyers in question rely in order confidently to minimize their search costs may be debased by a multiplicity of differing distribution channels offering differing degrees of product support. Second, even if not, 'the viability of the franchises may hinge on sales restraints' (p. 186) and, more uniquely, the policing, enforcement and identification costs of ensuring that the high service outlets do indeed exist and do indeed perform to claimed standards would be increased with parallel distribution channels. In a world of bounded rationality and opportunism there are incentives to invest in 'commercial reputation by surrounding transactions with institutional infrastructure' (Williamson, p. 186).

The institutional alternative of forward integration by the manufacturer may well often be less efficient since the distributors may well be highly diversified into slots alien to the manufacturer's expertise. Alternatively, similar products might not be readily available from other manufacturers if they in turn felt uneasy about possible opportunistic behaviour by the first (now vertically integrated forwards) firm. Finally, management of owned outlets may (or may not) have less incentive to provide the same standard of service that owner franchisors would have.

In a word, a case can be made to defend voluntary resale price maintenance. Consider again Figure 7.10. The demand curve for the price maintained product is $P_2 = f(Q_2, P_1^1)$ where $P_1^1$, the price of competing products is given. $AC_2$ is the average cost of sales and services of the independent retailers. They break even at $P_2^*$, $Q_2^*$ (inclusive of normal profits). CS is the welfare gain due to the practice of resale price maintenance.

(Contrarily, CS would be lost if fair trade laws banning voluntary resale price maintenance were enacted.)

4. Finally, advertising can be explained by transaction cost analysis while traditional analyses might merely see it as a market imperfection. Recall that Williamson (1985, p. 32) reminds us that the objective of any transaction is to '*economise on bounded rationality* while simultaneously safeguarding . . . against the hazards of opportunism' (emphasis in original). Stripped of the rather forbidding jargon, what this means is that if costs are minimized then advertising need no longer be subject either to accusations of providing limited and inadequate information, or of being misleading. To use more traditional language, if advertising was to be more informative and less persuasive, society would somehow suffer net costs. I have often referred to the economic benefits of advertising (e.g. Reekie, 1983). They include, for example, longer production runs and hence manufacturing scale economies, lower retail margins, and so higher levels of competition at all stages of distribution. Advertising also lowers the cost to the consumer of entrepreneurial alertness. As Kirzner (1972) pointed out, 'it's a tough job being a consumer' in an advanced society. The scope for choice can be bewildering. Advertising lowers the consumer's cost of selection while prompting him to be his own entrepreneur and so alert to new and better consumption opportunities. That such various benefits exceed the costs which would arise in the absence of advertising is not a complex argument. As Herbert Simon (1978, p. 6) pointed out, transaction cost analyses do not need elaborate use of calculus. 'Much cruder and simpler arguments will suffice to demonstrate an inequality between two quantities than . . . to show . . . [equivalency] at the margin.'

## 7.6 PRAGMATISM AGAIN

The above discussion has re-emphasized the wealth of understanding industrial economists now have while simultaneously reinforcing the point expounded time after time in earlier chapters that there is no easy answer. Perfect competition is a nirvana-like goal which, if achieved, would impose net costs on society. Its non-attainability, and the problems of measuring and assessing how far industry departs from it have been underlined. Whether such departures are beneficial or costly is not consistently clear and even pragmatic, case-by-case analyses require immense care in evaluation if all costs are to be taken account of. This chapter has expanded on the familiar concept of minimum efficient scale, and added considerably to the true concept of cost by introducing industry and firm, product and multiproduct costs, lifecycle costs and transactions costs, but this added richness of comprehension has been at the expense of still more desimplification and movement away from the SCP model which once seemed to serve us so well.

## REFERENCES

Alchian, A. (1963), 'Reliability of Progress Curves is Airframe Production', *Econometrica*, 31.

Baumol, W.J. (1982), 'Contestable Markets: An Uprising in the Theory of Industrial Structure', *American Economic Review*, 72.

Drucker, P. (1985), *Innovation and Entrepreneurship* (London: Pan).

Kirzner, I. (1972), 'Advertising', *The Freeman*.

Reekie, W.D. (1983), *The Economics of Advertising* (London: Macmillan).

Scherer, F.M. (1980), *Industrial Market Structure and Economic Performance* (New York: Rand McNally, 2nd edition).

Simon, H.A. (1978), 'Rationality as Process and Product of Thought', *American Economic Review*, 68.

Stigler, G. (1951), 'The Division of Labour is Limited by the Extent of the Market', *Journal of Political Economy*, 59.

Stigler, G. (1968), *The Organisation of Industry* (New York: Irwin).

Telser, L. (1960), 'Why Should Manufacturers Want Fair Trade?', *Journal of Law and Economics*, 3.

Telser, L. (1965), 'Abusive Trade Practice: An Economic Analysis', *Law and Contemporary Problems*.

Williamson, O.E. (1985), *The Economic Institutions of Capitalism* (New York: Free Press).

# 8.   Transaction Costs: A Closer Look

The discussion in Chapter 7 seemed to end on a note of despair. The volume of understanding about reality which is accumulating seemed about to implode under its own weight. Here we try to rescue ourselves from that fate by returning to the neoclassical analysis of Chapter 2 and grafting onto it the transaction cost framework of Chapter 7.

## 8.1   THE ENTREPRENEUR AND TRANSACTION COSTS

Consider Figure 8.1 (reproduced as Figure 2.3 above). There are two individuals, A and B, in a two-good, Y and X, world, with indifference curves as shown. Voluntarily negotiated trades are beneficial to both parties to an exchange, i.e. exchange does not benefit one party at the expense of another. Each currently possesses bundles of Y and X as indicated by the endowment point.

At E, since the indifference curves intersect, their slopes and hence their MRSs and the marginal valuations of X and Y held by A and B differ. The arrows indicate the trading process. When A moves from $Y_A$ to $Y'_A$ and gives up two units of Y, B acquires a corresponding amount. Similarly, A's positive acquisition of 1X from B is exactly counterbalanced by B's movement from $X_B$ to $X'_B$. T will be a point of mutually beneficial trading. No more trading will occur since, at this point, both A and B have identical valuations of Y in terms of X. Their respective indifference curves passing through T will be tangential to each other. A's minimum selling price for Y is the same as B's maximum buying price for Y (in terms of X).

Entrepreneurs can be regarded as middlemen — albeit very special types of middlemen. Here we shall try to conceptualize the entrepreneurial function by looking first at the simplest type of middleman — the middleman who facilitates trading between A and B in the situation detailed in Figure 8.1. In the illustration described above, A and B traded face to face. This is unusual. Normally trade takes place with a middleman. Why? The basic assumption of the earlier illustration was that A and B knew each other and could communicate at zero cost. But transaction costs (for example, information processing, transport, search by buyer and seller, etc.) are rarely zero.

Buyers and sellers do not normally know each other. They would have to search each other out and find out from each other what mutually beneficial exchange opportunities existed. These search and exchange costs could be diminished if a specialist third party undertook them, and collected information about bids and offers for a fee. Such a specialist could trade between A and B at less expenditure of time and effort than if they had traded directly.

For example, in Figure 8.1 a middleman could offer B 1.5Y for 1X, which is 0.5Y more than B's minimum supply price. He could take that X to A and offer it to him for 2.5Y which is 0.5Y below the maximum price A is willing to pay for 1X. The middleman

*Figure 8.1*

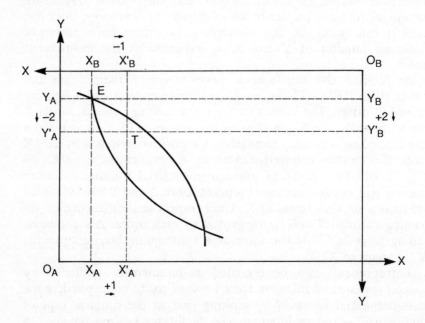

ends up with 1Y and both A and B are better off than they were (they are on higher isoquants). Without the middleman, and with heavy transaction costs (search, transport, bargaining), either the trade would not have taken place or exchange and transaction costs in excess of 1Y might have been incurred.

In Figure 8.2, had the initial endowment point been such that the difference between the MRSs was 0.5Y and, had the cost of engaging in trade, even using a low cost specialist middleman, been 1Y, then trade would not occur. A and B would remain at that endowment point and not move onto line GCDF.

*Figure 8.2*

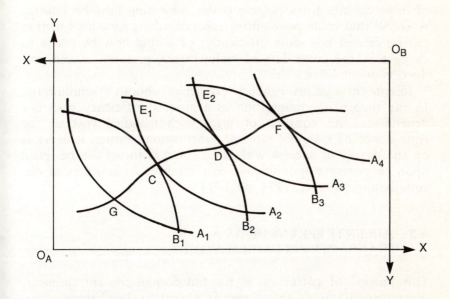

When a middleman spots the possibility to promote a trade between parties who have either previously been unaware that such a possibility exists, or who have been deterred by high transaction costs, then that middleman has spotted an entrepreneurial opportunity. When he promotes that trade he is acting entrepreneurially. When his transaction costs, including any reward for the bearing of risk and any (actual or imputed) interest he must pay to the providers of capital, have been deducted from his income the residual is entrepreneurial profits.

In the conventional theory of price the objective is to define the conditions of optimization in a given situation. For example, in terms of Figure 8.1 given endowment, given the tastes and preferences exemplified by the relevant isoquants for A and B, only definite and precise values of the quantity variables X and Y, and of the price variables (the MRSs), are consistent with an equilibrium situation. Conventional theory determines a point on the contract curve but it does not tell us how that point is arrived at. In a search for equality of the marginal rates of sub-stitution we are deflected from the more interesting and relevant tasks of asking why the entrepreneur/middleman arranges the mutually beneficial exchanges; of asking how he is made aware of opportunities for arranging trades; of asking how he informs A and B that trade possibilities exist; of asking how his function can be carried out more efficiently; of asking how he reacts to changes in the given data of endowments, preferences and pro-duction possibilities.

In conventional price theory 'efficiency' obtains in equilibrium. In the theory of competition as a process, efficiency does not depend on the equality of price with marginal cost or the equivalence of marginal rates of substitution, 'rather, it depends on the degree of success with which market forces can be relied upon to generate spontaneous corrections . . . at times of dis-equilibrium' (Kirzner, 1974, pp. 6–7).

## 8.2  THE ENTREPRENEUR AS A TRANSACTIONS FACILITATOR

This process of correction is the function of the entrepreneur. 'Entrepreneur means acting man in regard to the changes occur-ring in the market.' And when Mises (1963, p. 254) refers to the entrepreneur in this way he is not referring to capitalist or worker, to manager or employee, to producer or consumer. Any of these can be entrepreneurial: 'Economics, in speaking of entrepreneurs, has in view not men, but a definite function' (Mises, 1966, pp. 246–50). So by inference, any producer, consumer or resource owner who acts in response to change is, to a greater or lesser degree, an entrepreneur.

In the Pareto equilibrium of Chapter 2 there was no place for the function of entrepreneurship. In equilibrium, or what Mises called an 'evenly rotating economy' (Mises, 1966, pp. 246–50) there are no changes in the given data of endowments, technologies or preferences. In such an imaginary economy in which all transactions and physical conditions are repeated without change in each cycle of time there is no uncertainty. Everything is imagined to continue exactly as before, including all human ideas and goals. Under such fictitious constant repetitive conditions there can be no net change in any supply or demand and therefore there cannot be any changes in prices (or marginal valuations or marginal contributions). But as soon as these rigid assumptions of given data are abandoned it is clear that action must be affected by every data change. Since action is directed towards influencing the future, even if 'the future' is simply the next instant, then action is affected by every incorrectly anticipated data change between the initiation of the act and the period towards which the act is directed. 'Thus the outcome of action is always uncertain. Action is always speculation' (Mises, 1963, p. 252; see also p. 155 below).

This explains how every economic actor is an entrepreneur. There is no such thing as a perfectly predictable action. Moreover, this discussion can help highlight the differences and similarities between the Schumpeterian and Misesian concepts of 'entrepreneurship'.

In a chapter headed 'How the economic system generates evolution', Schumpeter (1939) identified innovation as one of the principal promoters of economic change and growth. Innovation was defined by Schumpeter to include not only the introduction of new products and techniques but also the opening-up of new markets and supply sources, the improvement of management techniques and new distribution methods. The person responsible for doing these and other 'different things' is the entrepreneur or innovator. The entrepreneur, to Schumpeter, is a factor input and like other factor inputs must be rewarded. It is the payment for entrepreneurial services which forms Schumpeter's well-known concept of profit as a reward for innovation. 'It is the premium put upon a successful innovation in a capitalist society and is temporary by nature; it will vanish in the subsequent process of competition and adaptation' (Schumpeter, 1948, p. 83).

Here are highlighted both the differences and the similarities between the Misesian and Schumpeterian entrepreneur. Mises' entrepreneur, like Schumpeter's acts for anticipated personal gain. But the Misesian entrepreneur is any human actor motivated by gain. In Figure 8.1 two individuals, A and B, gained from the process of trade. In discussion it was shown that the trade could also have been initiated by a middleman. The spotting of the opportunity for gain, the initiation of the necessary action, and the capturing of the (uncertain) profit are all the functions of an entrepreneur. At some stage of the exchange each of A, B and the middleman had to act entrepreneurially. It is possible that each incurred similar entrepreneurial effort and reaped similar rewards, but it is more probable that one of the three assumed the greatest part (but not the whole) of the entrepreneurial role. No one can be wholly passive, no one can take totally predictable actions, no one can opt out of entrepreneurship except in equilibrium.

So both Schumpeter's and Mises' entrepreneurs act in accordance with the 'invisible hand' in order to obtain profit or gain. In this way their notions can be reconciled. But the differences are more important than the similarities. Schumpeter's entrepreneur moves the economy away from one equilibrium towards another higher level equilibrium. Mises' entrepreneur, however, helps move the economy towards equilibrium, but that equilibrium is itself an ever changing and unattainable objective. Schumpeter's entrepreneur can be studied within the context of an evenly rotating economy where particular individual changes are initiated by the innovator and the logical effects of these particular changes deduced via the principles of marginal equivalency and comparative statics. This can be a valid and useful method of analysis but it tells us little of the market process itself.

The concept of the entrepreneur can now be seen to be much fuller and richer than it appears at first sight. The entrepreneur (be he producer, consumer, middleman or resource owner) does far more than merely bring together two parties and facilitate a mutually beneficial exchange between them (as in Figure 8.1). The entrepreneur is the person who is alert to the presence of such opportunities before anyone else perceives them.

The entrepreneur notes, *ex ante*, that the indifference curves of consumers are different tomorrow from what they are today. He notes *ex ante*, that the production isoquants of producers are not the same tomorrow as they are today.

The entrepreneur may make mistakes in his predictions, or he may be correct: in which case he makes losses or profits. The entrepreneur must choose which prediction he believes to be correct. But he cannot simply choose to facilitate a process which equates *current* marginal valuations. Professor Shackle (1970, p. 106) says:

> Decision is choice amongst rival available courses of action. We can choose only what is still unactualised; we can choose only amongst imaginations and figments. Imagined actions . . . can have only imagined consequences.

Even without changes in basic market data (consumer tastes, production possibilities and resource endowments) decisions made today generate a new series of decisions tomorrow. Today's decisions (the commencement of the market process) are made in ignorance of the basic market data. As the market process unfolds this ignorance is reduced and each market participant revises his bid and offer prices in the light of what has occurred and what he has now learnt about others to or from whom he may wish to sell or buy. The process is inherently competitive since each successive set of offers and bids is more attractive than the preceding one. That is, every individual offer or bid is being made with the awareness that all others are now being made with fuller knowledge of the advantageous opportunities available. Since that is so, each individual participant knows that he cannot offer less attractive trading opportunities than his competitors. He (and they) must continually inch ahead of his (their) rivals.

## The Transacting Process

Even without changes in basic market data this competitive movement towards equilibrium brought about by entrepreneurs must occur. If it did not, the potential traders would not trade. In terms of Figure 8.1, A and B would go to market and return home empty-handed. Would-be traders (would-be self-improvers motivated by the invisible hand) would fail to realize that they could exchange unless they (or a middleman) learn to alter their bid and offer prices, that is unless someone acts in an entrepreneurial manner. The competitive process is 'analytically inseparable' from entrepreneurship (Kirzner, 1974, p. 16).

Now let us examine changes in the basic market data. If technology and/or tastes change, or if new types of quantities of resources are discovered, then any of the information contained in Figure 8.1 relating to the indifference curves of either A and/or B and/or to the dimensions of the Edgeworth box itself, and so to the relative position of the endowment point E, will be affected. Market disequilibrium is not then simply a pattern of prices and quantities subject to change under competitive pressure from the entrepreneurial arbitrage function. It is not then simply a case of an actual or hypothetical middleman offering a seller a marginally higher price and a buyer a marginally lower price than would satisfy either, and pocketing the (net of costs) difference as profit. With changes in the basic data this same process is occurring as the 'middleman' offers buyers other marginal improvements (such as a wider product range, or a higher quality product) and/or as he provides sellers with conditions or opportunities for sale not previously on offer.

To accomplish these things the 'middleman' or entrepreneur must generally also incur costs. But his net-of-costs profit does not arise through him exchanging something he values less for something he values more. It comes about rather because he has been alert enough to discover sellers and buyers with such different valuations. Pure entrepreneurial profit arises from 'the discovery of something obtainable for nothing at all' (Kirzner, 1974, p. 144, emphasis in original).

Conceptually then, entrepreneurial profit is the reward which accrues to that unique someone who is alert enough to take it. The very act of grasping what is already there will alert less wakeful entrepreneurs to do the same so that over time the combination of arbitrage and entry ensures that such profits fall to zero. Such a process will work itself out competitively or begin again when another such opportunity appears and is noticed by the most alert to have emerged.

Of course, the entrepreneur in practice may well have to involve other market participants before he can grasp his profits. He may, but need not, combine the entrepreneurial role with that of one of these other participants. Other market actors include consumers, producers and resource-owners.

An entrepreneurial consumer, as an individual, may seek out improved exchange opportunities. So too might a producer. But it is worth pointing out that both production and consumption can be subsumed under exchange. For example, Robert Clower (1977, p. 33) argues:

An ongoing exchange economy with specialist traders is a production economy since there is no bar to any merchant capitalist acquiring labour services and other resources as a 'buyer' and transforming them (repackaging, reprocessing into new forms, etc) into outputs that are unlike the original inputs and are 'sold' accordingly as are commodities that undergo no such transformation. In short, a production unit is a particular type of middleman or trading specialist.

Austrians such as Mises, Hayek and Kirzner would agree with much of Clower's view. But they would disagree with him when he says 'that "capitalists" are just individuals who have the wit and forethought to exploit profit opportunities by . . . engaging in the "production" of both trading services and new types of commodities'. Those with the 'forethought' are the entrepreneurs. Capitalists are resource owners who may combine that function with that of entrepreneurship.

One needs to look no further than the nineteenth-century history of retail cooperatives in the United Kingdom to see how consumers, too, can perceive entrepreneurial opportunities and exploit them. The fact that the retail cooperatives came to employ resources of land and labour and have accumulated trading capital to purchase other forms of stocks and equipment may mean that some entrepreneurial acts in the modern, consumer cooperative are inspired by resource owners such as managers or capitalists but the proximate entrepreneurship was undoubtedly that of consumers.

At the individual level also, consumers seek out favourable exchange opportunities. But in the modern industrial economy the costs of entrepreneurial activity, the costs of generating alertness to the potential of gain, is more generally carried out by resource owners, producers and consumers of intermediate products rather than by consumers of final products. It tends to be firms which carry out competitive price adjustments in both a situation of static and of changing market data. Final consumers tend to buy or not to buy according to the valuations they place or will place on the offered commodities. The more complex the economy, the greater the variety of goods and services available, the more likely this is to be true. The consumer has only a limited timespan in which to carry out entrepreneurial search (there are a fixed number of hours in the day). Yet the range of purchase opportunities continues always to increase. It is not surprising, then, that more and more of the entrepreneurial role is being undertaken by producers.

Not only is the firm (or the entrepreneurial component of the firm) constantly adjusting or being forced to adjust its offered price to bring it closer into line with consumer wants, the firm is also constantly attempting to adjust its whole commodity offering. In the light of changing technologies, resources and consumer tastes, the entrepreneurial component in the firm will not only be attempting to bring bid and offer prices marginally closer together but will also be attempting to bring the range and quality of apparently and potentially tradeable goods and services closer together.

In this way product differentiation, research and development, selling cost and advertising will all be engaged in by competitive firms attempting better to satisfy consumer demand.

When a producer-entrepreneur incurs costs to satisfy what he perceives will be consumer demand, he is doing so to win antici-pated revenue in excess of his anticipated costs. He will gain that anticipated profit only if he competes more successfully than others in meeting demand. His costs will include the normally defined manufacturing costs and also the conventionally defined advertising costs. But no 'single penny of the outlay . . . [manufac-turing or advertising costs] . . . can be perceived as anything but costs incurred in order to "sell"' (Kirzner, 1974, p. 144).

If we turn to Figure 8.3 we can obtain a flavour, not only of how entrepreneurs can bring buyer and seller together, but of how their arbitrage profit is whittled away by the competitive process. Again we have two traders A and B, of goods X and Y, with initial endowments of E. We have already seen verbally how one entre-preneurial middleman can bring A and B together, offer B more than his current marginal valuation of Y (in terms of X), and A more than his marginal valuation of X (in terms of Y given up). Absent transaction costs all three parties would end up better off, or, given transaction costs trade would take place provided the entrepreneurial profit was less than these costs.

Figure 8.3 assumes the presence of an entrepreneur who we will call $a$. As usual the possibilities for A and B to improve their positions are enclosed by the unlabelled indifference curves emanating from the respective origins. Entrepreneur $a$ is alert to the fact that A and B are currently at point E and are unaware of any possibility of improving their positions, $a$ knows (or thinks he knows) the preferences of A and B, he requires the quality of alertness, and simply offers A what he buys from B and vice versa. The preferences of $a$ are indicated by (for example) the indif-ference curve $aa'$ lying on a map emanating from the origin $O_a$, a mini-diagram with axes parallel to and of the same scale as the main figure. His optimal strategy is to move $O_a$ along A's

*Figure 8.3*

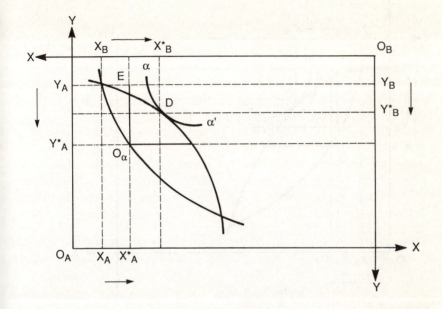

indifference curve until *aa'* is tangential to B's indifference curve at D. He then offers A just marginally more Xs than indicated by $X_A^* - X_A$ in exchange for a bundle of Ys just marginally less than indicated by $Y_A - Y_A^*$. B is offered just marginally more than $Y_B^* - Y_B$ in exchange for a bundle of Xs just marginally less than indicated by $X_B^*$. If we assume the marginal amounts required to induce A and B to trade with *a* are zero then the entrepreneur ends up at point D with a profit of Xs equal to $X_B^* - X_A^*$ and of Ys equal to $Y_A^* - Y_B^*$.

To introduce a competing entrepreneur, *β*, into the analysis we employ the same framework, the only difference in Figure 8.4 is the introduction of an additional indifference map for *β*. O'β must lie on a higher indifference curve than A's original one in order to encourage A to deal with *β* and not with *a*. Where *a* offered A $X_A^* - X_A$ in exchange for $Y_A - Y_A^*$, *β* offers fewer Xs but also obtains fewer Ys in exchange ($Y_A - \overline{Y}A$ instead of $Y_A - Y_A^*$). Because of A's preference this is a more favourable exchange and leaves him on a higher indifference curve at Oβ. Similarly, B gives

*Figure 8.4*

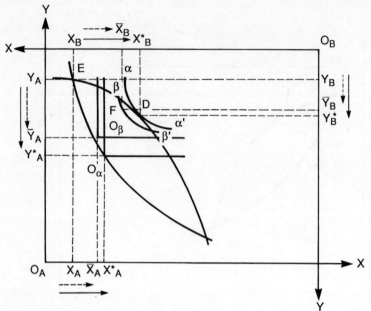

*Figure 8.5*

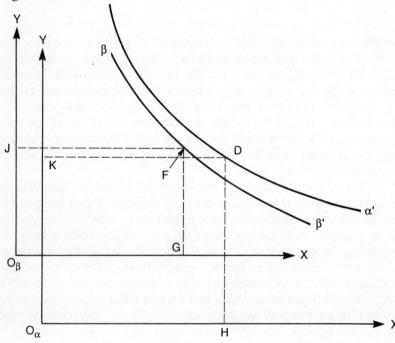

up fewer Xs ($X_B - \bar{X}_B$ instead of $X_B - X_B^*$) and gains fewer Ys ($\bar{Y}_B - Y_B$ instead of $Y_B^* - Y_B$) and the point F is more satisfactory to him than was D when he dealt with entrepreneur $a$. $\beta$ is now making all the entrepreneurial profits, and not $a$. But these profits have been reduced from $a$'s $X_B^* - X_A^*$ plus $Y_A^* - Y_B^*$ in Figure 8.3 to $\beta$'s $\bar{X}_B - \bar{X}_A$ plus $\bar{Y}_A - \bar{Y}_B$ in Figure 8.4. It is difficult to see at first glance that $\beta$'s profits are of necessity less than $a$'s were, although *a priori* it must be so and geometric measurement would indicate it was. Figure 8.5 abstracts from Figure 8.4 the relevant indifference axes for $a$'s and $\beta$'s consumption of goods A and B. There it can be more clearly seen that $a$'s consumption of both goods (i.e. $a$'s profits) would be greater than $\beta$'s consumption of both (DH > FG and KD > JF).

## 8.4  WHO IS THE ENTREPRENEUR?

This diagrammatic discussion is a useful expository device although it does run the danger of being over-mechanistic. It suffers from the defect that disequilibrium is deemed always to be noticed by entrepreneurs. And, if this is the case, then entrepreneurship is something which can be readily specified and defined, and entrepreneurs are not then 'different' from any other type of person except in so far as their training and expertise differs: a lack of uniformity common to all human beings who follow varying careers with different preparatory backgrounds. On this view an entrepreneur is no more different than a doctor, an engineer or a chemist from his fellow men. He has merely had different training from his fellows; as have his fellows from each other.

The above approach was developed in a recent and interesting book by Casson (1982). He defines the entrepreneur (p. 23) as *someone who specialises in taking judgemental decisions about the coordination of scarce resources* (emphasis in original). This definition enables Casson to concentrate on full-time decision-taking managers (and not just on any and all 'purposive human actors' as would Austrian economists) in their role as co-ordinators of means and ends which are known, albeit only with probabilities of unity or less. Casson thus assumes away ignorance but the resulting framework enables him, at least partially, to break away from neoclassical assumptions of perfect knowledge and equilibrium. This he does in his Chapter 7 and usefully exploits Edgeworth box analysis of the kind used above.

Unfortunately, this explicitly assumes that uncertainty can be removed by a search for information (Casson, 1982, p. 119). This neoclassical development is incomplete. Even if information is sought until the marginal costs of searching equal the marginal benefits the unknown will remain unknown. Further much of what is unknown is due not to lack of search but to an unknowability about alertness. Second it transforms the entrepreneur into a 'specialist' who can be trained or at least pre-selected and instructed into the science or art of 'taking judgemental decisions' with more or less success. This is at odds with both Marshallian theory and intuition. Finally, the Edgeworth box is positively misleading in the sense that it describes entrepreneurial activity *ex post* whereas the whole essence of Austrian entrepreneurship is that the indifference curves seen by the entrepreneur are not those extant today but those which he believes *ex ante* will exist tomorrow. Chapter 9 examines some of these defects in more detail.

## REFERENCES

Casson, M. (1982), *The Entrepreneur* (Oxford: Martin Robertson).

Clower, R. (1977), Private communication to Joan Robinson cited in 'What are the Questions?', *Journal of Economic Literature*, XV.

Kirzner, I. (1974), *Competition and Entrepreneurship* (Chicago: University of Chicago Press).

Mises, L., *Human Action* (1963 edition).

Schumpeter, J.A. (1939), *Business Cycles* (London: Harrap).

Schumpeter, J.A. (1948), *Socialism and Democracy* (London: Harrap).

Shackle, G.L.S. (1970), *Expectation, Enterprise and Profit* (London: George Allen and Unwin).

# 9. The Firm, the Manager and the Entrepreneur

Minimization of transactions costs and the spotting of arbitrage opportunities depend on entrepreneurs to initiate the transactions in the first place. Entrepreneurs are taken as given in the SCP analysis of industry. The difficulty with that approach is that it is what Hayek (1979) called 'scientistic'. That is, it adopts the methodology of the natural sciences in a field where it is both inappropriate and confusing. In contrast to physics or biology the raw materials analysed in economics are not phenomena capable of objective description. Rather, individual humans (producers and consumers), their actions and their perceptions make up the raw data. Attempts to explain the workings of markets without reference to the attitudes and motives of men themselves are, therefore, woefully incomplete. As Lachmann put it (1973, pp. 11, 53), 'there are millions of consumers and producers . . . [and] no two of them take their [economic decisions] in precisely the same way'. Yet it is at precisely the level of the individual firm that managerial and industrial economics should be at its most useful. What should any one firm do to maximize profits, and why do *collections* of firms take the *varying* decisions and adopt the *varying* behaviour patterns which they do? The answers must be tailored to the unimaginable number of simultaneous and successive actions by individual actual and potential competitors. Further, the action must ultimately satisfy a countless number of both known and as yet unrevealed individual consumer tastes.

Abstract scientistic models ignore these subjective complexities. They are mathematically muscle-bound. It is not even conceptually feasible that all the subjective information on consumer tastes and competitive behaviour be collected. Here we depart from Hayek's (1945) view that it is 'conceptually possible' to process all information centrally. The problem to Hayek was one of immense spatial dispersion between private individuals. It is

153

more. Decisions made by a firm today are made in anticipation of tomorrow's individual tastes, attitudes and competitive behaviour. As Shackle (1970, p. 106) put it: 'Decision is choice amongst rival courses of action. We can choose only what is still unactualized: . . . only amongst imaginations and figments.' Admit freedom of individual action tomorrow, admit future innovation and taste change and no model built today, even if fully provided with today's spatially dispersed and private information, could predict tomorrow's optimal actions.

## 9.1  THE MANAGER IS NOT (NECESSARILY) THE ENTREPRENEUR

The as yet unimagined is unknowable. So the need for data by such models far outstrips the possible supply of information, and predictive content is then often low or negligible. This is not to say that academic business economists are acting irrationally in producing a plethora of ever more esoteric theories. For the individual academic, to write a paper containing relatively minor mathematical rephrasings of existing models is a low-cost activity. It is relatively difficult and more costly to conceive of and develop novel theoretical departures and insights. But academic career advancement depends on publication. So we should not be surprised that the low-cost scientistic publication route is over-populated.

The obverse of this is equally discouraging, and again it is a symptom of scientism. This time the problem is one of holism, not objectivism: there is reliance on the notion that one can learn more from studying mechanized regression of statistical aggregates than one can from examining their teleological or individually motivated components. The temptation to be holistic is great.

Another low-cost method of producing publications is to take advantage of computerization. Vast quantities of data can be processed quickly and easily, and if we have to crank out 100 equations before one is obtained with coefficients significant at the 1 per cent level, then this is not a major problem. Only positive results need be published and the adversarial nature of much academic debate ensures that the evidence is duly selected. Hence the apparent conflict between economists. It is a dialogue of the deaf. The trouble here is not that the models are short on data, but rather that the types of data which do exist overwhelm the models.

So we have two basic problems in industrial economics. First, models may be built which are abstruse and remote from the reality of heterogeneous individual human actors; then the theory:data ratio is unhelpfully high. Second, analysts often demand more of theory than it can deliver; then the theory:data ratio is below optimum. Both problems have the same solution, namely to improve quality and applicability of theory. How can this be done?

Compliance with all of the complexities of reality is fortunately not necessary. Friedman (1957, p. 24) pointed out that all that is required is that theories contain 'the forces that the hypothesis asserts to be important'. Unfortunately, due to scientism, almost all managerial economics models ignore and assume away one crucial, ubiquitous and pervasive real-life phenomenon: heterogeneous ignorance. Not one of us knows today what tomorrow's variety of consumer tastes will be. None of us knows what tomorrow's range of production technology will be. All of us will guess, and some of us will guess better than the next man. It is to the 'best guessers' — those most alert to changing market conditions — that profits accrue. Those who make poor assessments incur losses.

A leading intermediate text (Brealey and Myers, 1981, p. 28), exemplifies exactly the scientistic position which assumes away heterogeneous ignorance: 'Our . . . lesson is a . . . general one and can be summed up by the precept, "There is no such thing as a money machine". In well-functioning open markets any potential money machine will be *eliminated almost instantaneously* by those who try to take advantage of it' (emphasis added).

But Brealey and Myers notwithstanding, there are many, many money machines and they are not 'eliminated . . . instantaneously'. All economic activity is 'money machine' in nature. As Mises (1949, pp. 14, 251) said, 'Individuals only act in the hope of gain'. And because they act in heterogeneous ignorance such 'Action is always speculation'. How do these insights highlight the theoretical deficiencies of modern managerial economies?

Managerial economics is the practical application of marginal equivalency. That is, all activities in the firm should be pursued until their hoped for marginal benefits equal their respective hoped for marginal costs. That is how, *ex post facto*, economic historians explain their operation.

If there were no money machines people would never act in the hope of gain. Further, people who act are more often correct than incorrect or increasing wealth and income would never be observed. If an extra pound of TV advertising generates additional profits of £2 while if spent on the press it would raise profits by £3 then, *ceteris paribus*, promotional expenditures should be reallocated to the press until expected marginal returns are equated. The logic is unassailable. The data are available to apply the logic and the textbooks have described the methodology for almost two decades (Reekie, 1975).

Nagging doubts remain, however. Not, to be sure, that there might not be a money machine, but that the machine's *modus operandi* can always be exploited as described. The give-away was the phrase 'hoped for'. If it had not been for this we could have equated, as many often wrongly do, administration with entrepreneurship.

The marginal equivalency principles of managerial economics can help the administrator optimize in a stochastic situation. They cannot help the entrepreneur act, decide or initiate when there is what Loasby (1976, p. 8) called partial or what we term heterogeneous ignorance. The adjective 'heterogeneous' seems more appropriate to our teleological, non-holistic approach. The marketing writer, Wroe Alderson (1958, p. 132) emphasized that 'To succeed in competition, each firm, like every blade of grass, must find a separate place to stand'. Alderson emphasized that real-life markets were not homogeneous on the supply and demand sides (as in perfect competition), nor even heterogeneous (as with monopolistic competition) but 'discrepant' with consumers, products and enterprises differentiated. For heterogeneous suppliers and demanders to have even partial congruence the question of 'how much information is enough?' must be answered. Tantalizingly, Alderson posed but failed to answer this question (Reekie and Savitt, 1982, p. 62). Managerial economics can be used only to train businessmen as coordinators of known scarce means, aiming for known ends.

This restricts us to situations of perfect knowledge; or to areas where partial ignorance can be removed by search; or to decisions where probability theory can provide 'most likely' proxies for perfect knowledge. Managerial economics cannot be used in situations of self-induced change under heterogeneous ignorance. It must be confined to the analysis of *ex post* data; to finding tangency points between existing budget lines and already discovered isoquants. But entrepreneurs do not act on the indifference curves extant today but on those which they believe *ex ante* will exist tomorrow. Moreover, different entrepreneurs have differing *ex ante* beliefs.

Compared to the entrepreneur the managerial economist is no more than a rather pompous inventory clerk. The inventory clerk looks at current consumption patterns, compares them with current productive capacity and concludes that the two do or do not equate arithmetically. He then advocates measures to maintain or remove any supply:demand mismatch. The entrepreneur, on the other hand, must deal with the fact that demand patterns today do not represent what consumers want tomorrow. Likewise, examination today of manufacturing plant, research facilities and numbers and skills of employees does not indicate what the firm can provide tomorrow (neither on a deterministic nor even on a stochastic basis). Only tomorrow's demand and supply behaviour can reveal that; and even then only in principle, since in practice tomorrow's preferred supply and demand will probably not achieve coordination. Lachmann (1973, p. 39) has long emphasized that 'not all plans can succeed', while Hayek (1937) describes the failure as continuous: it is an 'ever receding equilibrium'. The modest business economist should not presume infallibly to know before the event the most efficient way of producing a good. Nor should he presume dogmatically to know in advance what the consumer will in fact want.

The entrepreneur, however, must decide. He must act today as though he did know tomorrow's market conditions. If he is right in his estimate his action results in a profit; if not, he bears a loss. Who is this entrepreneur? He is not, as some writers argue, a 'specialist' who can be trained to take 'decisions' (e.g. Casson, 1982, p. 27). If so, as Sargant Florence (1972, p. 197) wrongly claimed, he is simply top manager who can be trained in modern managerial economics. Marshall avoided this trap. In Chapters 7 and 8 of Book VI of his *Principle* (1966) he contrasts what he calls the 'undertaker' or 'organizer' with the manager.

To Marshall the manager is an informed specialist decision-taker. Marshall's 'undertaker', however, is close to what more recent Austrian economists such as Kirzner (1973) call the entrepreneur. The entrepreneur or undertaker is not simply an informed managerial economist. A managerial economist earns a managerial salary. Nor is he a capitalist who earns interest. The undertaker's reward is over and above any 'interest' on capital and 'management' earnings. To the extent that there is such an excess ('from a considerable negative to a large positive quantity', p. 517) it is due, according to Marshall, to the 'organisation' which brought management and capital together in the first place. As Kirzner would put it, the reward or profit is due to the entrepreneur's alertness to an opportunity — the opportunity in question being the possibility of assembling resources at a cost less than consumers will pay for what these resources produce. Marshall's organization was thus not simply specialized decision-taking (which is his 'management'), but was very close to Kirzner's entrepreneurship.

So, there are money machines. They are operated by entrepreneurs who start them up in the speculative hope of profit. Marshall, like Mises, emphasizes the importance of speculative action as a cause of profit: in 'trades in which the speculative element is not important . . . the earnings of management will follow pretty closely on the amount of work done in the business . . . ' (p. 510). Marshall in that sentence does not distinguish 'management' from 'organization' so one could be accused of quoting out of context. Earlier, however (p. 495), he points out that 'gross earnings' is the reward accruing to both roles, and that 'net earnings' of management is what accrues to 'organization' alone. Marshall's taxonomy may not be consistent but his meaning is transparent.

The organizer earns his profits by discovering 'something obtainable *for nothing at all*' (Kirzner, 1974, p. 14, emphasis in original). As Marshall put it (p. 517), the organizer is alert to opportunities, since when 'profitable business opens out to him . . . he regards the harvest accruing from it as almost pure gain; . . . as a rule it scarcely occurs to him to set off his own extra labour as a deduction from these gains: they do not present themselves to his mind as to any considerable extent earnings purchased by extra fatigue'.

The question is not whether there are money machines but how they are identified and operated. This is the frontier which industrial economists still have to cross. Despite the ever-increasing sophistication of our decision tools, we have still not really identified entrepreneurship. Marshall (p. 503) implied that the necessary ingredients of entrepreneurship are very general. '[B]usiness power is highly non-specialized, because in the large majority of trades, technical knowledge and skill become every day less important relatively to the broad and non-specialized faculties of judgement, promptness, resourcefulness, carefulness and steadfastness of purpose.' Kirzner (1982, p. 149) defines this 'non-specialized power' as 'alertness' or 'the motivated propensity of man to formulate an image of the future'.

We do not talk about alertness in industrial economics, however. We assume people are technicians and take as given motivation. Nevertheless, surely it is the business of economics, and especially industrial economics, to determine the type of market environment most likely to foster and stimulate varying types of alertness? It is to this aspect of business economics, the organization of firms to which we now turn.

## 9.2   THE REASON THE FIRM EXISTS

If the entrepreneur carries out a function of 'speculative organization', if he does not act as a 'trained decision-taker' then who, in the modern corporation, is the entrepreneur and who are the trained decision-takers? Recent literature on the theory of the firm can help answer these questions although we shall find that in doing so still wider issues are raised. This literature, sometimes Austrian in origin, sometimes not, has one thing in common: dissatisfaction with the neoclassical view of the firm as a collection of resources solely at the disposal of an identifiable wealth-maximizing owner-manager. Berle and Means (1932) were the first to popularize the now familiar concept of a divorce of firm ownership from control, in that they alleged that modern corporate managers rarely (or at least decreasingly) held a legal property stake, in the form of common stock, in the companies they administered. This resulted in a plethora of theories of the firm acknowledging this apparent truism and each suggesting that managers had different motivations from owners. For example, Baumol (1959) argued that sales maximization was the prime managerial goal; Williamson (1964) delineated a more broadly-based managerial utility function; and Marris (1971) argued in favour of corporate growth. These views however, contrast with Austrian notions of the modern corporation. Kirzner (1972, p. 65) argues that if the divorce of ownership from control is such that shareholders cannot curb managerial behaviour to act exclusively in their, the shareholders' interests, then it is only because the shareholders believe, in their entrepreneurial judgement, that the benefits of continuing to be a shareholder in such a firm exceed the cost.

What role then does the modern firm play in economics? To

answer this question a large volume of recent literature is available, much of it stemming from the seminal paper by Ronald Coase (1937). In this section we shall also draw on the work of Williamson (1975), Jensen and Meckling (1976), Alchian and Demsetz (1972) and Fama (1980).

The fundamental question posed by Coase (1937) was to ask why on some occasions buyers and sellers transact in the market-place while on others they perform similar activities in a vertically integrated firm. Coase discounts the notion that it is the presence of uncertainty which is the reason for bringing firms into existence. All production is entrepreneurial in nature. But the entrepreneurial role is not the same as the firm's role. Entre-preneurs can be, and are, hired in the market to undertake uncertainty. For example, speculators buy stock for unpredictable resale in the commodity futures market. Again the question is left unanswered: why in some cases does entrepreneurship coincide with a firm's activities, and in others is carried on at arm's length in the marketplace outside the firm?

Coase concluded that firms come into existence because the costs of using the price mechanism vary. Transactions are not homogeneous. When transaction costs rise too high, when the costs of negotiating and contracting become excessive, firms come into being. A firm then is merely that area of activity within which the economies of internal organization exceed the economies of market relationships. To bring a firm into being, to assemble resources in anticipation of a reduction in transactions costs is an entrepreneurial act. To maintain a firm in being need not be entrepreneurship. The economies which can be obtained by replacing arm's length relationships with firms are also limited. Firms are groups or teams of people (and other resources) and groups must be coordinated. Coordination itself is not costless and may be subject to diminishing returns. Moreover, although firm or cooperative team production may result in an output which exceeds the total output which could be achieved by each team member if he operated in isolation, and although this excess may be greater than the costs of organizing the firm or team, there still remains the problem of monitoring.

Alchian and Demsetz (1972) view the monitoring of effort and the rewarding of productivity as the two major problems in firm production. They argue that the interdependence of team pro-duction means that it is difficult to ascertain what part of total output is attributable to any one team member's efforts.

Conversely, shirking may go unobserved. In individual efforts the individual reaps all the benefits of his efforts, and if he shirks he bears all the costs of shirking. But in team work, the total costs of shirking are not borne by the shirker, they are borne by the full team. Everyone admits that he is better off if no one shirks, but everyone also realizes that if he alone shirks, the cost to him will be small: he can get a 'free ride' on the efforts of other team members.

More shirking will therefore occur in firms than in individual market-related transactions. Shirking is cheaper in firms or teams and therefore each individual has a higher incentive to substitute leisure for productive work. The team members can get over the problem by hiring another member to monitor the productive activity of the total team. To be effective the monitor must have disciplinary powers over shirkers which can be used without disbanding the team. In short he must be able to fire a shirker. The monitor is the manager, or, more accurately in the large firm, the management group. But who monitors the monitor? How can it be ensured that managers do not shirk? The traditional legal answer is that there is a board of directors acting as shareholders' agents. The modern economic theory of principal and agent does not deny this but concentrates more (relatively) on the agency relationship between owners and managers on a general level. It sees each as having differing skills or expertise, each as having differing capital endowments, and each as having differing degrees of risk-aversion. Moreover, as well as being able to 'fire' the manager or the agent in the normal legal manner, newer theories show how the disciplining of the monitor can also be achieved through the market in corporate control. The owner can sell the firm to a new owner who will fire the dilatory manager. It is to these issues we now turn. We shall also see below that the economic discussion of transaction costs, an acknowledgement that the management group is not a monolithic structure, and a willingness to perceive the possibility of competition in unwonted places, can help answer this question in a far more satisfactory manner than an unreasoning acceptance of traditional legal structures *per se*.


## 9.3 TRANSACTION COSTS AND THE FIRM

Williamson (1975, 1979) complements and adds to Alchian and

Demsetz's (1972) view of why firms exist. The latter emphasized the concept of team production and monitoring but did not accept contractual relationships (and hence transaction costs) as important. Indeed they said: '[L]*ong term contracts* between employer and employees *are not the essence of the . . . firm*' (emphasis added). However, Alchian (1982, p. 20) now accepts that this 'assertion is incorrect' given Williamson's subsequent analyses. It is to Williamson's discussion of transaction costs, contractual relationships and hence the firm that we now turn.

Williamson's thesis commences by stressing the advantages of team activity over sequential spot contracting by market exchange. Indivisible physical resources are used for the maximum benefit of the group as a whole, and not for the benefit of a monopolistic supplier renting out time or space to individuals. Similarly, the learning-by-doing informational advantages gained by team members on the job accrue to the team as a whole. The costs of renegotiating with each worker (who is gaining ever more experience) the terms under which he will supply his (ever-changing and ever-scarcer) skills are eliminated or reduced. In brief, transactions costs are reduced and all reap net benefits individually as a consequence of team membership.

In addition, Williamson argues that simple, non-hierarchical teams can offer a more certain income than can individual effort coupled with insurance contracting in the market. One reason for this assertion is that *ex ante* recruitment to the team can limit membership to good risks. That is, although selection errors will be made, a policy of deliberately choosing or attempting to choose productive, well-motivated co-workers will result in the team being composed of members whose efficiency, on average, is higher than that of all individuals in the market. Insurance costs will consequently be lower in team effort than in individual effort.

Finally, Williamson takes issue with Alchian and Demsetz's (1972) view that the benefits of team production as such, namely the problem of non-separability of tasks, is the reason why groupings of workers emerge. Alchian and Demsetz use the example of manhandling heavy loads into trucks which, to be carried out efficiently, requires two men. Such examples are alleged by Williamson to be rare or, if division of labour by in-dividual workers is not feasible, then division of labour by small groupings certainly is. Work could pass from process to process by purchase and sale. But buffer-stocks would have to be held at each interval to facilitate coordination and so permit the drawing-up of meaningful contracts to cover the exchanges made at each stage. Thus internal organization comes about, Williamson argues, not only because of the benefits of team production arising from non-separabilities (the original Alchian and Demsetz view) but (as with Coase, 1937) to minimize transaction costs (of haggling and of carrying relatively high inventories).

But why should peer-group activity develop into hierarchical group activity? What are the specific costs which a non-hierarchical firm must meet, and what corresponding benefits accrue to a firm which removes its labour exchange activities from the extra-firm market to what Williamson calls the 'internal labour market'?

Williamson contends that non-hierarchical groups are limited by 'bounded rationality'. In other words the human mind, even if it has an objectively rational goal, is unable to process all of the complex and voluminous information which is necessary in order to take the required decisions. The information can neither be adequately received, processed nor transmitted. After a point the opportunity cost of wasted time by communicating everything to and from everyone for the purposes of reaching a collective decision becomes prohibitive. If scale economies of some type justify larger groupings of people then changes in organizational structure may be required. One person could, of course, be given the decision-taking role in a group so that diseconomies of communication be avoided and a peer-group relationship retained.

A hierarchy will almost certainly emerge, however, because of 'bounded rationality differentials' between the members of the group. Williamson justifies this claim on the grounds that unless leadership of the group is undemanding, or each member is equally well qualified with respect to administration, then either group productivity or group democracy must be sacrificed.

Alchian and Demsetz argued that hierarchies would emerge because of the need to monitor the performance of the group and so minimize shirking. Williamson agrees with this and gives it as the second main reason for the limitations to peer-group persistence. Malingerers, he argues, can be cajoled by their fellows to work harder; if that fails, rational appeals will be made; thirdly, the group will withdraw social benefits from the offender; and, finally, the group may resort to 'overt coercion and ostracism'. When these fail the free rider or shirker may be monitored and/or awarded discriminatory wages which is 'tantamount to introducing hierarchy'.

Once a hierarchy has emerged (*vis-à-vis* a non-hierarchical group) what benefits accrue? Williamson argues that the resulting structure, which in effect is what is commonly called the firm, is not rigidly authoritarian but is, in itself, an internal labour market, 'an employment relation', with distinct transaction cost advantages over external labour markets.

To understand the firm as an internal labour market (and so an entity which is not just a 'black box' but one to which economic or market analysis is applicable) it is necessary also to realize that, although property rights in specific tasks are relatively weak, 'job idiosyncracy' exists. Williamson argues that 'job idiosyncracy' or non-homogeneity occurs because workers acquire 'job-specific skills and related task-specific knowledge' comparable to the knowledge of Hayek's 'man-on-the-spot'. Thus workers progressively obtain more and more knowledge of the kind Hayek termed applicable to 'particular circumstances of time and place'. This results in asymmetry either in the information held by members of a firm and/or in the costs of acquiring that information. (Williamson defines this phenomenon as 'information impactedness'.) But information impactedness is precisely the reason why normal market transactions occur. Entrepreneurs spot opportunities for mutually beneficial exchange between buyers and sellers, help initiate a suitable transaction and so move the market towards equilibrium.

In analogous manner, within the firm, the firm itself is moved towards its objective (or equilibrium) as members enter into mutually beneficial trades or contracts. Such exchanges occur, even in a hierarchical situation, because the parties to the exchange place different marginal valuations on the commodities (for simplicity, say labour and cash) they are trading. The differing marginal valuations arise due to information impactedness. The superior has unique information relating to the income the firm can obtain from a given set of productive inputs. The subordinate has unique know-how, arising from experience, relating to the task he will be called upon to perform. This makes it easier (i.e. cheaper) for him to perform that task at the margin and so makes it easier for him to compete against a willing but inexperienced subordinate (for example, an outsider) who would have to incur training and learning costs.

What kind of contractual relationship then is the most efficient? Williamson examines five. Only one is regarded as sufficiently flexible to permit adaptation to changing internal and external market circumstances. Only that one is also able to overcome the problems of opportunism (for example, shirking), peer group organization, and task idiosyncracy. That one is the internal labour market. We shall initially survey the demerits of the other four.

First, a contract could be made now with a subordinate (or group of subordinates) to perform a specific task in the future. This, however, is impractical (i.e. too costly to implement) in complex and uncertain business environments and can be dismissed as of little practical interest. A second alternative is to draw the contract up in probabilistic or contingent terms to account for such uncertainties. An agreed wage would be paid now in return for future services which would depend on circumstances. Williamson argues that business life is too complex to write such employment contracts feasibly or cheaply *ex ante*. Bounded rationality would prohibit it. Even if it were feasible to write the contracts at reasonable expense, Williamson then argues that there would probably be problems of comprehensibility which would impede agreement. At least one party to the contract (probably the worker) would not fully understand the ramifications of the complex agreement to which he is being asked to accede. Information impactedness would be an obstacle. *Ex post*, the contract would face enormous enforcement problems. Opportunism could result in shirking. Information impactedness could result in disputes over which contingent state of the world had, in fact, come to pass. And resort to arbitration would not, by definition, reduce the information impactedness problem. The arbitrator himself would face the problem as to how much of the apparent or claimed knowledge asymmetry regarding the state of the world was real and how much was due to opportunism (lack of candour or honesty in drawing up or executing the transaction).

The third alternative is sequential contracting: i.e. a series of short-term contracts in the spot market. This concept permits continuous adaptation of the contract to changing circumstances and so overcomes the problems of uncertainty. Bounded rationality and information impactedness pose much less severe problems since no attempt is made to detail all contingencies in advance and so, *ex post*, there need be no dispute over which state of the world had come to pass. This was the original Alchian and Demsetz (1972) view of the firm. Williamson, however, denies that sequential spot contracting can be applied to the situation of the firm because of unacceptably high transaction costs. It is inefficient in that there is scope for opportunistic behaviour due to task idiosyncracy. This 'effectively destroys parity (with outsiders) at the contract renewal interval. Incumbents who enjoy non-trivial advantages over similarly qualified but inexperienced bidders are well situated to demand some fraction of the cost savings which their idiosyncratic experience has generated.' Such problems of opportunism can only be overcome if workers are either asked to bid for employment contracts by offering lump-sums to employers reflecting the present value of the monopoly gains which will accrue to them due to their idiosyncratic experience (but this re-introduces issues of bounded rationality and information impactedness); or if workers promise not to behave opportunis-tically when contracts come up for renegotiation, which assumes they will behave irrationally; or if workers submit to authoritarian monitoring.

Authority is the fourth form of contractual relationship. Simon (1957) suggests an authoritarian agreement exists if a worker is willing to accept a boss's authority in exchange for a stated wage. This type of agreement will be preferred to an extra-firm 'sales contract' provided that a deterministic (wholly certain) sales contract cannot be drawn up and that the area of uncertainty which does remain (what the worker will, in fact, be asked to do) will not prove unattractive to the worker. It will be advantageous to the boss to draw up such a contract if he wishes to postpone the precise selection of the worker's task until some time after the contract is made. Simon's authority contract is simply one in which the parties 'agree to tell and be told'. But, Williamson argues, 'the terms are rigged from the outset'. The 'sales contract' with which Simon compares his authority relation is merely our first contractual (and flexible) alternative. Our second and third possibilities (a contingent sales contract and a series of sequential spot contracts) both offered the advantages of flexibility in response to changing circumstances. Does the authority relation, then, offer anything in terms of efficiency? It is less costly than the contingent sales contract in that it does not impose the bounded rationality problem and so high transaction costs of generating knowledge of all alternative outcomes in advance. It is superior to the spot contracting mode in that transaction costs are lowered due to the decrease in frequency with which contracts are negotiated. Nevertheless, all of the problems of task idiosyncracy which were present in spot contracting remain to be faced. For example, how are terms of employment to be adjusted over time as circumstances change? How are the problems of disputes due to either opportunism or information impactedness to be resolved? With job idiosyncracy firms will either have to bear the high costs of continuous labour turnover or the high costs of meeting the demands of idiosyncratic workers with monopoly bargaining power.

The fifth possibility, the internal labour market is, if not optimal in terms of minimizing transactions costs between firms and employees, possibly the closest approach to optimality yet suggested. In particular, it overcomes the problems posed by task idiosyncracies. The essence of the employment relation or the internal labour market is that the individual contract is replaced by the collective bargain. This results, to cite Williamson (1975, p. 74), in a 'fundamental transformation . . . where wage rates are attached mainly to jobs rather than to workers'. The incentive to behave opportunistically which individual workers would have in individual contracting (due to their peculiar experience) is thus greatly reduced. The collective agreement also overcomes problems of uncertainty by being written in general terms which makes it 'an instrument of government as well as exchange'.

All individuals who collectively accede to the contract presumably do so because they feel it is to their individual net advantage. Each has an area within which he is indifferent as to what instruction he may receive from those to whom he has granted authority or powers of government. But any one individual whose area of indifference is opportunistically distinct from those of the rest of the group will not, provided the distinction is small, reject authority. Should he do so he would pose a threat to the benefits of all the other individuals who gain from the agreement. Thus group pressures would be exerted against such opportunistic behaviour and the authority relationship embodied in the contract be reinforced from below. Bounded rationality is attenuated by writing the contract in non-precise terms. Information impactedness, *ex post*, or disagreements in contractual interpretation resulting in disputes, are provided for by writing into the contract, *ex ante*, details of dispute-settling mechanisms. This allows the day-to-day running of the firm to be pursued while the grievance is tackled by the arbitration apparatus devised by the parties to the contract. Since this apparatus may be composed of some sort of elected group (such as a union committee) representing the workers as a whole, it will be more concerned with the interests of the total labour force. Thus, again, opportunistic behaviour due to task idiosyncracy is curbed.

But the acceptance of the employment relation does not ensure that the firm receives 'consummate' as opposed to 'perfunctory' cooperation from its labour force. The former is described by Williamson as an 'affirmative job attitude' including the 'use of judgement, filling gaps, and taking initiative in an instrumental way'. The latter, by contrast, 'involves job performance' of a minimally acceptable sort — where minimally acceptable means that incumbents who have idiosyncratic advantages, 'need merely to maintain a slight margin over the best available inexperienced candidate'. Consummate cooperation could be obtained by awarding individual incentive payments of a sequential spot contract kind but this is precluded in the collective bargains of internal labour markets. Williamson argues instead that the advantages of internal labour markets can be maintained, but consummate cooperation also obtained if, as part of the internal incentive system, higher-level positions are generally filled by internal promotions. If such practices are followed by most firms the internal labour market is strengthened.

Other implications follow. The firm can risk-avert by only employing newcomers at low levels in the hierarchy. This protects the firm against opportunistic job applicants who might represent themselves as more productive than they otherwise are. Promotion will only follow as experience warrants it. Restricting 'ports of entry' to low-level jobs reflects the advantages of the internal market over the external labour market in other ways as well. Any lateral transfer which could occur between firms at higher levels because an employee is motivated to move due to a (correct) denial of promotion in his original firm is less likely. Interim information impactedness might otherwise have resulted in such a transfer taking place. The new employer would not have had the advantage of the old employer's hierarchy to provide him with information relating to the defects of the new entrant. Moreover, opportunism by the old employer could have resulted in problems of veracity regarding the quality of the new entrant. The old employer might have been only too happy to be rid of the employee (who might have reached his existing level in the old firm as a consequence of a rating error in the first place).

In short, intra-firm labour markets, hierarchies, have informational advantages over extra-firm labour markets. They are less subject to bounded rationality, information impactedness, and to opportunistic behaviour. They are better than perfunctory cooperation as a consequence of their hierarchical structure. And a monitor, indeed a hierarchy of monitors, in the Alchian and Demsetz sense, is still required.

## 9.4 THE DIVORCE OF OWNERSHIP FROM CONTROL

We have now established that the divorce of ownership from control does not mean that the firm needs to be viewed as a 'black box'. The extent of the 'divorce' is, of course, an empirical question. But that it exists, even if the degree to which it exists is not a subject for consensus, is not in doubt. However, even if we can now apply economic analysis within the firm as well as between firms does this necessarily make any impact on the claim that managers can pursue objectives fundamentally different from those of wealth-maximizing shareholders?

The answer is no. Part of the apparent difficulty in seeing this is in the taxonomy of 'manager', 'worker' and 'shareholder'. The very words inculcate an image of antagonists rather than complementary team members. The Alchian and Demsetz notion of a team overcomes the problem. The firm is merely a team which exists (or, set of contractual agreements negotiated) for the benefit of all team members. Some are wealthier than others. Some are risk-preferrers. Others are more risk-averse. Some have talents of monitoring and selection. Others have a comparative advantage in energy, knowledge and skills as producers. Provided property rights exist in these interpersonal differences they can be freely exchanged. Each individual will still care only for his own personal benefit when negotiating the exchange (such is the restricted thesis of the divorce of ownership from control) but each will only enter into the contractual agreement known as a firm if each believes he will be better off thereby. The firm is simply another example of mutually beneficial exchange.

There is nothing authoritarian, dictatorial or exploitative in the relationship. Employees order employers to pay them amounts specified in the hiring contract just as much as employers order employees to abide by the terms of the contract. The team itself, however, is hired and fired with abandon in the (spot) marketplace by consumers. There are two types of team member who gain or suffer from satisfying or failing to satisfy consumers. One is the fixed reward claimant and the other is the residual claimant (or shareholder).

Fixed reward claimants are shielded in the short run from the exigencies of demand by the terms of their contract. They must be paid whether the residual claim is large or negative. Residual claimants do not have this cushion. In the long run, claimants with fixed payment contracts can move to other teams to preserve their contractual claims.

But does the modern firm permit more or less opportunism than alternative forms of organization? Williamson (1979) argued that cost economizing is of the essence in commercial transactions. Costs are of two kinds: productive expenses and transaction costs. In situations where transaction costs are negligible buying-in rather than making is optimal since scale economies can be fully exploited. When transaction costs are higher, or the potential for savings in production expenses is less then the balance alters. Economizing on transaction costs 'essentially reduces to economising on bounded rationality while simultaneously safe-guarding the transactions . . . against the hazards of opportunism' (Williamson, 1979, p. 246). Thus for recurrent transactions a make decision is more likely than a buy-in decision since bounded-rationality costs are minimized by saving the expense of continuously rewriting contracts. The more idiosyncratic or seller/customer-specific is the traded good the more complex must the contract be and so the greater is the potential attenuation of bounded rationality. On the other hand, Williamson points out that monitoring costs then rise as the contractor has now to ensure contract execution and guard against opportunism. Such monitoring (transaction) costs begin to exceed the benefits of economizing on bounded rationality (transaction costs) the less frequent is the execution of the relationship between the two parties. This is because of inadequate monitoring skills. Thus after a point, as a recurrent transaction becomes less frequent one aspect of transaction costs outweighs the other and a buy decision becomes more likely. Williamson (1979, p. 247) uses the phrase 'governance structures' to distinguish between market trans-actions, neoclassical contracting (where formal legal contracts are involved and a third party, the civil law, is used in both contract construction and execution) and relational contracting. Relational contracting is further subdivided into unified governance (the firm) and bilateral governance where two equal but independent partners buy and sell from each other. This analysis, however, only helps explain why the firm may be the most efficient structure in certain circumstances. We still have not definitely answered the question whether it has become more or less so since the alleged divorce of ownership from control came to the attention of some writers. We turn to these issues in Chapter 10.

Finally, while Williamson's classification of governance structures is useful, it subsumes both the firm (unified governance) and market transactions, and *other* relationships (e.g. bilateral governance) which other writers might well regard as a type of market transaction (namely bilateral monopoly). In doing this we can lose sight of the uniqueness of these characteristics related to all other transactions in whatever type of market or legal framework.

In a recent paper Demsetz (1987) accomplishes this, while showing how the Williamson and Alchian and Demsetz views can be reconciled. While Alchian (p. 162 above) has accepted the need for a long-term contract to be a factor of the firm, Demsetz has not. Demsetz still emphasizes that the distinguishing feature of a firm is the monitoring of shirkers in a situation where team production is more efficient than isolated and discrete activities with exchange. Shirking (in firms) is the key. The analogous key to identifying market related activities is the presence of 'shirking across markets' (Demsetz, 1987, p. 6) or, as Williamson terms it, opportunism. The requisite monitoring process in firms was attributed to and identified by Alchian and Demsetz with the individual who has the residual rights (i.e. after all other factors have been paid), who has rights to observe, to be the common contractual party with all other inputs, to alter team membership, and finally the ability to sell such rights. The 'monitoring process across markets' to paraphrase Demsetz is just as identifiable, the partners to the transaction may share more or less of the bundle of rights just described, but no one party has all of them. If a single party did possess all such rights and monitoring duties then a firm would exist.

In Chapter 10 we look further at these issues. We examine the notions of internal markets within firms for managers and workers and the rights of monitors to discontinue relationships. We will show how the different risk preferences of shareholders and managers are reconciled by principal/agent theory and how the market in corporate control permits a subdivision of the bundle of rights of the monitor identified above while simultaneously ensuring efficiency of firm operation when unified governance is the selected method of managing.

# REFERENCES

Alchian, A. (1982), 'Property Rights, Specialisation and the Firm', in J.P. Weston and M.E. Granfield (eds), *Corporate Enterprise in a New Environment* (KGG Productions).

Alchian, A. and Demsetz, D. (1972), 'Production Information Costs and Economic Organisation', *American Economic Review*, 62.

Alderson, W. (1958), *Dynamic Marketing Behaviour* (Homewood, Ill.: Richard D. Irwin).

Baumol, W.J. (1959), *Business Behaviour, Value and Growth* (New York: Macmillan).

Berle, A.A. and Means, G.C. (1932), *The Modern Corporation and Private Property* (New York: Macmillan).

Brealey, R. and Myers, S. (1982), *Business Finance*, 2nd ed. (Mondinhead: McGraw-Hill).

Casson, M. (1982), *The Entrepreneur* (Oxford: Martin Robertson).

Coase, R.H. (1937), 'The Nature of the Firm', *Economica*.

Demsetz, H. (1987), 'The Theory of the Firm Revisited' (mimeographed).

Fama, E.F. (1950), 'Agency Problems and the Theory of the Firm', *Journal of Political Economy*.

Florence, P.S. (1972), *The Logic of British and American Industry* (London: Routledge and Kegan Paul).

Hayek, F.A. (1937), 'Economics and Knowledge', *Economica*, 4.

Hayek, F.A. (1979), *The Counter Revolution of Science* (Indianapolis: Liberty Press).

Jensen, M.C. and Meckling, W.H. (1976), 'Theory of the Firm, Management Behaviour, Agency Costs and Ownership Structure', *Journal of Financial Economics*.

Kirzner, L. (1974), *Competition and Entrepreneurship* (Chicago: University of Chicago Press).

Knight, F. (1921), *Risk, Uncertainty and Profit* (New York: Houghton, Mifflin).

Lachmann, L.M. (1973), *Macroeconomic Thinking and the Market Economy*, Hobart Paperback No. 56 (London: Institute of Economic Affairs).

Loasby, B.J. (1976), *Choice, Complexity and Ignorance* (Cambridge: Cambridge University Press).

Marks, R., Marris, E. and Woods, A. (eds) (1971), *The Corporate Economy* (London: Macmillan).

McNulty, P.J. (1962), 'Economic Theory and the Meaning of Competition', *Quarterly Journal of Economics*.

Reekie, W.D. (1975), *Managerial Economics* (London: Philip Allan, Oxford University Press).

Reekie, W.D. and Savitt, R. (1982), 'Marketing Behaviour and Entrepreneurship: A Synthesis of Alderson and Avitsien Economics', *European Journal of Marketing*, 16.

Simon, H.A. (1957), *Models of Man* (London: John Wiley).

Williamson, O.E. (1961), *The Economics of Discretionary Behaviour* (New York: Prentice-Hall).

Williamson, O.E. (1973), *Markets and Hierarchies* (New York: Free Press).

Williamson, O.E. (1979), 'Transaction Cost Economics: The Governance of Contractual Relations', *Journal of Law and Economics*.

# 10.  Principal/Agent and Corporate Control

The theoretical reasons the corporate controllers (allegedly divorced from ownership) continue to work in the interests of residual claimants or owners are twofold. First, there is the presence of an active internal (and external) labour market for the agents or monitors (i.e. managers). Second, there is the market in corporate control. We examined in Chapter 9 why firms (as hierarchies as opposed to markets) exist. In this chapter we shall discover that introducing outside equity into a firm results in agency costs. Individual ownership of firms (to avoid agency costs) is unlikely, not just for the obvious reasons of scale (individuals could always borrow) but rather because of the incentive effects of borrowing on a highly geared owner-manager. Failure costs would be borne by the debt-holder rather than equity. Selling equity to outsiders, we shall see, does reduce firm value because of agency costs but there is an optimum point where these marginal agency costs to the owner equal the marginal benefits of a more widely diversified portfolio (which is a similar conclusion to Kirzner's view that if owners decide in their own best interests to hire managers, it must be because in their judgement they believe that is the best available alternative — see p. 159). First, however, we look at recent developments in principal/agent theory.

## 10.1  PRINCIPAL AND AGENT[1]

An agent carries out some function on behalf of his principal. (Thus this definition is at once wider but also less precise than the lawyer's where the agent can contract and legally bind his principal with third parties.) The basic objectives of principal/agent theory is to examine how explicit or implicit contracts can be drawn up between the two parties to take account of shirking, opportunism, bounded rationality and information impactedness; to allocate risk 'efficiently', to monitor agent behaviour and to construct an optimal incentive structure. The theory has many implications but here we restrict ourselves to two: the relationship between owner and manager, and that between employer and employee. First, however, we look at some generic issues.

Clearly, in risk-free situation, where the outcome of a relationship is directly observable and totally predictable any contract between principal and agent need merely specify the desired outcome and agency payment. Principal and agent will then agree to pay and be paid for delivery of a specified performance. No agency problems exist. A simple case of mutually beneficial contractual trading will occur.

When there is an *indeterminate outcome* and *attitudes to risk differ* between the two parties, however, then an agency problem does exist. (The analysis need not depend on which party is more or less risk-averse: we shall assume it is the agent, and that the principal, in our specific examples the owner or the employer who is risk neutral or preferring.) Consider the situation where an outcome will depend not only on the agent's effort but on a stochastic state of nature (market demand or the economy) then any contract will involve risk to both parties since the outcome is probabilistic. Assume the agent's effort, $a$, is readily measurable and that the state of nature, *ex post*, is readily measurable, then there is no shirking or monitoring problem and the issue is only one of efficiently allocating risk, *ex ante*, so that neither the risk-averse agent nor the risk-neutral principal could have been made better off by any other allocation of the expected monetary value (EMV) of the outcome.

Consider an agent and principal faced with two possible outcomes, $II_1$ and $II_2$ dependent on two states of nature $s_1$ and $s_2$ with probabilities $p_1$ and $p_2 = (1 - p_1)$ with $II_1 > II_2$. Assume no shirking and hence a given $a$. The outcomes $II_1$ and $II_2$ are divided between A and P such that $II_1 = II_{1_A} + II_{1_P}$ and $II_2 = II_{2_A} + II_{2_P}$. Assume that A can rank outcomes according to standard gamble, certainty equivalence theory, then his utility function showing indifference curves of constant expected utility can be constructed. The shape of such curves will, of course, be dependent on his attitude to risk. A risk-neutral individual will have a utility function with straight line indifference curves. (The mathematical expected monetary value of the outcome, EMV, anywhere along the line will be $p_1 II_1 + p_2 II_2$.) A risk-averse person, however, would require ever-greater compensation in terms of $II_2$ as the value of $p_1 II_1$ falls, given $p_1 = 1 - p_2$ (and vice versa if $p_2 II_2$ fell). His EUV (expected utility value function) would only be the same as the corresponding computed EMV at one unique, certainty equivalent point. Figure 10.1 illustrates the discussion to this point.

*Figure 10.1*

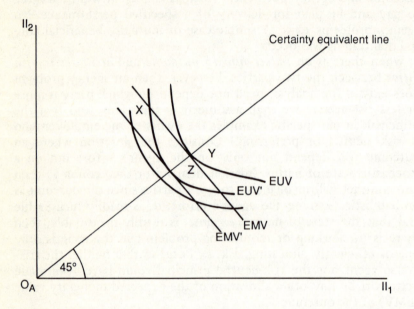

The 45° line joins points of equal values of $II_1$ and $II_2$ (which are denominated in the same units, say money). Through any point on this line an EMV straight line indifference curve of constant expected outcome can be drawn and it is at the intersection of EMV with the 45° line that the risk-averter's indifference curve (EUV) would also pass. Other (lower-valued) curves are also shown. Clearly, individual A located at point X would, if he is risk-neutral, be indifferent as to whether his claims on II were located at X or Y. If he is risk-averse, however, he would be indifferent as to whether his claims on II lay at X or Z. Z, however, has a lower EMV than Y. There is scope, therefore, for a risk-averse person at X, to relocate himself between Z and Y on the certainty equivalent line by exchanging claims on $II_2$ for claims on $II_1$, provided another party (the principal) is present also with access to $II_1$ and $II_2$, who is willing to trade claims. A risk-averse agent, in short, will always be willing to shed some risk until he arrives on the certainty equivalent line where, by definition, the slope of whatever EUV line he achieves has the value (negative) $p_1/p_2$. (Recall that EMV = $p_1 II_1 + p_2 II_2$.) Indeed, since at the limit, as Y approaches Z, a risk-averter would never be prepared to move from Y to X but would always be willing to move from X to Z we can assert that Z is, strictly speaking, preferable to X. In other words, in general terms, the outcome probability ratio provides the prices at which contingent claims will be traded, while in strict and specific terms, a risk-averse person would always tend to move to the certainty equivalent line passing through the same EUV curve.

So how can risk be shared efficiently between principal and agent (i.e. so that neither can be made better off)? We return, as does Ricketts (1987, p. 124), to an Edgeworth box diagram, recalling that $II_2 < II_1$, that over a run of events $II = II_A + II_P$, and imposing the condition that A is risk-averse while P is risk-neutral. $O_A$ is in the bottom left-hand corner while $O_P$ is in the top right. A's indifference curves are concave to $O_A$, while P's (because of risk-neutrality) are straight lines. Point X is where the agent receives $II_{1_A}$ if outcome $II_1$ occurs and $II_{2_A}$ if outcome $II_2$ occurs. At that point the principal receives $II_{1_P}$ or $II_{2_P}$ respectively, depending on the overall outcome. Clearly X is not Pareto optimal or efficient in the sense that both A and P could become better off (or at least one could without harming the other) by exchanging claims on the outcomes so that they arrived at a division of $II_1$ and $II_2$ between Y and Z. In fact, a move from X to Z could occur if each was going to retain the same EMV for his respective efforts. In other words, a risk-neutral principal could provide complete insurance to a risk-averse agent (or vice versa) provided only that s is observable and that effort incentives and monitoring provide no problems. (When both parties are risk-averse efficient claims allocation will occur at a tangency point of the two sets of indifference curves between the two certainty equivalent lines.) In other words, the principal would 'pay' the

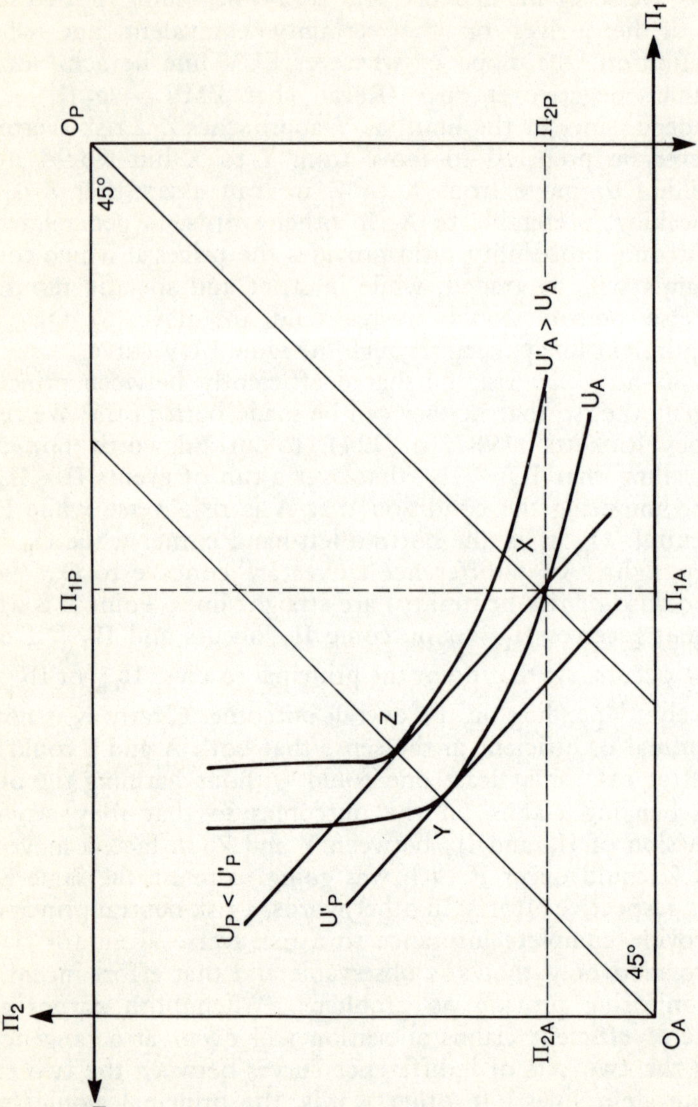

Figure 10.2

178

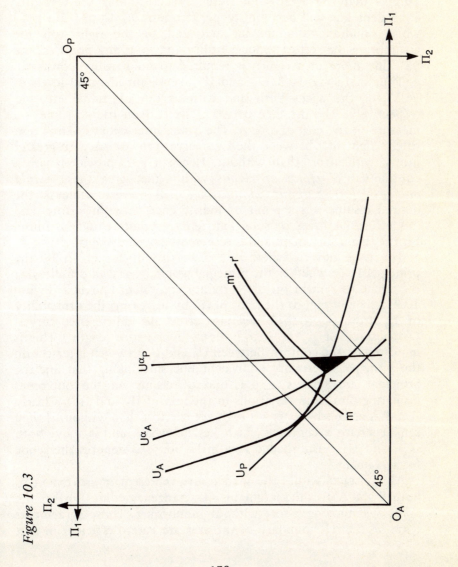

Figure 10.3

179

agent an amount which depended only on the state of nature and keep the rest of the output (the residual) for himself. The output resulting from any additional principal input would always go to P while the nature of s would enable risks to be divided according to individual preferences and aversions towards risk.

But *what if the outcome* II is *also dependent on a, the agent's efforts?* In particular, what if, given that $II_1 > II_2$, a rises to make $II_1$ more likely to occur? The impact on the conditions of Figure 10.2 is that the agent's indifference curves along the certainty equivalent line will become steeper (from $p_1/p_2$ to $p^a_1/1 - p^a_1$) while simultaneously moving out and to the right (on the assumption that effort reduces utility and so at any point on the 45° line more of a return is required to hold utility constant).

Thus in Figure 10.3 $U_A$ and $U^a_A$ represent identical levels of EUV for the agent with and without the additional effort a respectively. The distance between the two on the 45° line is a measure of the cost of a to A. The curves intersect at r. Any point to the right of r between the two curves provides A with greater utility with effort than without. Hence if A is provided with a contractual *portfolio of claims* within that area these *would induce effort without monitoring*. Self-interest achieves the desired results. r is a point of indifference between 'effort' and 'no effort'. A locus of such indifference points could be found for the two utility maps and is represented by the line $rr^1$.

The issue now is whether it is worth inducing effort by the principal P, or whether the principal would be as well off allowing the agent to remain on his certainty equivalent line as in Figure 10.2. Any contract to the right of $rr^1$ by increasing the probability of $II_1$ from $p_1$ to $p_1^a$ will also affect P's indifference curves. (To a slope of $p_1^a/1 - p_1^a$ along their entire length.) This is indicated by the contrast between $U_P$ and $U_P^a$ (which intersect on the principal's certainty equivalent line since along that line the principal aready has a portfolio of claims on the outcomes insulating him from variations in the mix of $II_1$ and $II_2$). Clearly P and A are both better off with agent effort than without if they can negotiate a contract which lies below $rr^1$ and is above both $U_A^a$ and $U_P^a$. The shaded area in Figure 10.3 denotes the scope for agreement.

All contracts within the shaded area represent improvement to both P and A over the original $U_P, U_A$ tangency point. Further the agent will provide effort without monitoring. Those agreements lying on the $rr^1$ boundary of the area are Pareto efficient in that any movement from a given point on that boundary to another point in the shaded set will harm either A or P. Conversely, it is possible to move from *within* the shaded set to *some* point on the $rr^1$ boundary which will benefit one or both of A and P without harming the other. Nevertheless, the indifference curves of A and P intersect (they are not tangential) along $rr^1$. (This complication has not been added to the figure but can be visualized by 'sliding' $U_p{}^a$ to a new position passing through r.) In other words, because of the provision of effort incentives, both parties are better off, but they are not in the efficient risk-sharing situation they were in Figure 10.2 where they moved from point X to Z. *There is a conflict between sharing risks and providing incentives.* This will be so provided only that A's effort is not too costly and/or provided the impact of $a$ is not too low. (Diagrammatically either of these conditions could 'squeeze' the shaded area in Figure 10.3 out of existence.)

The above argument, however, assumes no observability of effort. *If the agent's efforts can be observed it may enable some risk-sharing benefits to be recaptured.* The problem now is whether the information about effort would be accurate, free from opportunism and bounded rationality and so usable in contract construction. Can information about effort containing errors (due to random sampling monitoring, for example) be incorporated into a mutually beneficial contract? For example, an unlucky shirking agent who puts in a lot of effort might be 'spotted' by a monitor, while an idle agent might be 'working hard' at the time of a monitor's check. In short, monitoring adds yet another probabilistic variable into the situation.

Recall Figure 10.3, where $rr^1$ is the agents' locus of indifference between 'effort' and 'no effort' in a non-monitoring, no-observability situation. If observability and hence the possibility of effort monitoring is introduced the boundary $rr^1$ would alter, say, to $mm^1$. In other words, monitoring, by providing effort incentives, can permit recapture of some of the risk-sharing benefits.

Consider Figure 10.4 and take any point r on the $rr^1$ frontier as the starting point of our analysis. Both parties can become better off with rather than without monitoring even given the presence of opportunism and bounded rationality provided the probabilities of accurate monitoring are such that the agent and principal can embody them in appropriate contracts. The cost of effort to the agent falls (given observability and monitoring) since now a monitoring linked reward is provided (hence $\bar{U}_A^a$ intersects A's certainty equivalent line to the left of the intersection of $U_A^a$ with that line). Analogous to Figure 10.3's comparison of $U_A$ and $U_A^a$ $\bar{U}_A^a$ has a steeper slope on A's certainty equivalent line than $U_A$ had (effort directed at the greater outcome $II_1$ is more likely) but has a gentler slope than $U_A^a$ (since outcome is now dependent not only on $a$, effort; on $s$, the state of nature; but also on the probability that $a$ is actually incurred which is partly dependent on A's perceptions of monitoring accuracy). The normal arithmetic of multiplying together probability factors of less than unity results in a smaller likelihood that outcome $II_1$ will result. Hence $\bar{p}_1^a/1 - \bar{p}_1^a < p_1^a/1 - p_1^a$. In addition $\bar{U}_A^a$ (which provides the same utility as $U_A^a$ in the absence of monitoring) intersects $U_A^a$ to the left of r (at point x). Any point to the left of x between the two curves provides A with less utility-absent monitoring, and any point to the right of x between the two provides A with greater utility in the presence of monitoring. x is a point of indifference between monitoring as acceptable and undesirable to the agents. It lies to the left of r since monitoring does not have a probability of unity of successful implementation. Or, in other words, all other things remaining the same, $II_2$ becomes more likely an outcome than $II_1$, given the imperfections of monitoring. mm[1] is the locus of all such intervention points x where the agent is indifferent as to the presence or absence of monitoring.

Analogously to Figure 10.3, in Figure 10.4 the principal's indifference curves also change slope along their entire length. That curve which passes through r, $U_P^a$, in Figure 10.3 provides a given portfolio of claims on $II_1$ and $II_2$. With the new probabilities $U_P^a$ pivots to $\bar{U}_P^a$ (at the same level of utility). Thus any contract within the shaded area of Figure 10.4 provides scope for agreement on monitoring, and furthermore moves both P and A closer to the optimal risk-sharing situation where $U_P$ and $U_A$ could be tangential. (Optimal risk-sharing, of course, with x on A's certainty equivalent line is still not accomplished, as with all transaction costs analyses, the question at issue is not the gaining of 'perfection' but rather the optimal economizing of bounded rationality and the optimal attentuation of opportunism.) Again, whether x is more attractive than r will depend on the reliability of the monitoring and its cost (both of which factors could influence the shape and position of $\bar{U}_A^a$ and $\bar{U}_P^a$) which could squeeze mutually agreeable monitoring contracts out of existence.

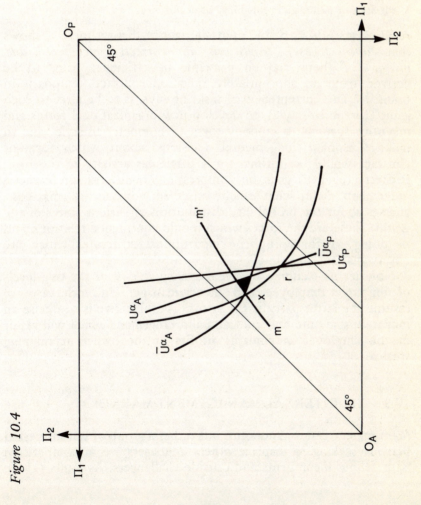

*Figure 10.4*

183

## 10.2 AGENCY THEORY AND INDUSTRIAL ORGANIZATION

The theory's institutional significance will become apparent below when we discuss Fama's view of the firm as a 'nexus of contracts' (which can be implicit or explicit) and Jensen and Meckling's measure of agency cost when owners cease to be controllers. The predictions of the theory depend on:

the nature of the risk preference of the principal and agent
observability of outcome and ease of agreement on its measurement
observability of behaviour during contract execution (effort)
monitoring costs and credibility of monitoring
the state of nature and probability of occurrence.

As Ricketts (1987, p. 147) puts it, agency theory 'merely' shows that *once [these] conditions are correctly recognised and interpreted* there may in principle be efficiency gains to be derived from an appropriately specified contract' (emphasis in original). The entrepreneurial task, he says, is to be alert to such gains (Kirznerian style), to develop new organizational forms and inventive systems to embody them (Schumpeterian style) and to make Cassonian 'judgemental decisions' about which form of contract would be optimal for a particular activity in the firm. Ricketts (p. 148) goes on: 'impressions about risk preferences; judgements about what can be observed, how, and at what cost; guesses about the probability distribution of various states of the world: these are the forces which mould contractual relations, and in doing so throw up the institutional structures which are observed at any one time.'

Now let us examine principal/agency theory at the two levels of employer/employee and owner/manager. In each case we assume the latter party is the agent. The objective is to devise an incentive structure and contractual arrangement which will result in the employer maximizing profits or the owner maximizing wealth.

## 10.3 THE INTERNAL MANAGEMENT MARKET

Management is not a monolith but rather a group of self-interested persons seeking to displace others. Managers are in competition with fellow incumbents and outside challengers. As Fama (1980, pp. 291–4) points out, managers rent their wealth or human capital, to the team and the 'rental rates . . . signalled by the management labour market . . . depend on the success or failure of the firm'. How do the pressures work?

Managers are 'sorted and compensated' (Fama, p. 292) according to performance. Since the firm is always in the market for new managers it must be able to explain to potential recruits how they will be rewarded. If the reward system is not responsive to performance the firm will not be able either to recruit or retain the best managers. Conversely, but by the same argument, managers, especially top managers, have a stake in the firm's performance since the external market uses that as a means of determining his opportunity wage. In the internal management market monitoring is part of a manager's role. Part of his talent is the ability to monitor lower levels of management, gauge their performance and reward them accordingly. And, as Fama (p. 293) points out, this monitoring process operates from lowest levels upwards as well. 'Lower managers perceive that they can gain by stepping over shirking or less competent [seniors] . . . [while] in the nexus of contracts . . . each manager is concerned with the performance of managers above and below him since his marginal product is likely to be a positive function of theirs.' Furthermore, given 'competition among the top managers . . . to be the boss of bosses' (Fama, p. 293) they are perhaps 'the best ones to control the board of directors'. Their specialized knowledge plus their market-determined opportunity wages may render them 'the most informed and responsive critics of the firm's performance'.

Managerial compensation packages indeed are often structured to minimize any principal/agent conflict with shareholders. Conceptually managerial rewards can have three components: (1) unconditional compensation (e.g. salaries, pension benefits); (2) compensation conditional on stock market performance (e.g. stock options); and (3) compensation conditional on accounting performance (e.g. profit sharing). Fama (p. 298) argues that managers and shareholders use these monitoring techniques as forms of 'ex post settling-up' devices that depend on satisfactory contract execution and which substantially alleviate incentive problems. Furthermore although accounting based-performance measures are subject to managerial manipulation, such compensation tools are used mainly for middle and lower managers (who are least able to manipulate reported profits) while senior managers are most likely to be rewarded with stock market based performance measures which they in turn are unable directly to control since in efficient markets share prices reflect all available information.

Compensation packages for managers are also tailored to ensure coincidence of time horizons between the agent and principal. Thus the fact that managers' time horizon may be too close can be alleviated, for example, by favourable current salaries which would be lost if the manager were to be fired, or the inclusion of stock options in retirement packages.

Williamson (1983) has also highlighted the role of the board of directors. Originally, the board was seen as the monitor of the management team. This was and is the legal perception. However, Berle and Means, in their analysis of the modern corporation saw it as acquiescing with management's divergence from owners' interests rather than acting as the owners' representatives. Williamson, and other writers, however, see the board as yet another form of task specialization carried out to alleviate the costs of agency. The argument runs as follows.

Strategic decision taking is becoming ever more separated from day-to-day management as a consequence of the decentralization of large firms into multidivisional (M-form) organizations. The M-form firm is characterized by self-contained operating divisions separated from the general corporate office which handles strategic planning. Each division is separately monitored by the central office while it is itself monitored by externally observable variables such as stock prices and published profits.

Fama and Jensen (1983) justify these arguments as follows. In the M-form firm control is delegated to specialists by function where *decision management*, initiation and implementation of strategic plans is carried out by senior managers. *Decision control*, the ratification and monitoring of strategy formulation and its implementation, is the function of the board. Agency problems are reduced by linking compensation to these specialized activities. The board of directors has as one of its functions the selection of the optimal structure of governance contracts with managers to avoid shirking by them. So conflicts over horizon times are alleviated by appropriate stock options and pension plans. Similarly if managers are anticipated to be unduly risk averse dividends will fall (see p. 188 below), stock prices will fall and the managers' job will again be at risk in the corporate control market.

The corporate agency relationship states that managers select the contractual terms offered to potential investors. To raise capital at the lowest price (the highest share value) shareholders must be offered evidence (including the presence of intra-firm incentive structures) that convincingly demonstrate the minimization of agency costs. But even more important may be the corporate control market itself, which is beyond the reach of managers and forces them to consider their shareholders' interests.

The chances of collusion by such senior managers to expropriate the wealth of shareholders by not pursuing wealth-maximizing goals is minimized by the managerial market mechanism already described and by the market in corporate control. This latter is the market in which another group of specialists in the team operate. These are the specialists who are willing to accept risk and engage in residual claim contracts with the remainder of the team. It is the shareholder's willingness to bear the costs and benefits of the changing value of the firm which makes him the owner of the firm. Alchian (1982, p. 25) points out that there are four separable tasks in exercising property rights: (a) selecting resource use, (b) monitoring input performance, (c) revising contracts or replacing inputs, and (d) bearing the value changes of resources. 'The first three can be delegated to fiduciary agents acting as specialists, but the fourth cannot.' (This is not to deny the existence for some commodities of future markets where owners can hedge to minimize risk of loss. But the operation and successful outcome of such hedging activity is the direct consequence of the resource owner bearing a value loss on one bundle of resources and an offsetting value gain on another. Futures markets permit this type of activity to 'reduce or control risk' but it is still the resource owner who bears the value changes. Similarly, the resource owner may delegate the monitoring task to a specialist to 'reduce or control risk' but he still bears the value change of the resource consequential to the delegation.)

## Entrepreneurship and the Market for Corporate Control

The market in corporate control was most eloquently described by Manne in 1965. Like the managerial market this market also ensures that the divorce of ownership from control is more apparent than real. Directors and managers cannot long depart from the wealth-maximization objectives of shareholders or they will be displaced by the takeover mechanism (the corporate control market). Information on management performance is disclosed by the price of the firm's shares. The stock market thus provides not only price signals about where to 'invest' and disinvest financial resources but it also provides information about management which can be used to allocate rewards and penalties. A poorly managed firm will suffer from a declining share price. Stockholders will sell to higher bidders who perceive that replacing the management team will improve the firm's performance and so share price. Hence poor managers will either be removed or stimulated to improve their performance by the operation of the stock market. 'Without a stock market, information about performance of managers would be more difficult to obtain' (Alchian, 1982, p. 27) and the advantages of specialization within the team (risk-bearing and monitoring respectively) could then appear to be outweighed by the costs of opportunism resulting from delegation. So task specialization and resulting efficiency is encouraged by the presence of a stock market, and those who bewail the 'divorce of ownership from control' have failed to see that what the modern joint stock company permits is a marriage of productive convenience between internal labour markets and entrepreneurship. It is not a device which results in an autonomous Galbraithian technocracy responsible to no one but itself.

Marriage partners, however, as the Bible tells us 'are no more twain, but are one flesh'. In analytic or legalistic terms it may in many situations be impossible to distinguish husband from wife. So, analogously, in the marriage of convenience which is the modern corporation it may be impossible to ascertain who is the entrepreneur.

Mises (1949, pp. 303–11) argues that the entrepreneurial function can exist at all levels in the hierarchical firm, but warns that it is a serious error to confuse the entrepreneur with any particular category in the hierarchy. 'The manager is a junior partner of the entrepreneur . . . [whose] own financial interests force him to attend to the best of his abilities to the entrepreneurial functions which are assigned to him within a limited and precisely determined sphere of action.' In a firm which is subject to what Mises terms 'profit management', entrepreneurship can be delegated. Profit centres can be set up within a business and the entrepreneur can allocate tasks to each and appraise each centre according to the profits it contributes to the total business.

Each division can be regarded as an autonomous business buying and selling to other divisions and to the outside market. Thus the entrepreneur can assign to each section's management a great deal of independence. Within circumscribed limits divisional managers need merely to be told to make as much profit as possible:

> Every manager and sub-manager is responsible for the working of his section or sub-section . . . . If he incurs losses, he will be replaced . . . . If he succeeds in making profits his income will be increased or at least he will not be in danger of losing it . . . . His task is not like that of the technician, to perform a definite piece of work according to a definite precept. It is to adjust — within the limited scope left to his discretion — the operation of his section to the state of the market.

Thus employees in a firm at any level in the hierarchy can exercise an entrepreneurial role. The area within which that role can be carried out increases the more authority the employee has. But the manager, no matter how high, can never be the entrepreneur since he 'cannot be made answerable for the losses incurred'. In the final analysis, Mises argues, the entrepreneur is the owner. He alone determines the grand strategy of the business. He may call on managerial advice but the decisions are his. Decisions as to 'what lines of business to employ capital [in] and how much capital to employ . . . [decisions as to] expansion and contraction of the size of the total business, and its main sections . . . [decisions as to its] financial structure' fall upon the entrepreneur alone.

The mechanism used to ensure this is the market for corporate control, the stock market. The prices of stocks and shares 'are the means applied by the capitalists for the supreme control of the flow of capital . . . [this] decides how much capital is available for the conduct of each corporation's business; it creates a state of affairs to which the managers must adjust their operations in detail'.

Not only is this a positivist description of the industrial firm it is also, Mises argues, normatively desirable:

> Society can freely leave the care for the best possible employment of capital goods to their owners. In embarking upon definite projects these owners expose their own property, wealth and social position. They are even more interested in . . . success . . . than is society as a whole. For society as a whole the squandering of capital invested in a definite project means only the loss of a small part of its total funds; for the owner it means much more . . . . But if a manager is given a completely free hand,

things are different. He speculates in risking other people's money. He sees the prospects of an uncertain enterprise from another angle than that of the man who is answerable for the losses . . . he becomes foolhardy because he does not share in the losses too.

Thus, the entrepreneurial function can be partially delegated, as Alchian suggested, to a fiduciary agent or manager. In the ultimate, however, the entrepreneur himself remains the owner of the property rights whose value can rise or fall. To ensure that he retains these property rights the market in corporate control must be subject to effective competition. So too must the internal management market. These two conditions hold most obviously when there is a stock market with a diffusion (or potential diffusion) of ownership. And secondly, when the transaction costs of hiring managers by a firm (to Williamson, a 'unified, relational contract') are less than those of other governance structures. By this analysis, if society is to be optimally served by the entrepreneurial function, the divorce of ownership from control must be a fiction. The reality should be a marriage of convenience between the internal management and labour markets and the entrepreneur.

At first glance we seem to have two mutually exclusive answers to our attempt to identify the entrepreneur. The first is that he is everywhere. This is simply a restatement of the general principle of human action that man acts in anticipation of gain. Employees, managers and shareholders were all seen to behave entrepreneurially. The second answer is that the entrepreneur is restricted to the shareholder, in which case much of the above discussion is redundant.

The paradox is resolved and the conflict removed if we bear in mind that anticipated gain is not synonymous with anticipated corporate profits. The latter is only a subset of the former. Everyone acts for anticipated gain but only shareholders act unambiguously to acquire corporate profits. The role of internal labour markets and the market in corporate control is simply that of ensuring that the conflict of interest between non-shareholder entrepreneurs and shareholder-entrepreneurs is minimized. If this is achieved then delegation of the shareholder-entrepreneur's function can be achieved successfully without removing from him what Knight (1921, p. 271) identified as the essential roles of control and responsibility.

The above discussion has also highlighted, *inter alia*, that the terms 'entrepreneur' and 'firm' are not synonymous. Although traditional neoclassical textbooks often use the words inter-changeably they are misleading (as the proponents of the notion of the concept of the divorce of ownership from control have pointed out, albeit from a different stance from the above arguments). As McNulty (1968) said, in a *cri de coeur*, 'although economic activity encompasses both production [in the firm] and exchange [in the market], the concept of competition has been generally associated only with the latter'. Competition within the firm, although written about by Mises, has only become overt in the literature since Alchian, Demsetz, Manne and Williamson have emphasized the nature of the firm, transaction costs, property rights and the markets in corporate control and in management. The entrepreneur is he who brings together resources into an entity known as 'the firm'. He sells the output of those resources using the firm as his production instrument. The firm is instigated by the entrepreneur. The original entrepreneur may die or be replaced, as may the firm. But entrepreneurial elements within the firm, as a team, can arise and prevent this. They themselves can earn rewards of a supra-normal level either as workers, managers or shareholders. Given the workings of the markets in corporate control and in manage-ment, shareholders as the ultimate capitalists cannot long be deprived of such entrepreneurial rewards. And if they are so deprived it is because, in their own entrepreneurial view, it is less costly continuing to employ the other team members than to carry out the latters' functions themselves.

## The Management/Shareholder Contracts

The relationship between 'owners' and 'managers' is a special example of 'agency'. That is, it is a contract where principals (owners) engage agents (managers) to perform services on their behalf and in so doing delegate considerable decision making authority to them. Assuming both principals and agents are utility maximizers, it is likely that an agent will act in such a way that, whilst maximizing his own utility, he will not maximize that of the principal. The monetary value of the benefits forgone by the principal because the agent does not maximize the latter's utility is called the 'residual loss' from the relationship. The word 'residual refers to the total agency costs borne by the principal less 'bonding' (e.g. contractual conditions and writing) and 'monitoring' costs.

Jensen and Meckling (1976) represented the magnitude of the residual loss diagrammatically as follows. Assume that the manager gains utility from both money wages and the present value of perks. Given technology and demand, any combination of policy variables will result in particular cash inflows in future periods which in turn will determine the market value of the firm. Given the manager's money wage, if he took the value maximizing level of perks and chose the value maximizing level of price, etc., the firm's value would be maximized at, say, point $\bar{V}$ in Figure 10.5. But a manager may take more perks than the level which maximizes the firm's market value. If he does, actual market value will decrease because, by definition:

$$V = \bar{V} - P$$

where $V$ = market value of firm
$\quad\quad P$ = PV of perks
$\quad\quad \bar{V}$ = maximum market value of firm

Therefore, for each additional £1 by which the manager increases the PV of his perks, the market value of the firm decreases by £1.

*Figure 10.5*

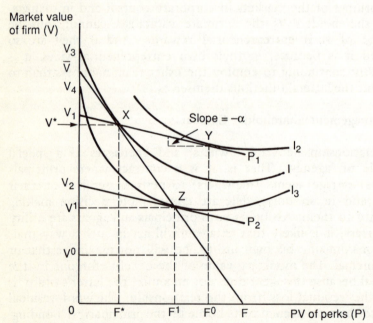

Similarly, we can deduce that if the manager takes all of the PV of profits as perks, the value of the firm would be reduced to zero: point F in Figure 10.5.

The magnitude of the agency 'residual loss' is found by comparing the value of a firm where the owner is also the manager (and hence there is no agency relationship) with a case where there is such relationship. Suppose, first, that the manager owns 100 per cent of the equity of the firm. Then the maximum market value of his (100 per cent) share in the firm, given any level of perks, is shown by $\overline{V}F$. This is because, if he increases the PV of his perks by £1 and the market value of the firm decreases by £1, the latter is his loss of wealth: he owns the entire firm. Suppose also that his indifference curves between utility and perks are as shown. To maximize his utility he will choose to take the PV of perks equal to F* and correspondingly the value of the firm will be V*:point X.

Secondly, suppose the owner (already at point X) sells some of his shares in the firm to an outsider but retains a proportion, $a$, of the firm's equity. In this case, if he — still being the manager — increases the PV of perks taken by £1, the market value of the firm decreases by £1. But, since he only owns $a$ of the firm, the cost to him of taking extra perks is now lower than it was when he was the owner. The market value of his share decreases only by $a$ £1, and $a$ is less than 1.0. Hence the constraint which the manager (and now only part-owner) faces in his choice of $PV_{perks}$ and $MV_{firm}$ has a slope of $-a$, not $-1$ as had $\overline{V}F$. This constraint $V_1P_1$, however, must also pass through point X. This is because, if the individual wishes, he can still have that combination of perks and MV which he had before selling his shares.

The share sale provides him with cash receipts $(1 - a)V^*$, the MV of his remaining shares $aV^*$ and perks corresponding to F*. The new constraint is shown as $V_1P_1$. If the manager's indifference curves are unchanged, he will choose a greater PV of perks, $F^0$, (point Y) than when he owned the whole firm. Since the PV of perks has increased, the actual market value of the firm will decrease by this amount, i.e. from V* to $V^0$.

However, share purchasers are not naive. If they believe that after purchase the manager will take perks in excess of F*, and consequently that the value of the firm will then fall below V*, they will only, at most, be prepared to pay $(1 - a)$ times the new expected value of the firm. They will not be willing to pay as much as $(1 - a)V^*$ for the shares. Similarly, the owner/manager is aware that, with chosen perks of $F^0$, the firm would only have a value of $V^0$ and, while he is willing to sell for $(1-a)V^*$, he is not prepared to sell for $(1-a)V^0$. He will only be prepared to sell for $(1-a)$ times the new expected value of the firm, or above.

Given that the owner/manager wishes to sell $(1-a)$ of the firm, what price will be satisfactory to both parties to the trade? Jensen and Meckling show that it must be $V^1$, on a constraint line $V_2 P_2$ which passes through Z, a particular point on $\bar{V}F$ where the owner/manager has an indifference curve $I_3$, tangential to it.

To understand that this is mutually acceptable, consider Figure 10.6. If the point of tangency between $V_2 P_2$ and an indifference curve were to the left of B, say A, the manager would take perks of $F_x$. If $(1-a)$ of the shares were sold for $(1-a)V^1$ but after their sale their value were $V_x$, the original owner would have sold the shares for less than he could have received for them. Alternatively, if the point of tangency were lower than B on $V_2 P_2$, say C, the manager would take perks of $F_{xx}$ causing the firm's value to be $V_{xx}$. If a new owner paid $(1-a)V^1$ for his

*Figure 10.6*

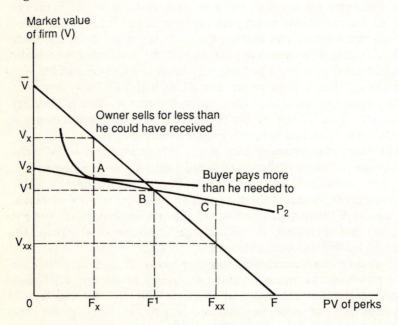

shares, he would have paid more than he need have. But if tangency occurred at B, the perks taken and firm value would be $F^1$ and $V^1$. In that case the buyer would pay a price and the original owner would receive a price reflecting what the shares were worth to each respectively.

In summary, we see that when a manager owns all the shares of a firm, the firm's value is $V^*$ (in Figure 10.5). But when he owns only $a$ of the shares, because he takes more perks than the sole owner, the value of the firm and of his wealth is less than $V^*$: it is $V^1$. This reduction in the value of the firm is the 'residual loss' of the agency relationship which was created when the owner/ manager sold some of his shares. In terms of utility the agency cost to the owner/manager is $V_3 V_4$ since this represents the reduction in market value which gives the same utility loss as the movement from point X to point Z in Figure 10.5.

Of course, as Jensen and Meckling point out, this 'loss' is perfectly consistent with economic efficiency since the owner/ manager would only incur it if he believed he could make himself better off by using the cash receipts $(1 - a)V^1$ elsewhere. Similarly, shareholders will only pay for the shares purchased if, in their judgement, this is the best alternative use of their resources.

This paper by Jensen and Meckling as well as conceptualizing agency costs also answered two of the riddles posed by much modern finance literature. These riddles were the outcome of articles by Modigliani and Miller (1958 and 1961). The first paper demonstrated that given certain assumptions (including perfect information and zero transaction costs) the capital structure of firms is a matter of indifference in minimizing a company's cost of capital. The second paper similarly 'proved' that the level of dividend payouts was irrelevant. Yet debt:equity ratios and dividend distribution policies do vary across firms. Why?

Jensen and Meckling's paper described above, showed that an all-equity structure would give substantial discretion to managers to use owners' assets for their own benefits (limited only by their broad fiduciary duties). But managers in fact do have an incentive to minimize the weighted average cost of debt and equity capital since failure to do so would make them vulnerable to takeover and hence job loss. In order to raise equity at the lowest cost, managers must convince potential shareholders that agency costs will be minimized. A high gearing ratio encourages risky invest- ment behaviour by managers (and owners) since rewards could be high and any losses would be (mainly) carried by debt holders. Different capital structures are not irrelevant. They rather represent different responses to variations in agency costs.

The notion that the Modigliani–Miller theorem and its derivatives are theoretical curiosities which mislead rather than enrich our understanding of corporate behaviour also holds for their 'dividend irrelevancy' result. Firms continue to pay dividends even given that their payment is costlier (to shareholders) than would be other methods of returning assets to their owners (dividends are subject both to tax on corporate profits and on personal income). Further, even assuming firms have optimal investment policies, dividend payouts require the raising of new debt or equity to finance such policies. Raising new capital is costly and such behaviour would therefore seem to be irrational if retentions are an option. Agency theories explain such behaviour (for example Easterbrook, 1984). First, dividends may be paid because the issuing of new capital signals that the firm's finances and behaviour will be scrutinized by expert financial intermediaries such as issuing houses and merchant bankers. That is, shareholders have implicitly agreed that the monitoring involved in flotation of new stock has lower costs than does direct monitoring and supervision of managers. Dividend payments require that managers subject themselves to such scrutiny by capital markets when issuing new securities. Second, managers may be more risk averse than owners. In the absence of dividend distributions retentions will decrease the gearing of the firm thus decreasing the managers' (and the debt holders') risks at the expense of owners. Dividend payments maintain the gearing of the firm and so encourage managers to take risks in line with equity holders' preferences.

Agency theory thus improves upon the earlier 'signalling' view of dividends of the 1960s and 1970s, namely that they indicate the firm is in sound health. This was an unsatisfactory explanation since dividends can be paid in bad years as well as good. The agency explanation rather signals that specialists in the capital markets have monitored the firm's performance and they have indicated to owners that new securities are backed by adequate earnings potential.

Our later chapters have shown how theory has advanced beyond the analyses of the structure/conduct/performance models based on Pareto optimality as discussed in the earlier section of the book. Nevertheless there are still major gaps in our understanding which must be plugged. The several approaches to understanding industrial organization are far from reconciled or fully developed and as a consequence dogmatism, as we have repeatedly stated, would be misplaced. Regulation of industry should be based on an eclectic view of theory. The next two chapters examine respectively competition policy and general regulation and observe each in the light of our discussions to this point.

## NOTE

1. This section relies heavily on the recent integrative exposition of Ricketts (1987).

## REFERENCES

Alchian, A. (1982), 'Property Rights, Specialisation and the Firm' in J.F. Weston and M.E. Greenfields (eds), *Corporate Enterprise in a New Environment* (Los Angeles: K.G.C. Productions).

Berle, A.A. and Means, C.G. (1932), *The Modern Corporation and Private Property* (London: Macmillan).

Brealey, R. and Myers, S. (1982), *Business Finance*, 2nd edn (Maidenhead: McGraw-Hill).

Casson, M. (1982), *The Entrepreneur* (Oxford: Martin Robertson).

Easterbook, F. (1984), 'Two Agency Cost Explanations of Dividends', *American Economic Review*, 74.

Fama, E.F. (1980), 'Agency Problems and the Theory of the Firm', *Journal of Political Economy*, 88(2).

Fama, E.F. and Jensen, M.C. (1983), 'Separation of Ownership and Control', *Journal of Law and Economics*, 26.

Florence, P.S. (1972), *The Logic of British and American Industry* (London: Routledge and Kegan Paul).

Hayek, F.A. (1937), 'Economics and Knowledge', *Economica*, 4.

Hayek, F.A. (1945), 'The Use of Knowledge in Society', *American Economic Review*, 35(4).

Hayek, F.A. (1979), *The Counter Revolution of Science* (Indianapolis: Liberty Press).

Jensen, M.C. and Meckling, W.H. (1976), 'Theory of the Firm, Management Behaviour, Agency Costs and Ownership Structure', *Journal of Financial Economics*, 7.

Kirzner, I. (1973), *Competition and Entrepreneurship* (Chicago: Chicago University Press).

Kirzner, I. (1982), *Method, Process and Austrian Economics* (Lexington, Mass.: D.C. Heath).

Knight, F. (1921), *Risk, Uncertainty and Profit* (Chicago: Chicago University Press).

Lachmann, L.M. (1973), *Macroeconomic Thinking and the Market Economy*, Hobart Paperback No. 56 (London: Institute of Economic Affairs).

Loasby, B.J. (1976), *Choice, Complexity and Ignorance* (Cambridge: Cambridge University Press).

Marshall, A. (1966), *Principles of Economics*, 8th edn (London: Macmillan).

McNulty, P.J. (1968), 'Economic Theory and the Meaning of Competition', *Quarterly Journal of Economics*, 82(4).

Miller, M.H. and Modigliani, F. (1961), 'Dividend Policy, Growth and the Valuation of Shares', *Journal of Business*.

Mises, L. von (1949), *Human Action* (Cambridge, Mass.: Yale University Press).

Modigliani, F. and Miller, M.H. (1958), 'The Cost of Capital, Corporation Finance and the Theory of Investment', *Amercian Economic Review*, 48.

Reekie, W.D. (1975), *Managerial Economics* (London: Philip Allan, Oxford University Press).

Ricketts, M. (1987), *The Economics of Industrial Organisation* (Brighton: Wheatsheaf).

Stigler, G.J. and Friedland, C. (1983), 'The Literature of Economics: The Case of Berle and Means', *Journal of Law and Economics*.

Williamson, D.E. (1983), 'Organisational Form, Residual Claimants, and Corporate Control', *Journal of Law and Economics*, 26.

# 11.  Competition Policy

This chapter is deliberately superficial. Partly because to cover the main areas of policy thoroughly would require several volumes, and partly because the legal system in many countries is in a continuous state of flux. To attempt to be definitive in one short chapter would consequently be presumptive. Nevertheless it is hoped that the following pages will be a useful *aide mémoire* both on the history of competition policy (which helps explain where we are) and some current issues (which helps suggest where we might move). The two countries examined are the USA and the UK with obeisance made to European Community legislation given the intended goal of a Single European Market by 1992.

## 11.1  MONOPOLY POLICY IN THE USA

American anti-trust policy has tended to emphasize the structure of an industry. 'Unreasonable' and 'undue' concentrations of market power are discouraged either by merger prevention or by divestiture of assets (e.g. in 1982 American Telegraph and Telephone, AT & T, was compelled to sell off its interests in 22 regional telephone and cable companies). The objective has been to maintain a 'substantial' number of competing firms and hence to minimize monopolistic behaviour as such. In brief the traditional rationale for the policy rested on market structure rather than on market conduct or performance.

The Sherman Act 1890 was the first manifestation of this approach. It was limited to two brief provisions:

1. It condemned as criminal every contract, combination in the form of trust or otherwise, or conspiracy in restraint of trade or commerce among the several states, or with foreign nations.
2. It condemned monopolies, or attempts or conspiracies to monopolize any part of that trade or commerce.

Although the Federal Trade Commission was established in 1914 to improve anti-trust enforcement it was not a court where infringements of the Sherman Act could be tried. The main enforcement agency was and remains the ordinary (criminal) federal courts.

Until around 1920 almost all cases which reached the Supreme Court were decided in favour of the government. During this period, however, the case experience, precedents and rulings which were accumulating were focusing on the word 'every'. In lower courts verdicts were being arrived at which bore little apparent consistency, because different judges interpreted the law in different ways. The controversy was resolved in a typical legal manner. 'Every' was to be interpreted 'reasonably'. This judgement was handed down from the Supreme Court in 1911 in the Standard Oil case. And since this case the *rule of reason* has been used implicitly or explicitly in most anti-trust cases.

The rule of reason, however, was riddled with potential for ambiguity. It did attempt to move the law away from a purely structural approach to assessing monopoly (i.e. a sort of crude 'bigness is bad' *per se* attitude). In the 1911 case, the court said, both common law and statute were concerned with one question only. The question was 'does the restraint, viewed in its market setting, constitute a . . . significant limitation on competition?', or is the practice before the court 'clearly anti-competitive'? If so, the court's discretion under the rule of reason is exhausted. The Act therefore, seemed to forbid bad trusts, and condone good ones.

Under the Sherman Act the Standard Oil trust was dissolved, although as McGee points out (1987, p. 464): 'even today, more than 75 years after dissolution, who knows whether [the firm's] efficiency outweighed its power to fix price.' In short, economic trade-offs were not made, 'guilt' was determined by structure not performance. Ironically, the dissolution resulted in several regional near-monopolies. In the same year the American Tobacco trust was dissolved, in this case (McGee, p. 465) the rule of reason applied, a trade-off was made, the court decided that economic performance had improved, yet ordered dissolution none the less. The 1920 US Steel case continued this swing away from condemnation of size *per se*. The court did not order dissolution. It claimed that US Steel had not exerted its market power and therefore committed no offence despite its size. Indeed the judgement praised the 'industrial statesmen' (including Elbert Gary of the notorious Gary Dinners where price agreements were reached over formal meals away from the public eye but not explicitly in secret) while criticizing price competitors such as Andrew Carnegie who undercut the cartels.

The next main milestone was the 1945 Alcoa case where again dissolution was rejected as a solution for size, and in return the firm was condemned, and had to agree to 'compete less hard' (McGee, p. 470) in the future, as it had done in earlier years, by expanding capacity in expectation of demand. (In effect, consumers would then have to pay more for what they wanted while awaiting supply increases.) The 1982 AT & T case has already been alluded to, dissolution by consent was adopted by AT & T probably because it was deemed by the company to be less costly than continuing to fight in the courts for a case which it might lose. Conversely, the IBM case of 1982 was dropped by the authorities after thirteen years of litigation, most of the government's complaints being that IBM had reduced prices and increased outputs which McGee (p. 476) points out are 'not exactly the stuff of which real monopolizing and consumer injury is made'.

In short, size leads to visibility and hence to increased vulnerability from litigation. The 'rule of reason' is flexible but hardly predictable in its application.


## 11.2  MONOPOLY POLICY IN THE UK

Why was US legislation some sixty years ahead of any equivalent activity in Britain? Rostow argues that several reasons can be given:

1.  There was no overt and dramatic merger movement in the UK in the 1880s and 1890s as there was in the USA. In Britain buccaneering equivalents of Carnegie (steel), Rockefeller (oil) and Morgan (banking) did not exist. One trust which did come into being, the Players and Wills formation of Imperial Tobacco, was mainly a defensive move against the entry into the UK market by American Tobacco.
2.  Competition in Britain was, in any event, far greater than in America. British firms had to compete in export markets, and against foreign imports. America, partly due to tariffs, partly to self-sufficiency, was far less exposed to foreign competition. There was thus a more overt 'need' for anti-trust laws.

3. The late nineteenth-century depression was deeper and more prolonged in the USA. Big business there was regarded as a convenient scapegoat.

4. British political philosophy has never placed so strong an emphasis on the devolution of power as has the American tradition. The USA even fought a civil war over the issue of states' rights. Thus the notion of a few large businesses controlling the economy and located in a few urban centres, such as New York, appeared more repellent to Americans than a similar situation would in Britain, which in any event is geographically only the size of many American states.

5. Politicians saw little mileage in Britain from anti-trust legislation. The Labour Party was more interested in reform through socialism than through competition. The Whig tradition of economic liberalism, which would have been interested, had been submerged in the Liberal and Conservative Parties, both of whom were concerned with other issues of public importance (social welfare spending, Imperial trade preferences, the 'Irish question' and the Boer War and its aftermath).

6. Academic economists, although they would have been favourably inclined towards the US legislation, were at the time more concerned with issues of international free trade or monetary policy.

In both Britain and the USA the 1930s was the nadir of anti-monopoly policy. The excess industrial capacity which existed was interpreted by many, rightly or wrongly, as a result of over-expansion due to excessive competition. The National Industrial Recovery Act of Roosevelt's new deal authorized — and the tacit encouragement of cartels in Britain and Europe permitted — industries to fix prices and limit output. The rationale was that cartelization, by increasing profits, would induce production and investment and so stimulate employment. Certainly cartelization increases cartel members' profits, irrespective of general demand conditions, but profits do not induce investment *per se*. Investment is induced by the expectation that a high return will be obtained. If money is to be invested but expected profits are low (as they would be during a depression) then the investment will not take place. Instead of expanding, firms will first, take the increased profits due to cartelization out of the industry; second, reduce output from the competitive level to the monopolistic level; and third, increase price. Although shareholders' income would be increased by government-encouraged cartelization, and so their spending power would rise, it seems unlikely that this would be sufficient to offset the reduced spending of consumers generally, owing to both the higher prices and the lower employment caused by the monopoly and the overall depression.

Why, then, did Britain eventually adopt and develop some form of competition policy? To answer this question we again turn to Rostow. During the 1920s and 1930s the Depression resulted in economic policy concentrating on mitigating the effects of the slump in world and domestic trade. The remedies selected were the abandonment of free international trade and the encouragement of industrial rationalization, including British participation in some existing continental cartels. Whether these remedies were right or wrong is irrelevant here: the time was not propitious for policies that discouraged monopolistic practices and encouraged competition.

The 1944 White Paper on Employment Policy took a different view, however. It argued that competition would assist in mitigating any post-war inflation by encouraging firms to hold prices down. This argument was strengthened by the view that exhortation to the monopolists of labour, the trade unions, to hold down the price of labour and not press for excessive wage demands was unlikely to be successful if business was not controlled in some fashion. It also argued that a competitive framework for industry was more likely to result in greater flexibility towards innovation and productivity-increasing technical change than a monolithic structure would be.

In the succeeding period, disillusion with nationalization in the Labour government itself resulted in a swing towards a belief in the attractions of anti-monopoly legislation as an alternative. This resulted in the Monopolies and Restrictive Practice Act being passed in 1948. It is often said that this legislation is conduct-oriented rather than structure-oriented, as is the Sherman Act (at least as far as monopolies are concerned). In other words a firm or group of firms will be condemned if its behaviour is deemed to result in some specific 'abuse' or poor performance detrimental to the public interest. Clearly 'abusive' or poor performance need not be associated automatically with market dominance. Thus, again, British policy is often alleged to be more pragmatic in intent than its US equivalent.

Certainly the British approach emphasized, until recent years, the concept of the 'public interest', while the US rule of reason stressed the 'market setting' and 'competition'. Are the approaches conflicting? Is it fair to dub the American 'structural' and dogmatic and the British 'conduct'-oriented and pragmatic? These demarcation lines are probably too strict. Moreover, as noted below, the 'public interest' is difficult to determine. (So too is 'reasonableness', but it was then defined in the economic terminology of markets and competition, which even if interpreted variously by lawyers and judges does have clearer-cut meanings for economists.)

Professor G.C. Allen (1968, p. 116) (a former member of the Monopolies Commission) has argued that the guidance provided by the 1948 Act as to the public interest 'consisted of a string of platitudes which the Commission found valueless, and it was left for the members themselves to reach their own conclusions by reference to the assumptions, principles or prejudices which their training and experience caused them to apply to economic affairs'. Only after the passing of the Fair Trading Act 1973 did anti-monopolies policy explicitly specify that 'competition' should be regarded as a normative goal. Even in the 1973 Act, however, the guidelines as to the public interest include as a preamble the need to take account of 'all matters which appear . . . in the particular circumstances to be relevant'. For example, 'the balanced distribution of employment' is a guideline which would seem to be more relevant to an Act relating to regional than to monopolies policy. It can only confuse the workings of the Commission, and in certain circumstances may place it in a position where there is a need to take a decision favouring either more or less competition subject to providing less or more regional assistance. For reasons of both fairness and efficiency such decisions should be left to politicians, not their specialist advisers in unrelated areas.

It is often claimed that the strength of British monopolies' policy lies in its 'pragmatism' and flexibility (particularly in comparison with the 'dogmatic' approach of the US anti-trust laws, where size alone is often regarded as a sufficient ground on which to produce an unfavourable judgement). In Britain, market conduct has been examined rather than mere size. With the accumulation of case law over the years, charges of a lack of consistency have been made as often as has praise for the prag-matism of the Commission. In some cases, no doubt, this pragmatism had the advantage of providing flexibility and discretion which enabled the judgement to vary with the circumstances. In others, businessmen have been provided with judgements which must have been totally unexpected.

In the first two decades of the Commission's life many apparently contradictory judgements were made. British Oxygen earned a return on capital of 23–25 per cent which was 'unjustifiably high', while the Molins Machine Company's 36 per cent was acceptable. Turner and Newall's drop in profitability from 42 to 13 per cent was disapproved of as indicating inefficiency, while Kelloggs' fall from 70 to 37 per cent was approved of on the assumption the declining trend would continue. At the level of market predominance Lucas with 95 per cent of the car dynamo market escaped censure, while Roche, with 60 per cent of the tranquillizer market was argued to have abused its position. The two main detergent powder firms were condemned for entry deterring levels of advertising expenditure while holding 96 per cent of the market. Their (higher) advertising expenditures in the liquid detergents market where they held a 66 per cent share escaped censure.

This list could be extended but suffice it to say that the economic trade-offs of deadweight welfare loss, scale economies, X-efficiency and scale economies or diseconomies were never explicitly attempted and that what was deemed to be 'in the public interest' in the UK was as unpredictable as what would be deemed to be 'reasonable' in the USA.

## 11.3  RESTRICTIVE PRACTICES LEGISLATION

In both the USA and UK restrictive practices, collusion and anti-competition devices were either deemed illegal from the days of the original Sherman Act (1890) or, in the case of the Monopolies and Restrictive Practices Act (1948) at the very least, subject to investigation. The UK legislation was strengthened by the Restrictive Trade Practices Act 1956 which deemed that all agreements between firms (not just the 'legal' monopolies which held 33 per cent (later 25 per cent) of the relevant market) had to be registered officially and were presumed to be against the public interest unless the non-criminal Restrictive Practices Court deemed them to be acceptable against a list of prescribed criteria (which included a final, 'catch-all' public interest yardstick).

The two main additional pieces of US legislation are the

Robinson–Patman Act 1936 and the Federal Trade Commission Act's ban on false and misleading advertising which resulted in major (but indecisive) investigations in the 1970s (Ornstein, 1985). The Robinson–Patman Act was passed because of perceived weaknesses in the Clayton Act 1914 which prohibited price discrimination which 'substantially' lessened competition or tended 'to create a monopoly'. It excludes from this prohibition discrimination owing to differences in grade, quality or quantity of the good sold; discrimination which makes 'due allowance' for differences in cost; and third, discrimination 'carried out in good faith' to meet a competitor's price. Small traders were not protected since the quantity clause provides an easy escape, and second the courts refused to apply the law when the discrimination resulted from the pressures of large traders on their suppliers. These issues became increasingly apparent with the advent of large-scale retailing during the 1920s and 1930s. The Depression coincided and the problems of small and medium-sized buyers were compounded by the tendency of manufacturers to shade prices and give less than overt rebates in the face of declining demand. The trend towards government approval of cartelization (see pp. 202–3) was embodied in the National Recovery Administration in the USA and the Robinson–Patman Act was passed against that background.

Its main purpose was to prevent powerful retailing groups obtaining 'undue' favours from their suppliers relative to small and medium-sized traders. It prohibits the charging of different prices to different purchasers of 'goods of like grade and quality' if the effect 'may be substantially to lessen competition or tend to create a monopoly . . . or to injure . . . competition'. Another section renders it illegal for a buyer 'knowingly to induce or receive a discrimination in price'. The refunds allowed relate to perishability, obsolescence, 'due allowance for differences in the cost . . . resulting from the differing methods or quantities' specific to the transaction in question, and third, that it was done 'in good faith to meet an equally low price of a competitor'.

Neale (1960, pp. 252–3) summarizes the case law history of the Act's application as follows:

> [it] will be met with frank unbelief. The idea that a manufacturer may break the law by granting a wholesaler's discount to a wholesaler who also runs retail shops, or by selling goods direct to retailers at a price higher than one of his wholesalers may be charging, or by beating an offer made

to an important customer by a rival manufacturer or even by matching the offer unless he is satisfied that his rival can justify his low price by cost savings . . . may simply seem incredible.

But incredible or not that is the US law. The muddle is inevitable given the conflicting objectives of the Act. It is attempting to protect small business against price disadvantages on the one hand, while simultaneously attempting to combat price discrimination as anti-competitive.

The difficulty industry has with the law is illustrated by the 'good faith' price-matching defence. For success the seller must show that the matched price is itself lawful. This necessitates knowledge of the competitor's own price and cost structure (which if shown to be possessed could well be used for prosecution as a conspiracy in restraint of trade under the Sherman Act). Further confusion is caused by the phrase 'price differences' which is used in the legislation, not 'price discrimination' (which is a technical term indicating disproportionality of price:marginal cost ratios). Thus identical prices with different costs (uniform price discrimination) cannot be reached by the legislation.

In 1980 the US Department of Justice recommended repeal of Robinson–Patman, and that section of the Clayton Act which it had amended. But to date this has not happened. In the interim it may be falling into disuse but prior to 1980 it certainly had anti-competitive effects by deterring firms from engaging in selective price-cutting (which is one main reason why economists argue cartels cannot survive absent government regulatory support). The Act is essentially more concerned with protecting particular competitors, rather than competition.

As in the US the UK's Restrictive Trade Practice legislation is also under review. In 1988 the Department of Trade and Industry put forward new proposals in a Green Paper.

The 1956 Act required that details of any agreement concerned with the supply of goods and involving two or more businesses operating within the UK had to be notified for registration (since 1983 to the Director General of Fair Trading (DGFT)) if the agreement contained any restriction on freedom of action in commercial matters. The Act applied even to informal, verbal, agreements which might not be legally binding. Once an agreement was placed upon the register it was the duty of the Registrar (later the DGFT) to refer the agreement to the

Restrictive Practices Court for adjudication. The Act itself did not prohibit any agreement except collectively enforced resale price maintenance. But it did presume that agreements were against the public interest and it put the onus upon the parties to an agreement, if they wished to continue to operate it, to show to the satisfaction of the court that it yielded benefits positively in the public interest.

In the majority of cases brought before it, the court found the agreements to be against the public interest and struck them down. In the face of these judgements, the parties to many other agreements abandoned them rather than defend them before the court.

Nevertheless parties to agreement may still decide not to notify. It is not an offence to fail to do so. The restrictions in an agreement that has not been notified are void and unenforceable but there is little disadvantage in this if the agreement is operated in secret. If an unnotified and therefore unlawful agreement is uncovered, anyone who has suffered loss can sue for damages but this right of private action — almost the only such right under UK competition legislation — has been virtually unused. Moreover, the Office of Fair Trading's powers to uncover secret agreements are limited and are confined to serving a statutory notice requiring the recipient to declare whether or not he is party to any registrable agreement.

The DTI's proposals are intended to deal with this weakness and to focus the law more explicitly on agreements which have a damaging effect upon competition. The registration system would be done away with. Any agreement or concerted practice between firms, which had the purpose or effect of preventing, restricting or distorting competition in any market would be prohibited. The parties would be able to seek exemption if competition was not entirely eliminated, on the grounds that the agreement improved efficiency or innovation so long as consumers shared in any such benefits. Exemption could be obtained on the 'individual merits' or by reference to 'block exemptions' for particular types of agreement meeting specified criteria. Candidates for block exemptions include exclusive distribution and purchasing agreements, patent licensing agreements, franchising and R & D cooperation agreements. However, exemptions from the present law will not automatically receive exemption under the proposed law.

Operation of unlawful agreements (i.e. agreements that prevent, restrict or distort competition which have not been granted an exemption) will be liable to punishment by fines of up to 10 per cent of turnover.

Decisions on whether an agreement is to be prohibited, whether an exemption should be granted and what fine should be imposed would be taken by the OFT subject to appeal to the Restrictive Practices Court. The new authority would be given new powers to investigate secret agreements, not only powers to require the production of information and documentation but also (more controversially in the context of UK national law) powers of entry and search without advance warning. Administrative enforcement would be supplemented by rights of action for third parties.

These proposals are closely modelled on Article 85 of the Treaty of Rome. The coexistence of domestic and community law does mean that there may be conflicts and that industry suffers a degree of double jeopardy; although conflict can be minimized by close liaison between London and Brussels, and further there is possibly good reason why a similar approach should be followed in all EEC states.

How should we assess the success of monopolies policy? In the case of the USA spectacular divestitures have occurred (albeit sometimes simply resulting in the replacement of a near national monopoly with several smaller but complete local monopolies). In the UK although there have been no major divestments, Shaw and Simpson (1986) investigated 28 industries reported on by the Commission between 1959 and 1973. They contrasted the experience of leading firms in this group with leading firms in a non-investigated group of industries. The evidence pointed to a modest erosion of market share for leading firms in the test group, but this was not significantly different from the decline recorded by firms in the control. Within the test group, however, in a sub-group which had been subject to some remedial entry barrier reduction there was a larger erosion of dominance (but still not a statistically significant one) than in either the test group as a whole or the control group. Whether or not the US policy has done some good, it appears the UK policy, also despite apparently perverse decisions, has at least done little positive harm.

## 11.4  MERGER POLICY IN THE USA

Mergers are evaluated under the Clayton Act and a merger is considered illegal if it 'substantially decreases competition or tends to create a monopoly'. The Act was further strengthened by the Celler–Kefauver Anti-merger Act 1950. The wording can be and has been interpreted very broadly. Thus the words 'tends to' have produced what is known as the 'incipiency doctrine'. That is, where a merger need not itself result in a monopoly but nevertheless any succeeding mergers would as a consequence be that much closer to producing one, for reasons of incipiency, a merger is prohibited. Two famous cases illustrate this. In the 1962 Brown Shoe case Brown and Kinney Shoe were prevented from merging, one ground being that 'if a merger achieving 5% control were now approved, we might be required to approve future merger efforts by Brown's competition seeking similar market shares'. In 1966 Von's Grocery and Shopping Bag, which would have achieved 7.5 per cent of retail grocery sales in the Los Angeles area were also prevented from merging because of the incipient 'trend towards concentration' it would have instigated. (This despite the ease of entry into grocery retailing and the existence of several thousand independent retailers.)

Only in 1974 was this strict doctrine relaxed and other variables than concentration and market shares were given weight in Department of Justice and Federal Trade Commission analyses. The turning point was the General Dynamics case of that year where two coal companies were permitted to merge despite their apparently high aggregate combined market shares. The reason was that one firm's share was based on contractual commitments to supply most of its already known coal reserves. Given that the contracts already existed adding these figures in to the combined market share of the two gave a misleading impression of total market power.

Whatever the validity of this claim (accepted by the Supreme Court) it did establish the precedent that other evidence should be examined in merger decisions, and not just crude concentration and share data. The Department of Justice consequently drew up Merger Guidelines in 1982 (modified slightly in 1984) to reflect the state of the law, and to embody more of the thinking available from the economic field of industrial organization. The underlying philosophy of the guidelines is that small numbers facilitate collusion, as does the presence of entry barriers and also the presence of market or product characteristics which make price shading or chiselling difficult. The possibility of cost savings from mergers as a trade-off with their anticompetitive effects should also be considered. With these philosophical underpinnings five steps are then suggested for investigators to take:

(a)  A 'relevant anti-trust market' should be defined to evaluate competitive effects. The definition should be constructed for a set of products and geographic area on the basis of elasticity of demand. Specifically a market is 'relevant' for anti-trust purposes if a 'hypothetical monopolist' could profitably raise his price by some percentage above the 'current' (which need not be the competitive) price for a 'non-transitory' time period. In assessing the profitability of this price rise the Guidelines direct investigators to evaluate the cross-elasticity of both demand and supply and how such substitution by consumers and other producers would occur within twelve months in response to the price rise. (The 1982 Guidelines suggest a 5 per cent price rise, the 1984 modifications suggest the possibility of bigger values such as 10 per cent.)

(b)  The market, once defined, is then assessed for its concentration level using the Herfindahl–Hirschman Index. (This is the same as Herfindahl Index discussed on p. 47 but the absolute percentage numbers not the decimal equivalents are used in the summation: thus a firm with 80 per cent of the market contributes $80^2$ (6400) not $0.8^2$ (0.64) to the Index. White (1987, p. 16) claims that any merger with a market HHI (*ex post*) of under 1000 is unlikely to be challenged, while unless there are mitigating circumstances such as easy entry, any merger likely to produce a HHI of over 1800 (if the partners have market shares that cause the Index to rise by over 100) will be questioned. Mergers within the 1000–1800 lower and upper bounds 'require further analysis before a decision is made whether to challenge'.

(c)  Ease of entry is assessed in a way similar to that of market definition. 'Easy' entry exists if in response to the hypothetical price increase discussed above (where supply and demand cross elasticities and the 'non-transitory' time period are already defined to assume a twelve-month adjustment period by consumers and competitors) enough new capacity would be brought on line within 24 months to render the price rise unprofitable.

(d)  Other competitive factors which might make collusion more or less likely and successful are evaluated (e.g. information exchanges, contracting practices, product heterogeneity, discount structures, etc.).

(e)   The 1984 Guidelines suggest that mergers likely to raise prices will nonetheless be allowed if the firms can demonstrate 'clear and convincing evidence' that the merger is 'reasonably necessary' to create significant cost savings or other efficiency benefits such as scale economies or innovation encouragement. This last guideline is similar to the Williamsonian 'trade-off' discussed above (p. 25).

Scherer (1980, p. 124) shows how the 'incipiency doctrine' and the Celler–Kefauver Act 1950 slowed the trend towards growth in one's own market (or a related market) by merger. The consequence was a dramatic increase of merger activity into non-related markets (conglomeracy). Thus in 1948–57 only 3.2 per cent of assets acquired by merger were takeovers of unrelated firms. As the provisions of Celler–Kefauver began to bite, related activity mergers became less likely to pass unscathed through the courts and between 1956–63 15.9 per cent of acquired assets represented totally unrelated conglomerate merger activity. By 1963–72 this figure reached 33.2 per cent and in 1973–77 the figure was 49.2 per cent. Whether it is desirable to divert corporate growth activities away from areas where they would naturally be expressed into other areas such as unrelated diversification is another issue we discuss below.

## 11.5   MERGER POLICY IN THE UK

Just as US anti- (associated interest) merger activity resulted in an increase in conglomerate mergers, the success of the UK anti-restrictive practice legislation (some 2500 agreements had been outlawed or, more often, abandoned by 1963) may have resulted in formal mergers as a legalized alternative to non-legal agreements. Be that as it may, it was only in 1965 that the Monopolies and Mergers Commission replaced the previous Monopolies Commission. In the following twenty years only 85 (non-newspaper) mergers were referred to the Commission and 27 were found to be 'against the public interest'. The number is not large and again the few judgements showed the almost predictable unpredictability we have come to expect of anti-trust bodies.

Thus, for example, in 1981 Lonrho was debarred from acquiring

House of Fraser whilst in 1979 Lonrho (which then held 19 per cent of Fraser shares) was permitted to acquire a third company, SUITS (which held 10 per cent of Fraser shares). The earlier report stated that this would result in a 'merger situation', but if consummated, as attempted in 1981, it 'may be expected not to operate against the public interest'. Even more confusing was the acceptance by the Commission that if either of the competing takeovers for the Royal Bank of Scotland in 1982 were to take place this would have *increased competition* by introducing a significant 'fifth force' into British banking. The bid by the Hongkong and Shanghai Bank was rejected for chauvinistic reasons (it was not a registered member of the UK clearing system). The bid by the Standard Chartered Bank was rejected for even narrower reasons of Scottish regionalism (career prospects for Scots would be threatened).

British policy is also under review, however, and the Department of Trade and Industry published a discussion paper on the topic in March 1988. Events such as the merger bids for Rowntree Mackintosh by Nestlé (outside the EEC) and the increased probability of more mergers within the EEC itself due to probable increased international trading after 1992, plus attempted Community harmonization of rules for mergers (as well as restrictive practices) suggest we conclude this section with at least a cursory glance at what the future could hold.

A draft regulation for the control of mergers has been available since 1973 but Member States have so far been unable either to agree that a regulation is necessary or desirable or to agree to the successive drafts that have been produced.

The UK provisions for the control of mergers since 1965 arose out of the belief that insufficient protection for the public interest could be given after a merger had been completed. This is the basic argument for pre-merger control.

The 1965 legislation empowered Ministers to refer merger proposals as well as completed mergers to the Commission if the assets acquired were more than £5 million (now £30 million) or if the merger resulted in or enhanced a share of any UK market of $33\frac{1}{3}$ per cent or more (now 25 per cent or more). On a reference, the Commission investigates and reports to the Secretary of State for Trade and Industry whether or not the merger does, or could be expected to, operate against the public interest. If they conclude that it does, or would, they can make recommendations as to remedial action and the Secretary has statutory powers to prevent such adverse effects, including preventing a merger or breaking it up if it has already taken place.

The Fair Trading Act 1973 makes no presumption that mergers are likely to be against the public interest. Indeed, Lord Young, the Secretary of State, has confirmed that the effect of a merger upon competition in the UK is his primary consideration in deciding whether he should refer a merger to the MMC, and that if a merger appears detrimental to competition it is likely to be referred even if efficiency improvements or other benefits are claimed by the parties. Hence the decision to refer British Airways' bid for British Caledonian despite BA's claim that an increase in the scale of its operations was essential if it was to compete successfully with American 'mega-carriers' and despite British Caledonian's pleas that a merger was essential in view of its financial difficulties.

As we saw, few mergers are actually examined by the Commission. The 1988 policy review, 'Mergers Policy', rejects the arguments for a more interventionist approach. It also rejects the suggestion that the law should be changed so that parties to mergers would have to show, like the parties to a restrictive trading agreement, that their merger was positively in the public interest. 'This would make takeovers much harder to carry out, and would have a damaging effect on efficiency by weakening the discipline of the market over incumbent company managements.'

There is also a concern to speed up the procedures involved in merger control. 'Mergers Policy' proposes changes in the law designed to improve the efficiency of the procedures.

First a voluntary system of pre-notification is to be introduced. Under present law, there is no such obligation although many are and other mergers come to the OFT's attention from the financial press. Relevant information currently supplied with the notification would produce assurance that correctly notified mergers would be automatically cleared by the end of a specified period (four weeks — unless the OFT called for more information). Non-notified mergers would not only receive no such assurance but they would be liable to possible reference to the MMC for up to five years after completion rather than the present six months.

Thus the DGFT would have the power to accept from parties to a merger undertakings which would have statutory force in order to avoid the need for a reference. Assurances are often

currently offered but their enforceability is doubtful. Statutorily-
based undertakings would be a different matter. An obvious
circumstance where they would have value is where only part
of the merging companies produce competing products. If the
bidder is willing to divest part of the overlapping activities
competition concerns may be eliminated. Examples in the
past include Guinness's agreed divestment of some of DCL's
whisky brands during merger (admittedly after a decision to
refer had been taken). In all divestments allowed to end-1987,
the OFT secured a legally binding commitment to sell to
known third parties before the merger was completed.
Statutorily-backed undertakings would be a protection where
divestment cannot be completed until after the merger has taken
place.

The details of the proposed EC merger control are currently
the subject of discussion. The basic provisions are that any
merger above a certain size with a 'Community dimension' as
defined in the regulation (usually but not exclusively cross-
frontier mergers) would be prohibited as incompatible with
the Common Market if it significantly reduced competition
within the EEC or a substantial part of it. However an exemption
from this prohibition could be granted if the merger con-
tributed to some other policy objective of the Community such
as improving the efficiency and international competitiveness of
Community industry. Merger proposals within the scope of
the regulation would have to be notified and could not be
proceeded with until cleared by them. The current draft regulation provides for automatic clearance if the EEC has not
indicated within a period of two months that it proposes to
investigate the merger. If the EEC proposes to investigate then it
will have a further four months in which to decide whether to
prohibit or approve the merger.

The EEC Commission has already shown in the settlement
reached with British Airways on its merger with British
Caledonian (using existing powers under Article 86 to attack
a completed merger as an abuse of an existing dominant position)
that competition, at least as measured by firm numbers, is an
important goal. (BA had to give up several British Caledonian
routes before EEC approval was granted. It is interesting
that this was a case where double jeopardy existed and the
UK MMC treated the merger more leniently than did the
EEC.)

## 11.6   ASSESSMENT OF INDUSTRIAL POLICY

Governments can prevent mergers or encourage them. They can permit cartels or prohibit restrictive practices. Indeed, it can be argued that only with government backing can cartels persist because only governments have the ultimate power to prohibit new entrants or outlaw 'chiselling' on agreements. Conversely, by outlawing trade agreements, governments may deprive firms of market information (not of monopoly profits, since entrants and free riders will soon dissipate such rents). There is a distinction to be made, first, between outlawing a restrictive practice, second, providing a framework to enforce it (as with, say, the IATA airline cartel) and, third, refusing to provide the sanction of the law of contract to a restriction. This last option is often overlooked and was most prominent in the work of G.B. Richardson (1960). As we have seen, banning restrictive practices makes sense in a perfectly competitive, perfect information framework. Sanctioning restrictive practices by legal means makes sense in a world of natural monopoly if and when government can be expected to outperform the market. But when neither situation holds, when perfect information does not exist, when governments are swayed by pressure groups and not consumers, then the job of efficiently bridging the knowledge gap between two market participants or groups of participants depends on the Kirznerian entrepreneur. There is then a case to be made that the relevant entrepreneurship is more likely to emerge where information can be freely and readily exchanged without fear of prosecution. The dangers of an active anti-restrictive practices policy are that the information which lubricates market transactions will be suppressed. The dangers of government-enforced cartelization as occurred in the 1930s (and to a lesser extent today) are well known. The benefits of a benign approach to information exchanges, which presume the existence of and desirability of effective competition, but not its perfectability, are still little discussed, however. There are also arguments which suggest that when the government engages in merger or anti-merger activity it will also err.

Consider first merger prevention. The 'failing company' defence is often difficult to employ if the failing company has not, at the time of the proposed merger, failed enough. Yet mergers can be regarded as a civilized and efficient alternative to bankruptcy and voluntary liquidation. Certainly if a large firm is doing the acquisition, the *prima facie* reason will often be apparently one of merely raising market power. Perhaps if mergers were not so actively discouraged there would be fewer bankruptcies. To assess the true situation, the market which should be examined is not only the market for the goods in which the merging companies trade, but the market in what Manne (1965) has called 'corporate control' (since developed further by Jensen and Meckling (1976) as discussed in Chapter 9 above).

If this market is imperfect then managers can deprive owners of higher income from their shares for substantial periods, either through inefficiency or by pursuing non-profit-maximizing objectives. If it is working well this cannot happen, otherwise the share price of the firm will decline relative to other firms in the same industry. In so far as a low share price reflects poor management it also indicates what it could be if efficient management was installed. As a consequence, a merger or takeover attempt will occur in order to transfer the inefficiently utilized assets into the hands of those who can manage them more effectively. The potential capital gain in the share price will be the attraction which initiates this event.

Now consider merger encouragement (an activity engaged in by most governments in the 1930s and by the UK government in the 1960s and 1970s). If the market in corporate control is working smoothly then mergers to gain scale economies, and the extra profits which go with them, will automatically and smoothly take place without government encouragement. If such mergers do not occur then imperfections in the market for corporate control are enabling inefficient managers to pursue courses of action not in the best interests of their shareholders or of the nation as a whole.

This raises two questions. Is the market in corporate control working well? If not, should not the attention of government agencies be devoted to that market rather than the markets in products?

Certainly, if it is working smoothly then there is much less need for government interference, and there are reasons why such interference may be more harmful than helpful.

This argument can be clarified by asking two further questions. First, who loses most from poor decisions? If two firms refuse to merge in order to gain scale economies then their joint output is produced at a higher cost in resources than it need have been. This is a social loss, but is borne *entirely* by the owners of the firms in their lower incomes (we ignore tax losses to government from higher profits, and social losses due to monopolistic output reduction and higher prices if the firms had merged). Alternatively if, say, a conglomerate merger takes place in order to save costs but, in the event, managerial judgement is proved faulty and costs rise, then again the loss is borne solely by the owners of the firms who made the mistake in the first instance.

The second question to be asked is, who has the information to make pro- or anti-merger decisions which will be closest to optimal? The answer is and must be those most intimately involved with the decision situation, namely the members of the industry itself. The members of the industry have considerably more knowledge of a firm's and industry's cost and demand conditions and prospects than any outsider. This will hold for both horizontal and vertical merger situations, since knowledge of customers and/or suppliers is part of a manager's stock-in-trade. In other words, it is the members of the industry who have the most to lose from poor merger decisions and, therefore, who have the greatest incentive to take correct ones. It is they who know most about the decision situation they are involved in; it is they, therefore, who have the greatest ability to take the correct decision. Under these circumstances is it probable that outside legislators, however benevolent, know best? They have neither the incentive nor the ability to take the optimal decision. The assumption of benevolence must also not be made lightly.

This discussion depends on the smooth operation of the market in corporate control. What evidence is available that this market is or is not working well? Fortunately, since Manne's (1965) paper and Jensen and Meckling's (1976) article much empirical research has been done. Two main results are evident. First, the conglomerate merger wave of the 1960s and 1970s encouraged in the US by the successful governmental discouragement of horizontal and vertical mergers and by the 'pro-bigness' lobby of British governments in the middle to late 1960s, has produced what Meeks (1977) calls 'disappointing marriages'. The result has been a fairly high degree of voluntary 'unscrambling' and divestiture of unrelated activities by large firms. The market in corporate control is correcting governmentally induced errors. Second, takeovers of a voluntary nature do tend to be producing the benefits predicted and are exercising a disciplinary influence on managers who depart too far from the objectives of shareholder wealth maximization.

Jensen (1988), in a large-scale review of the literature to date, concludes that the 'market for corporate control is creating large benefits for shareholders and for the economy as a whole by loosening control over vast amounts of resources and enabling them to move to their highest-value use'. Between 1977 and 1986 the gains to shareholders of acquired firms totalled $346 billion. Jensen's estimate of the gains to shareholders of acquiring firms of previously non-fully utilized assets is much less, at $50 billion (a total equal to roughly one half of all dividends paid in the period). Thus it is target firms' shareholders who benefited most (that is, those whose agents were performing least satisfactorily). Shareholders whose managers were performing relatively more satisfactorily gained from their managers spotting of takeover opportunities but to a much lesser degree. (There is no reason why a trade in an Edgworth box should end up on the contract curve exactly 50 per cent of the way from each endowment point.)

Jensen shows how takeovers are most frequent in either declining industries (where it is an orderly alternative to bankruptcy) or in industries undergoing rapid change (technological, demand or regulatory) where more nimble-footed management is required than may exist in established firms where expert managers have ties or commitments to current sectional interest groups. Furthermore, with financial innovations such as 'leveraged buy-outs' small firms can now more readily obtain the resources for acquisition of much larger firms by 'issuing claims in the value of the venture', so such giant firms are no longer immune from 'corporate control' change.

Jensen discounts the view of those who say that takeover raiders sacrifice long-term benefits to increase short-run profits. Certainly, it is possible that managers may take such an approach (managerial myopia). The evidence, however, suggests that markets do not. Managerial myopia is followed by declining share prices and takeovers, not the reverse. Markets tend to value fully future costs and benefits. Hence the high prices at which (initially) zero-yielding biotechnology stocks can be issued. Jensen cites the study of the US Securities and Exchange Commission which shows that large institutional shareholdings are not associated with high takeover activity (thus disagreeing with the view that institutions are only interested in a 'quick buck' and are not loyal, long-run shareholders); that share prices rise on announcements of increased R & D expenditure; and that firms with high R & D expenditures are not more likely to be subject to takeover (again providing evidence against the notion that stock market activity will push management in the direction of short-run at the expense of long-run gains).

Jensen's concern is rather that well-run firms generate 'free cash flow' — that is, cash in excess of that required to fund all of a firm's projects, which have a positive net present value. To maximize shareholder wealth this should be distributed. But any motivation by managers to engage in corporate growth will result in a conflict of interest between them and the owners. Thus the problem is how to mobilize the market in corporate control (a takeover threat) to get such managers to act in shareholders' interests. One such means is the 'golden parachute' whereby a severance payment is made to managers who leave after takeover. Companies who implement such contractual obligations with their managers tend to see their stock price rise when the contract is announced. (In short, the conflict of interests between owner and manager is mitigated: the owner is telling the manager that he accepts that a takeover will impose heavy personal costs on him and this being so he will compensate him if and when he negotiates a takeover sale acceptable to the shareholder.) Of course, such contracts can be faultily designed. If they extend beyond members of management not likely to be directly involved in negotiating a takeover they may simply make the takeover unacceptably costly to a buyer and so be counter-productive.

Other activities that have recently been engaged in (particularly in the US) by firms attempting to avoid hostile takeovers include 'poison pills' and 'greenmail'. Both are intended to raise the cost of acquisition by outsiders. Provided the costs are willingly agreed to by existing shareholders there seems little reason for concern. They would then be a method of assuring (existing) management that owners are satisfied with their actual and expected performance and are prepared to make some sacrifice to give managers that assurance in order to obtain their consummate cooperation. However, in both cases, 'greenmail' and 'poison pills', the activities often tend to be initiated *after* a takeover bid is announced, and shareholders are then harmed by the loss of the takeover premium. (The remedy is obvious and does not require legislation as it simply means that the articles of association or incorporation of a firm must be drafted to permit or prohibit such activities.) 'Greenmail', sometimes known as a 'targeted repurchase' is the repurchase by management of a subset of shares at a premium from a takeover raider in exchange for withdrawal of the takeover threat. 'Poison pills' have many variants, all intended to make the target firm 'indigestible' to the takeover bidder. (For example, purchase by the victim of un-wanted assets at a high enough price to make acquisition appear unprofitable to the bidder. Or, more legalistically, the provision of convertible loan stock or accumulative rights issues to equity which are 'triggered' for conversion to equity or for take-up of rights if a takeover bid is announced.)

None of these arguments, or reviews of the evidence to date, suggests that the corporate control market does not work, or cannot be made to work to minimize agency costs.

One piece of empirical evidence by Scherer (1988) sounds a note of caution, however. Most studies have used stock market data, contrasting pre-takeover stock prices with bid prices. (They are 'event' studies.) Scherer reports on a major two-decade study examining how in-firm use of assets improved or deteriorated after the diversifying mergers of the 1960s and 1970s. As with Meeks' 'disappointing marriages', Scherer found that 'with few exceptions' they were 'much less than a resounding success'. Profitability tended to fall 'sharply on average relative to premerger levels'. This suggests that the takeover market or corporate control market does not 'work' in the benign way suggested. On the other hand, the takeovers examined occurred at a time when growth was channelled through anti-trust rules towards non-related lines of business. That the errors were 'regulation-induced' and not market-induced is not denied by Scherer's further evidence that by 1981, 'one third of the units required had been sold off . . . typically . . . from a conglomerate . . . to a horizontal or vertical relationship' where the management expertise was more relevant. By the 1980s then, when horizontal and vertical anti-trust legislation was becoming more lenient the efficiency-inducing effects of the corporate control market may have been correcting the regulation-induced errors of earlier decades.

Some remain unconvinced, however. The calls for a more directive approach to the management of capital by 'expert' outsiders rather than by the market will no doubt continue and only continued empirical and theoretical advances can help decide which route is optimal.

# REFERENCES

Allen, G.C. (1968), *Monopoly and Restrictive Practices Legislation* (London: George, Allen and Unwin).

Fisher, F.M. (1987), 'Horizontal Mergers: Triage and Treatment', *Journal of Economic Perspectives*, 1.

Jensen, M.C. (1988), 'Takeovers: Their Causes and Consequences', *Journal of Economic Perspectives*, 2.

Jensen, M.C. and Meckling, W.H. (1976), 'Theory of the Firm, Management Behaviour Agency Costs and Ownership Structure', *Journal of Financial Economics*, 7.

Manne, H.M. (1965), 'The Market in Corporate Control', *Journal of Political Economics*, 73.

McGee, J.S. (1987), *Industrial Organisation* (New York: Prentice-Hall).

Meeks, G. (1977), *Disappointing Marriage: A Study of the Gains from Merger* (Cambridge: Cambridge University Press).

Neale, A.D. (1960), *The Antitrust Laws of the USA* (Colchester: Utrecht).

Richardson, G.B. (1960), *Information and Investment* (Oxford: Oxford University Press).

Rostow, E.V. (1960), 'British and American Experience with Legislation Against Restraints of Competition', *Modern Law Review*, 9.

Salop, S.C. (1987), 'Symposium on Mergers and Antitrust', *Journal of Economic Perspectives*, 1.

Scherer, F.M. (1988), 'Corporate Takeovers: The Efficiency Arguments', *Journal of Economic Perspectives*, 2.

Schmalensee, R. (1987), 'Horizontal Merger Policy: Problems and Changes', *Journal of Economic Perspectives*, 1.

Shaw, R.W. and Simpson, P. (1986), 'The Persistence of Monopoly: An Investigation of the Effectiveness of the UK Monopoly Commission', *Journal of Industrial Economics*, 35.

Varian, H.A. (1988), 'Symposium on Takeovers', *Journal of Economic Perspectives*, 2.

White, L.J. (1987), 'Antitrust and Merger Policy: Review and Critique', *Journal of Economic Perspectives*, 1.

# 12.   The Consumers' Interest

We began by noting the welfare benefits of a perfectly competitive market where resources were allocated optimally by and for the interests of market participants. Market 'failures' such as natural monopoly, collusive behaviour, the departure from price and marginal cost equality necessitated by the presence of scale economies and the impact of the divorce of ownership from control have all been examined. The problems of possible divergences of social and private costs and benefits and that of 'public goods' have not been addressed but the interested reader is directed to discussions elsewhere on these issues (Reekie, 1984). The response of governments through anti-trust regulations and their attitudes to specific issues such as advertising have been either discussed in detail or alluded to. What has not been done is:

(a)   to present and assess the case for and against regulation *per se* (the choice for industrial organization policy advisers may well not be between perfect markets and no regulation and imperfect markets with regulation but rather between markets with all their 'imperfections', costs and benefits, and regulation, with all its imperfections, costs and benefits);

(b)   to ascertain the role of information in correcting or encouraging market failure; and

(c)   to examine if motivations for running a firm not answerable to capitalist managers (even given a divorced or ownership from control) suggest that alternative systems of economic management might overcome the diagnosed market failures of conventional economics.

These omissions will be examined here and conclude our discussions.

## 12.1 THEORIES OF REGULATION

There are two broad groups of theories. One is the 'public interest' group, the other is the 'sectional interest' group of theories. The public interest group advocates intervention in the marketplace at times of market failure such as when there is an inadequate supply of public goods (then government provision may be called for); or when natural monopoly or scale economies exist (when industrial regulation or control of prices and outputs of industries such as telecommunications or broadcasting may be demanded); or when there is a divergence between external and private costs and benefits which the private unregulated market has not internalized (when taxes, subsidies or controls of such things as pollution levels or gas cleaning equipment may be called for) but which would have been internalized had transactions costs been sufficiently low (see the discussion on the Coase theorem in Reekie and Allen, 1983, pp. 147–69); or when depletion of a non-renewable resource is progressing at a pace dissimilar to the conservation rate which the 'public interest' required then government may be called on to specify maximum rates of usage (again, this has been discussed in Reekie, 1985). Finally, we have seen that the 'public interest' is frequently used as a rationale for the various aspects of competition policy.

The sectional interest or self-interest groups of theories of regulation, however, suggest that regulation is not primarily engaged in for reasons of market failure but rather is an activity practised for the achievement of private gain of particular vested interest groups. This group is essentially one that argues that the regulators are 'captured' by those regulated. The terminology was popularized in a seminal paper by Posner (1974). He argues that those regulated may initially object but that they eventually come to accept the regulation and ultimately find it conducive to their own well-being. After a time, they become so familiar with the legislative and administrative process that they can use it to influence their 'captors' to pass legislation or use the administrative machinery in a way which obtains them higher returns or prices directly, or indirectly by restricting entry.

George Stigler's (1970) paper, four years earlier, and Peltzman (1976) gave the flesh of the 'capture theory' some economic bones. Stigler and Peltzman regard regulation as a commodity for which there is a demand, and for which, like any other good theme is an equilibrium price determined by demand and the supply of regulation. The demanders of regulation do so in order to receive benefits. For example, regulated industries often receive monetary subsidies and 'unless the list of beneficiaries can be limited by an acceptable device . . . [the subsidy] will be dissipated among a growing number of rivals'. As a corollary the regulated firms will also seek to request 'control over entry by new rivals'. As Stigler points out, governmental control of entry (by quota, occupational licensure schemes, e.g. taxis, physicians, TV broadcasting licensing) is far more 'efficacious' than the normal devices open to firms such as the competitive actions of price cutting, advertising, vertical integration, and so on. Third, the regulated will seek to have governmental policies 'directed to price fixing'. This is so since even if entry is precluded, price chiselling by existing firms will be possible and government-imposed price controls are far more effective than any private restrictive agreement could ever be in perpetuating above normal rates of return. Finally, Stigler argues, the regulated will also try to ensure that complements and substitutes are also regulated in their favour. Stigler and Peltzman both provide significant amounts of case evidence in support of their propositions (from inter-state trucking to commercial banking, from lawyers to retail pharmacists, from architects to airlines, from TV broadcasters to oil refiners).

Who are the suppliers of the benefits obtained by regulated industries? None other than the politicians and bureaucrats at various levels of government. And they are interested in supplying for a 'price'. The price is 'success in election and the perquisites of office' (Stigler), in other words votes, campaign contributions and lobbying support.

Stigler's main case evidence came from the US trucking industry in the 1930s. The railroad industry was concerned about incipient substitute competition as both better roads and more powerful lorries became available in the mid-1920s. They therefore lobbied for protection (against substitutes) by encouraging state regulation of maximum truck weights. By the early 1930s all 48 states had passed regulations which varied between limits on a four-wheel truck of 13,000 and 34,000 pounds (Louisiana and New York respectively) and on six-wheelers of 20,000 and 45,000 pounds (New Hampshire and Michigan). To protect itself the railroad industry would prefer regulation which would benefit it most. Lorries were most competitive on short hauls and in less than full car-sized loads. Stigler therefore postulated that protection would be least where hauls were longest (where railroads had less to fear) and that 'heavy trucks would be allowed in states with a substantial number of farms' (where railroad interests would have relatively less political power). Using regression analysis Stigler found that the weight limits in force (by state) were significantly and positively associated with the average length of railroad haul and with the number of trucks owned by farmers, and that both of these explanatory variables were statistically more powerful for six-wheel rather than four-wheel trucks. His hypothesis was not rejected.

Stigler's aim was to show how regulation, if in fact sectional interest motivated, is not therefore necessarily in the public interest. And if that is so then the corollary that an imperfect market (unregulated) may be more advantageous to the public than a regulated one. Profit-seekers attempt to operate in markets and entrepreneurially arbitrage between two parties whose MRSs differ. Buchanan (1980) has called this profit-seeking behaviour 'rent-creation'. However rent-creation is the result of exploiting unsatisfied demand through changes in production or distribution methods. It is eventually competed away in the absence of artificial market constraints. Rent-seeking, however, is the attempt by an individual or group to exploit a particular form of institutional arrangement (e.g. regulation), earn an amount over and above the normal supply price, and use the institutional arrangement to hinder the rent being competed away. In a sense, a transfer rather than a creation is taking place.

Stigler emphasizes this when he claims that even if a regulation which grants an industry power from the state benefited the industry only to the extent of the damage to the rest of the community, it would still be refused by a democratic vote (unless the industry controlled a majority of the votes). Monetary voting in markets is continuous and cumulative. The political decision process is 'fundamentally different' in that it is coercive not voluntary. There are two other major differences, namely, simultaneity and universality. Decisions must be made simultaneously (e.g. whether or not to legalize a satellite television channel) otherwise the voting process would be 'prohibitively expensive'. Accumulation of opinions is not possible, and opinion changing is not allowed for either. It is costly enough to make any purchase, it is conceptually impossible to ratify every other person's purchase as well (even if the 'purchases' are limited only to regulatory issues). Thus discretion at the margin by elected or employed representatives is the only feasible way of meeting the simultaneity condition. The universality condition means that everyone votes on everything, whether involved or not. In the commercial market, on the contrary, 'votes' (purchases and sales) are made only of what each has an interest, knowledge and motivation in. The non-purchaser of air travel will never 'vote' (buy) an air ticket. The uninterested voter on any given issue in the political process must, however, be included. (Local, regional and national tiers of government make a gesture towards attenuating this difficulty but it remains a gesture.) And if he is uninterested he will not be motivated to learn about the issues. Again the route set is for the voters to employ full-time representation organized in political parties.

The representative and his party are rewarded with success if they discover and fulfil the political desires of their constituency. If re-election depended on voting against socially injurious industrial regulation the representatives would vote against it. But since political decisions (elections) are infrequent and global the individual voter will have little incentive to learn about the merits and demerits of individual policy proposals. The cost of doing so in the political arena are greater than they would be in the commercial market 'because information must be sought on many issues of little or no direct concern to the individual, and accordingly he will know little about most matters before the legislature'. The preferences expressed at elections will thus be much less accurate than those expressed in a commercial market. Many uninformed people will be voting and affecting the decision. 'If everyone has a negligible preference for policy A over B, the preference will not be discovered or acted upon. If voter group X wants a policy that injures non-X by a small amount, it will not pay non-X to discover this and act against the policy.' Thus the regulatory process will notice and act upon all strongly felt preferences of majorities, many strongly felt preferences of minorities (if they care to indulge in lobbying costs) but will tend not to register lesser preferences of majorities and minorities. Thus a regulated industry might well find it worthwhile to expend resources to gain rent (on a straight, private investment appraisal basis) through regulation. The costs of that regulation, the rent would be transferred from, or dissipated across the rest of society in such a way that the costs would be barely perceptible, and not worth the while of any individual voter to query the why and the wherefore of his bearing the burden of the cost in the first place.

Certainly, as Stigler argues, those demanding regulation must deliver votes and resources. These costs of regulation will rise the bigger and more noticeable the industry. The more other groups are affected, and especially if noticeably affected, the higher will be the costs of successful lobbying. The universality and simultaneity conditions result in the need for representatives. This is also demonstrated by the 'Paradox of Voting'. Any majority has a technical flaw. Suppose persons A, B and C have to choose between alternative policies, X, Y and Z which are ranked by each as indicated:

| Policy/votes | X | Y | Z |
| --- | --- | --- | --- |
| A | 1 | 2 | 2 |
| B | 3 | 1 | 2 |
| C | 2 | 3 | 1 |

In a vote between X and Y, the former would win by 2 votes to 1. Between Y and Z, Z will win by the same margin. So X is preferred to Y is preferred to Z. But if an election is now held between X and Z, Z is preferred. Kenneth Arrow's General Impossibility Theorem has shown that virtually any collective choice rule will be inconsistent in this way. If regulation and voting distort what is the way out of the maze? Can, for example, the attributes of perfect markets be regained by providing greater information to market participants?

## 12.2 INFORMATION AND MARKET IMPERFECTIONS

One major source of market imperfections is incomplete information. It could be argued, as on pp. 139–51 above, that this is simply the state from which the market process begins as alert entrepreneurs notice information deficiencies and arbitrage them away. Alternatively, it could be argued that advertising provides consumers with sufficient information with which to make trades. Yet at the very least advertising must be regarded as biased information (a fuller discussion of these issues is provided in Reekie, 1988). Third, regulations could be passed requiring that market participants provide and receive some predetermined information. This option, of course, is open to all of the problems raised in the unfinished debate on regulation referred to in the previous section.

Utton (1986, pp. 39–51) provides a useful summary of the current state of the literature. Consumers have an incentive to demand information to optimize their spending patterns and minimize cognitive dissonance. Sellers also have incentives to provide information since absent information all brands would be presumed to be of average quality. Higher quality sellers will thus have an incentive to disclose these facts. These two facts, of themselves, do not guarantee optimal information provision, however. First, the benefits of information disclosure (like any public good) will go to all consumers, those who wish for it to make informed purchases and those who do not and buy indiscriminately. Under-supply of information is therefore probable since suppliers will not wish to pay for information provision for those who do not use it. In addition, there is the free-rider problem. Information, once supplied, can be transferred at zero cost and those who pay for its supply cannot recoup the total value of its benefits. The institutional method evolved to minimize these transaction costs is to provide information as a joint product with the good supplied, namely, and in particular, advertising.

So we come full circle to the advertising issue with its problems of selectivity of claims, and the oligopolistic minimax possibility of an oversupply of rivalrous claims. There is a frustrating indeterminancy about the information issue. As a public good it is under-supplied, as a joint product tied to a particular brand it may be subject to oversupply, especially given the two arguments of oligopoly rivalry on the one hand and advertising to 'signal' higher quality on the other.

Not only is there theoretical indeterminancy over the optimal amount of information, but unpredictable distortions can arise in the associated product markets from privately provided information. Utton highlights this dilemma by contrasting non-prescription (over-the-counter medicines) with second-hand cars. The former is his own example, the latter is a well known one used by Ackerloff (1970).

With products such as OTC medicines, Utton says (p. 42), 'information about the quality of product is sketchy and costly to obtain . . . [so] firms have an incentive to differentiate brands of what are physically the same product, with a consequent rise in the average price'.[1] This example is at odds with the previous statement that higher levels of information provision highlight better than average products (a view first put forward by Nelson (1970)). It also contradicts the Ackerloff result that if there is information asymmetry between buyer and seller, if price is more readily discernible than quality, then competition will be focused on the cheaper end of the market.

Thus Ackerloff argues, for new cars, buyers cannot tell which ones are the trouble-free majority and which are 'Friday-afternoon cars' or 'lemons' with a high propensity to throw up unpredicted faults after purchase. New cars, therefore, all sell at the same price. Second-hand cars, however, will sell at an average price well below the level expected from physical depreciation since demand will depend on price and lemon probability. 'Lemon probability' will be high in second-hand cars (say under one year old) as consumers will be highly suspicious of them being offered for sale. A low price will contract the quantity supplied, as owners of non-lemons will not offer them for sale because they cannot obtain the 'correct' price. The average quality of second-hand cars falls, and even in those cases where consumers would be prepared to pay more to obtain the information necessary to ensure that the vehicle they are buying is not a lemon they cannot.

The difficulty with these two examples (medicines and cars) is that the first is at least debatable and the second has seen (in the twenty years since the Ackerloff article) many devices introduced by the market to remove the 'lemon' problem (for example warranty schemes for second-hand cars by both dealers and manufacturers, free or inexpensive product checking by experts from the voluntary motoring organizations, and advertising-backed guarantees from manufacturers of new cars emphasizing that *their* second-hand products retain their 'correct' price levels if serviced, maintained or retraded through approved outlets).

As Utton (1986, p. 44) points out, however, by internalizing these externality problems in the way the Coase theorem predicts, over-compensation may occur. Consumers may exploit the guarantees, and producers in turn may be open to opportunistic behaviour. In short, transactions costs do exist, markets do tend to internalize externalities, and while regulation is available to remedy imperfections the costs involved in framing regulatory remedies suggest as Sherwin Rosen once put it orally (at the American Economic Association meetings in 1985), 'what is, is optimal'.

## 12.3 THE LABOUR-MANAGED FIRM

There are, of course, alternatives other than regulation. Unfettered capitalism as traditionally understood in the perfectly competitive model or as explained by the theory of the modern corporation where competition in markets in products and in corporate control ensure that it operates optimally in consumers' and owners' interests within the constraints imposed by transactions cost analysis may or may not be superior to regulation. But what of more radical alternatives such as Marxism and its variations? Marxism, as such, is more properly discussed in political economy than in industrial economics. Comparisons of the mechanics of a command economy *vis-à-vis* a market economy are not wholly relevant in discussions of the firm. Furthermore we have already made passing obeisance to the economics of politics in our discussion of regulation. Here we shall restrict ourselves to a brief glance at the theory of the labour-managed firm.

The theory has received its most elegant presentation in the work of Vanek (1970). Workers have the ultimate decision-making authority in Vanek style firms. Their objective is assumed to be income-maximization per worker. Interestingly, the long-run outcome is the same as that in a perfectly competitive capitalist system. There are differences in short-run behaviour, however. Consider Figure 12.1. The curves ARP and MRP are the conventional average and marginal revenue product curves of a competitive firm. $WW^1$ is the wage rate and the firm will hire L units of labour where MRP = $WW^1$. The function $CC^1$ is a rectangular hyperbola (analogous to a demand curve of unitary elasticity) at any point beneath which the area bounded by the axes is constant. Such areas represent the (given fixed) monetary value of capital employed and the points on the function show the capital cost per worker at different employment levels. With capital and labour as the only two inputs, income per worker is represented by the vertical distance between ARP and $CC^1$. This is represented by $YY^1$ which is maximized at the market wage rate of $WW^1$, leading both types of firm to employ at level L.

Now if the price of the final product rises, the short-run adjustments made by the two firms will differ. The labour-managed firm will increase wages, the capital-managed firm will increase employment. (In the long term, of course, new firms will enter the market competing away the higher wages — of the former; and the higher capital returns — of the latter.) Figure 12.2 replicates Figure 12.1

*Figure 12.1*

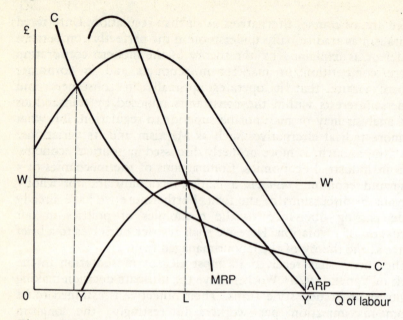

*Figure 12.2*

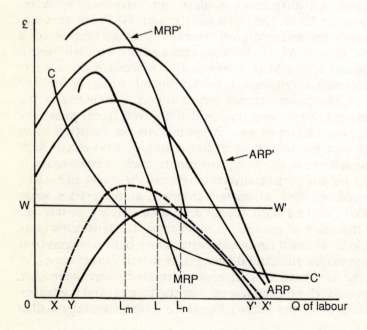

with revised ARP, MRP schedules reflecting the new, higher final product price. The traditional firm moves from L to $L_n$ where $MRP^1$ intersects $WW^1$ while the labour-managed firm reduces employment to $L_m$ where the income hill $XX^1$ has its summit.

This discussion is highly truncated and skeletal but it again suggests that legal forms do not impact greatly on the consumer, capitalist or worker. Rather markets and societies appear to evolve institutions which do satisfy members' aspirations (be they consumers, workers or capitalists) in such a way as to do so at minimum cost while providing curbs on the exploitation of one party by another. (In transactions costs language, given bounded rationality, and limited information, markets and institutions are developed and chosen which minimize transactions costs and attenuate opportunism.)

## 12.4  CONCLUSIONS

The above foray into the theory of the labour-managed firm may seem somewhat unsatisfactory in a chapter on the consumers' interest and indeed disappointing in a book on industrial organization in general. After all were not the SCP paradigm and Pareto optimality themselves directed at understanding, if not consumer, certainly social welfare? This is true but two useful factors have emerged from the discussion. First, the forces of supply and demand have been again seen to operate, irrespective of legal ownership entitlements (just as they did in the market for regulation). Second, we have again had it underlined that the firm is a nexus of contracts and that the initiator may be the capitalist, the worker or the consumer depending on the legal framework of the country and the least transactions costs approach to assembling resources (e.g. contemporary Yugoslavia encourages labour-managed firms; late nineteenth-century Britain with its relatively concentrated manufacturing industries, unconcentrated retailing industries and relatively educated populace was a fertile ground for the establishment of consumer-initiated retail co-operative stores).

The firm is in reality a nexus of contracts between financiers, entrepreneurs, labour, management, customers and suppliers. Some of the contracts which exist are long-run, others are spot. The consumers of the various resources come together as a firm because their value as a team exceeds the aggregate of the market values each could obtain separately. (Even a spot exchange involves mutually beneficial gain.) Departure (i.e. premature departures in terms of any explicit or implicit contract) of any team member will lower the team's value. (Thus the resignation of a skilled, experienced manager, the withdrawal of custom by a hitherto loyal client, the sale of a large block of equity will all lower the value of the firm.) Alchian and Woodward (1988, p. 70) argue that the desire to protect this value will encourage contracts designed to minimize the likelihood of such withdrawal. Further, those team members who own capital (human or other) whose value depends heavily on team performance (i.e. is 'team-specific') will 'pay the most for the right to control the team. By definitional consequence of being owners of such resources, they own the residual value.' They are the 'legal owners' albeit no one owns all the resources used in the firm. The equity owners, to protect against moral hazard will be partners to all contracts made by the firm, and will bear the residual loss or gain in value. The more general, less team-specific, more substitutable a resource is, the more likely it is to be rented, employed, or subject to a spot contract. 'Because their value . . . is independent of the fortunes' of the firm they will be paid no more than their opportunity cost.

Thus the difference between the summed opportunity costs (market values) and team value is the entrepreneur's return. Not all of that team value excess will be reflected in equity prices since several other parties to the contracts could well be earning in excess of their opportunity returns or wages given team specific investments and absent collusion. Thus we have 'golden parachutes' for certain managers and stock option schemes as managers try to protect their firm specific investments. Similarly, as Alchian and Woodward (p. 71) point out, the 'high' incomes (relative to opportunity wages) which owners as partners receive in legal, architecture, accounting, engineering consulting, and economic consulting firms, advertising agencies, restaurants, computer software creative houses and so on reflect returns to firm specific inputs, albeit the owners are generally 'labour' and not 'capital'. The issue is not whether labour or capital is the owner or the boss or that one hires the other or vice versa. The 'basic forces that shape the firm' (p. 72) are merely that the team leader (the manager) has a comparative advantage in deciding what the team should be and how it should operate and second, ownership is 'the residual claimancy on the most team-specific resources', be they labour or capital, tangible or intangible.

# NOTE

1. For an alternative view see W.D. Reekie and H. Otzbrugger (1985), *Competition and Home Medicines* (Institute of Economic Affairs).

# REFERENCES

Ackerloff, G.A. (1970), 'The Market for "Lemons": Quality Uncertainty and the Market Mechanism', *Quarterly Journal of Economics*.

Alchian, A. and Woodward, S. (1988), 'Review of Williamson's *The Economic Institutions of Capitalism*', *Journal of Economic Literature*.

Buchanan, J.S. (1980), 'Rent Seeking and Profit Seeking' in Buchanan, J.S., Tillison, R.D. and Tublock, G. (eds), *Toward a Theory of the Rent Seeking Society* (Texas: A. & M. Press).

Nelson, P. (1970), 'Information and Consumer Behaviour', *Journal of Political Economy*.

Peltzman, S. (1976), 'Towards a More General Theory of Regulation', *Bell Journal of Economics and Management Science*.

Reekie, W.D. (1985), *Markets, Entrepreneurs and Liberty* (Brighton: Wheatsheaf).

Reekie, W.D. (1988), *Issues in Advertising* (Cape Town: Juta).

Reekie, W.D. and Allen, D.E. (1983), *The Economics of Modern Business* (Oxford: Basil Blackwell).

Stigler, G.J. (1970), 'The Theory of Economic Regulation', *Bell Journal of Economic and Management Science*.

Utton, M.A. (1986), *The Economics of Regulating Industry* (Oxford: Basil Blackwell).

Vanek, J. (1970), *The General Theory of Labour Managed Economy* (New York: Cornell University Press).

# Index

(Author listings are given at chapter ends)

adverse selection 130
advertising 62, 137, 148, 227–9
agency theory 174–91
aggregate concentration ratios 82–5
Alcoa 201
allocative efficiency 4, 32, 38
American Tobacco 200f
Austrianism 2, 4, 65, 147
authority 166
average cost curve 21, 92–3

Bain index 54–5
bilateral monopoly 171
board of directors 186f
bounded rationality 130–7, 167, 181
Bowley-Edgeworth box 10–11
    see also Edgeworth box
British Airways 214–15
British Oxygen 205
bureaucracy 1, 222–8

capture theory 224
Carnegie 201
cartels 216
Celler–Kefauver Act 212
Clayton Act 206, 209
Coase theorem 230
collective bargaining 167
collusion 38–44
common costs 26f
community indifference curves 13, 16
comparative advantage 3, 97–9

comparative statistics 130, 144
comprehensive contracts
    see contracts
concentration measures 42, 45f, 53, 85–8
conglomeracy 221
consumers' sovereignty 20
consumer surplus 20, 25f, 133–4
consummate cooperation 168
contingency claims 164–6
contractability 118
contracts
    comprehensive 130
    neoclassical 170
    relational 170
    sequential 165
    spot 162, 166
corporate control 161, 174–91
cost of capital 35
costs 116–28
Cournot assumption 39–41, 58
cross-elasticities 52, 212
cumulative share curve 45

deadweight loss 23, 28f, 59–65, 205
debt equity ratios 195f
Department of Justice Merger Guidelines 210f
Department of Trade and Industry 207
Director General of Fair Trading 207
distributive efficiency 5

diversification 52, 221
dividend policies 195f
divorce of ownership from control 3, 159–73, 174–91

Edgeworth box 145, 152
   *see also* Bowley-Edgeworth box
elasticity 30, 42–5, 60f
endowment point 11, 141
entrepreneur 2, 4, 139–44, 151–6, 187–90
entry barriers 25f, 56, 211
European Economic Community 199, 215
experience curve 128–9
externalities 4, 224, 230

'failing company' defence 203
'fair trade' laws 135
Federal Trade Commission 53, 200, 206
firm 159–73
foreign direct investment 96–115
franchising 133
free cash flow 220f
free riding 133, 163
fundamental transportation 131, 167

Gary Dinners 201
General Dynamics 210
Gini coefficient 48
'golden parachute' 210, 234
governance structures 130
   bilateral 170
   unified 170
'greenmail' 230

Heckscher-Ohlin theorem 97–9
Herfindahl index 42, 47f, 211
Herfindahl-Hirschman index 211
hierarchies 163–4, 168
holism 156
Hongkong and Shanghai Bank 217
House of Fraser 213
Hymer-Pashigian index 49–50

IATA 216
IBM 201
Imperial Tobacco 201
impossibility theorem 228
incentives 180–91
'incipiency doctrine' 210
indifference curve 7, 10, 139, 156, 176
industrial organization 5, 37
industry life cycle 123–5
information 153, 228–30
information impactedness 164, 168
innovation 143
input–output analysis 98–9
instability index 50
internal labour market 167–8
internal management market 184–6, 191–8
inventive incentives 69–71
inverse elasticity rule 29–31
isoquants 7, 144, 156

job idiosyncracy 164, 166
   *see also* task idiosyncracy

Kelloggs 205

labour management 231–3
labour supply curve 19
leisure–work trade-off 17–19, 32
'lemons' 229
Leontief Paradox 98–9, 103
Lerner index 54
'Line of Business' data 53
long term contracts 162
Lonrho 212–13
Lorenz curve 48
Lucas 205

M-form organization 181
managerial objectives 159
managerial slack 33
marginal cost 10, 20, 21, 27–30, 54
marginal cost pricing 25f
marginal product 35

marginal rate of product transformation 5, 8
marginal rate of substitution 5, 7–8, 19, 139, 141
marginal utility 145
market concentration 38–54
Marshall, 2, 4, 67, 157
mergers 209–23
*Mergers Policy 1988*, policy review 214f
minimum efficient scale 3, 87–9, 91–7, 118, 120–1
mixed economy 73–7
Molins Machine Co. 205
monitoring 160, 169–71, 174–91
Monopolies and Mergers Commission 92
Monopolies and Restrictive Trade Practices 203
monopolistic competition 21
monopoly 1, 23
monopoly policy 199–222
monopoly profit 38, 62–5
moral hazard 130
multinational enterprise 1, 3, 96–115
multiplant costs 3, 121–3
multiproduct costs 3, 116–20

National Industrial Recovery Act 202
neoclassical contracting 170
    see also contracts
Nestlé 213
nexus of contracts 185

oligopoly 23
organizational slack 33, 65
organizer 157–8
opportunism 130–7, 165, 170, 181
opportunity cost 32

Pareto optimality 1, 8–23, 142
perfect competition 8–23, 27–35, 38, 42
perfunctory cooperation 168

plant size distribution 84–6
'poison pills' 220–1
ports of entry 168
price discrimination 133, 206
probability 156
product differentiation 56
product life cycle 3, 103–5, 125–9
profits 1, 57, 146
proprietary knowledge 106–7, 110
public choice 1
public goods 224
public interest 205

Ramsey pricing 28
rate of return 32–5, 200
'reconciliation of the optima' 94–5
regulation 1, 63, 223–7
relational contracting 170
    see also contracts
rent 3, 62–5, 107, 226
representative firm 67
resale price maintenance 135–7
reservation price 21
residual claims 187, 234
Restrictive Trade Practices Act 205
retail cooperatives 147
risk preferences 171, 174–91
Robinson–Patman Act 133, 206–7
Roche 205
Rothschild index 55–6
Rowntree–Mackintosh 213
Royal Bank of Scotland 213

scale economies 23, 26
scientism 155
second best 35
sequential contracts 165
    see also spot contracts
Sherman Act 199–200, 203
shirking 160, 163, 165, 171
small business 89–91
social costs 223
social justice 17
social welfare 5

spot contracts 162, 166
    see also contracts
Standard Chartered Bank 213
Standard Industrial Classification
    53, 78–83
Standard Oil 200
structure/conduct/performance
    paradigm 2, 4, 20, 27, 38–56
survivor technique 92

tariffs 107–9
targeted repurchase see 'greenmail'
task idiosyncracy 165, 167
    see also job idiosyncracy
team production 160, 162, 169
technical efficiency 5, 57
teleology 156
trade point 7

transactions costs 1, 3, 103, 129–
    36, 139–52, 230
Turner and Newall 205

undertaker 157
US Steel 200
utility maximization 67

value added 51
vertical integration 51, 123–5, 176,
    221
Von's grocery 210
voting 227–8

welfare loss 3
welfare trade-off 25f

X-inefficiency 3, 33, 65–9, 205

$$3000 \times \frac{5}{100} \times \frac{1}{12} = \frac{25}{2} \times 3 = \frac{75}{2} = 37.5$$

# Industrial Economics